The Ministry of Shepherding

A Study of Pastoral Practice

THE MINISTRY OF SHEPHERDING

by
Eugene L. Stowe

Beacon Hill Press of Kansas City
Kansas City, Missouri

Copyright, 1976
Beacon Hill Press of Kansas City

Library of Congress Catalog Card No. 76-28859

ISBN: 0-8341-0443-1

Printed in the United States of America

Dedication

To my dear wife

FAYE

Who has contributed immeasurably to the shepherding ministry of her husband and has endeared herself as an ideal shepherdess to the flocks which we have served.

Contents

Preface

At first glance this volume might well elicit the response "Not another book on the ministry!" In recent years a flood of offerings on various phases of this subject has poured off the presses of religious and secular publishers. Could anything new be left under the sun to say? Probably very little. What then would prompt a preacher to take up his pen and write one more book on this topic?

FIRST, THE PROFOUND CONVICTION AFTER 30 YEARS OF MINISTRY THAT THE PASTORAL OFFICE IS' STILL THE MOST BASIC, BIBLICAL MODEL FOR MINISTERING. Twenty of these years were spent in pastorates which ran the gamut of sizes of congregations and types of communities. The last decade has been spent in ministerial training and church administration—the preparation and supervision of pastors. From each of these vantage points it has become increasingly clear that with due respect to other ministries, no other type of Christian service quite equals the pastoral ministry in its vital contribution to the Kingdom enterprise. The most determinative human factor in the growth and development of the church is the effectiveness of its pastoral practice. The production of a greater number of highly motivated, more expertly skilled pastors must therefore be one of our highest priorities.

THEN, IT SEEMS THAT THE TIME HAS COME TO RESTATE AND REAFFIRM THE BASIC CONCEPT OF SHEPHERDING AS THE PATTERN FOR PARISH MINISTRY. Bishop Wilson T. Hogue's *Homiletics and Pastoral Theology* was the text used in my practics classes in the early 1940s. Ten years later Dr. G. B. Williamson authored *Overseers of the Flock*. Both of these classic works on practical theology placed special emphasis upon the pastor-shepherd image. However, in recent years there has been a tendency to cloak the man of God in more modern garments. By some he has been cast primarily as a counselor. Others have seen him as a coach. Certainly there is an element of truth in these and other designations. But no other name describes his fundamental role and total task quite like the word *pastor*, which literally means "shepherd." Nothing else quite embraces the whole scope and spirit of this unique ministry like the term *shepherding*.

This is not intended primarily to be a textbook and certainly not an exhaustive treatise on this subject. It is my prayer that it may contribute some foundation stones to the ministerial life which some future pastors are beginning to build in their college and seminary years. And may it be a refresher course of things both old and new to some who have served long and well but who have the commendable desire to serve even longer and better.

May I acknowledge a debt of gratitude to M. A. "Bud" Lunn, the manager of Beacon Hill Press of Kansas City, who supplied the original impetus for the writing of this book and whose constant encouragement has been so heartening. Also, my heartfelt appreciation to my secretary, Mary Ann Wagner, who not only accepted the extracurricular responsibility for typing the manuscript but endured the endless revisions with unfailing good cheer. "Of such [Buds and Mary Anns] is the kingdom of God"!

—Eugene L. Stowe

*Our Lord Jesus, that great shepherd
of the sheep* (Heb. 13:20).

*I was made a minister, by God's
gift* (Eph. 3:7, NEB).

CHAPTER 1

Where Shepherding Starts

Ministry means service. This concept is basic in either the secular or sacred realm.

In the Judeo-Christian tradition, while all of God's children are His servants, some have always been chosen for special ministries. The first of these was the *priesthood.* Early in the Genesis account we are introduced to Melchizedek, the priest of God, who blessed Abram in His name and received tithes in return. Later priests and Levites conducted the sacrifices and ceremonies of Tabernacle and Temple worship as professional ministers.

The other ministerial office set apart in the Old Testament was that of *prophet.* While on occasion he was given special gifts for foretelling future events, his primary task was that of forth-telling, or preaching as we think of it today. Though their service went largely unappreciated by their hearers, the prophetic ministry of such stalwarts as Amos and Isaiah stands as a timeless example of fearless proclamation of divine truth.

The New Testament pattern of ministry is a Person rather than an office. In Christ the priestly functions and the prophet's role are perfectly melded in His ministry of reconciliation.

But something new is added. Embracing the best in both of these traditional forms of service, Jesus introduces the concept of *shepherding*—the most comprehensive model of Christian ministry. It is so profoundly simple that it is simply profound—utterly timeless and yet the ultimate in relevance.

The Sheep

Before one can intelligently grasp the fundamentals of the ministry of shepherding, he must have a basic understanding of the nature and needs of the sheep. There are some very striking similarities between the natural temperament and tendencies of these animals and those of their human counterparts in the church flock. While Christian men and women may be highly intelligent and possess expertise in professional and cultural areas, in personal, spiritual matters they consistently demonstrate sheeplike weaknesses and infirmities.

One of these prominent characteristics is *defective vision*. It is estimated that the maximum limit of a sheep's effective sight is no more than 15 yards. This inability to recognize enemies except at very close range makes it easy prey for predators. When it seeks to escape by resorting to flight, it may plunge off a cliff to its death by failing to see the precipice before it is too late. What a picture of the ecclesiastical flock! A pitiful lack of spiritual insight and foresight renders all too many Christians helpless victims of the teachers of false doctrine whom Paul aptly describes as "wolves." Running scared from other real or imagined terrors, church members have too often been stampeded to their serious injury or even death because they have not seen the yawning abyss which lurked ahead.

Phillip Keller spent a number of years as a professional shepherd. Out of this experience he identifies several other likenesses between four-legged and two-legged sheep.

A hungry, ill-fed sheep is ever on its feet, on the move, searching for another scanty mouthful of forage to try and satisfy its gnawing hunger. Such sheep are not contented, they do not thrive, they are of no use to themselves nor to their owners. They languish and lack vigor and vitality.[1]

Small wonder that parishioners whose pastor does not feed them well wander off into the deceptively green pastures of "charismania," faith healing, and exotic Eastern religions.

Still another unique quality of sheep is described by Keller in these words:

> Owing to their timidity, they refuse to lie down unless they are free from fear . . . to be at rest there must be a definite sense of freedom from fear, tension, and aggravations . . . it is only the sheepman himself who can provide release from these anxieties. . . . A flock that is restless, always agitated and disturbed never does well. I came to realize that nothing so quieted and reassured the sheep as to see me in the field.[2]

And human "sheep" are no less subject to a variety of pressures and fears which keep them upset. If they are not calmed and reassured by the kindly ministrations of their shepherd, they are no good to themselves or to others.

Sheep being what they are, it becomes increasingly evident that the shepherd's role is a vitally important one.

The Shepherd

In and out of the Scriptures all shepherding starts with the Chief Shepherd. Jesus forthrightly declared, "I am the good shepherd" (John 10:11). This statement sets a standard of excellence for the ministry which is more easily understood than attained.

FIRST AND FOREMOST IS THE REQUIREMENT OF MORAL AND ETHICAL GOODNESS. Christ's character was unimpeachable. So virtuous was His life that He enjoyed the total confidence of those to whom He ministered. Completely selfless, He left no room for honest questions regarding the purity of His motives. Pilate confirmed this when he rendered the

---

1. W. Phillip Keller, *A Shepherd Looks at Psalm 23* (Grand Rapids, Mich.: Zondervan Publishing House, 1970), p. 46.
2. *Ibid.*, pp. 35-37.

verdict, "I find no fault in him." And shepherding in this day or anytime must begin with this same spiritual qualification. It is more than coincidental that in his classic catalog of the qualities of the successful minister, Paul heads the list with "of blameless reputation" (1 Tim. 3:2, Phillips). President Woodrow Wilson, who was the son of a minister, once said that the minister's work consists mainly in "being," not in doing or speaking. No more succinct statement of this biblical standard can be found than this: "The perpetuity and efficiency of the [church] depend largely upon the spiritual qualifications, the character, and the manner of life of its ministers."[3] No amount of professional skill or achievement can compensate for a lack of godliness in the man of God. William Barclay points up the imperative necessity of this vital piety by quoting the eminent philosopher Kierkegaard: "Order the parsons to be silent on Sundays. What is there left? The essential things remain: their lives, the daily life which the parsons preach. Would you then get the impression by watching them that it was Christianity they were preaching?"[4] None should essay to enter this ministry until he can humbly but confidently affirm with the saintly apostle, "For to me to live is Christ" (Phil. 1:21).

Anything less than the baptism with and the continued leadership of the Holy Spirit is insufficient spiritual preparation for shepherding. The crisis experiences of regeneration and entire sanctification constitute one righteous. Subsequent growth in grace is contingent upon careful obedience to the light and direction supplied by God's Spirit. Satan brings no more insidious temptation to the minister than a kind of clerical Calvinism which suggests that *once* a good shepherd, *always* a good shepherd. The preacher's piety is no more unconditional than the layman's!

A consistently cultivated devotional life is every bit as

---

3. *Manual, Church of the Nazarene* (Kansas City: Nazarene Publishing House, 1972), par. 401, p. 219.

4. William Barclay, *In the Hands of God* (New York: Harper and Row, 1966), p. 99.

essential to the parson as it is to his parishioners. Feeding *upon* the Word is a necessary antecedent to ministering *from* the Word. And how can one lead his congregation into a productive prayer life if he has not first practiced it in his own closet? "No man can give what he does not have,"[5] observes Walter Russell Bowie.

From this quiet cloister the shepherd ventures forth "a wholly holy man . . . not some harmless hermit in retreat but one who, standing in the sweat and muck of life, is burnished bright; a man who in Robert Frost's words is, 'Something like a star' and 'asks of us a certain height.'"[6] Dr. Lewis T. Corlett devoted his life to the training of preachers on the undergraduate, seminary, and in-service levels. As a fledgling pastor I heard him set the standard for the minister: so to live in the conscious presence of the Holy Spirit that his contacts with people would be a touch of heaven. This is the spiritual level of life for the pastor-shepherd!

His Call

REAL SHEPHERDS ARE CALLED, NOT HIRED. Jesus points up this truth in the passage immediately following His identification as the Good Shepherd (John 10:11-15). When the real cost of shepherding becomes apparent, hirelings are more interested in saving their own skins than in saving the sheep. Because His shepherdship was a divine vocation—literally, "calling"—Christ was ready to lay down His very life for the salvation of the flock.

A good Christian may or may not be a good shepherd. It is true, as Luther stated, that there is a priesthood of all believers. Elton Trueblood correctly speaks of the "ministry of the laity."[7] However, scriptural evidence is conclusive that the Christian ministry must have its genesis in a defi-

---

5. Walter R. Bowie, *Where You Find God* (New York: Harper and Row, 1968), p. 114.
6. David A. Redding, *What Is the Man?* (Waco, Tex.: Word Books, 1970), p. 22.
7. D. Elton Trueblood, *The Future of the Christian* (New York: Harper and Row, 1971), pp. 28-29.

nite, divine call. Simon Peter heard the clear summons to forsake his nets and begin fishing for men. Paul's tentmaking became merely a means of livelihood after he received the mandate by which he was "made a minister" (Eph. 3:7). The sobering certainty of that call rings out in his testimony: "Necessity is laid upon me; yea, woe is unto me, if I preach not the gospel!" (1 Cor. 9:16).

And none should settle for less than this same assurance. To some the call may come in a dramatic encounter with the Caller accompanied by deep, confirming emotions. The setting may be a commitment service in a youth camp. Or perhaps a missionary has presented the crying need for laborers in the vast harvest fields. Others may sense a growing awareness that this is God's will, culminating in the quiet certainty of divine vocation. In any event the call should be so clear that the passage of time only serves to amplify it.

The church and the Christian home may render valuable assistance in fostering such calls. A conducive atmosphere in which young people may hear the voice of God is vitally important. The sympathetic counsel of pastor and parent may serve a providential purpose. But the court of final appeal must always and inevitably be "I the Lord have called thee" (Isa. 42:6).

ANYTHING LESS THAN THIS CERTAIN SENSE OF CALLING IS INADEQUATE PREPARATION FOR SUCCESSFUL SHEPHERDING. James S. Stewart comments,

> That the ministry should be regarded as a profession—a career whose main qualifications are a certain amount of organizing ability, tact, and culture, the reputation of being a good "mixer" and a shrewd judge of men, some measure of facility of speech, and a decent level of piety—this is shocking and deplorable. No ministry is worth anything which is not first and last and all the time a ministry beneath the Cross. Let a man reckon the cost ere he closes with the call.[8]

---

8. James S. Stewart, *Heralds of God* (New York: Charles Scribner's Sons, 1946), pp. 199-200.

This Cross-cost is not imaginary. Financial sacrifice is still entailed in the ministry. Preachers' salaries are notoriously low, and there are no prospects that union organizers will effect a closed shop for the clergy! Job security leaves much to be desired when the pastor's future is left to the caprice of periodic congregational votes. Many a good pastor has laid down his ecclesiastical life for his sheep when he has dared to take an uncompromising stand on vital issues at the cost of bringing down the wrath of influential rams and ewes of the flock.

Small wonder that "ministerial 'camp-followers,' snatching at crumbs of glory and recognition"[9] without a sure and sustaining call will become dropouts when pastoral pressures mount. But the good shepherd, buoyed up by the constant assurance of the Divine Presence and enablement which accompany the Lord's call, will discover continuing challenge and unhoped-for remuneration as he perseveres in his assignment.

H. Richard Niebuhr suggests that there are four component parts to a call to the ministry:

1. The Call to Be a Christian
2. The Secret Call
3. The Providential Call
4. The Ecclesiastical Call.[10]

The latter two are confirmations of the private, personal call and have to do with the gifts which are corollary to the necessary graces for this service. There is considerable question whether a wise God calls individuals with inferior intelligence, poor judgment, or no capability for public speaking. Formal training can make up some shortfall in these and other areas, but the rising level of proficiency in the pew calls for above-average ability in the pulpit.

---

9. Gene E. Moffatt, *The Anatomy of the Ministry* (Atlanta: Pendulum Books, 1966), p. 50.

10. H. Richard Niebuhr in collaboration with Daniel Day Williams and James M. Gustafson, *The Purpose of the Church and Its Ministry: Reflections on the Aims of Theological Education* (New York: Harper and Brothers, 1956), p. 64.

Dr. Mark Gibbs is very penetrating in his analysis of this problem:

> Is the church getting its share of sharp, able young men? There is danger ahead if clergymen are more and more recruited from merely worthy, conscientious, but rather "average" types who may indeed in sheer defensiveness about their modest abilities resent the great strengths of some of the laity and feel at home in the company of their weaker, more insecure, more easily helped members.[11]

While the candidate for the ministry must be finally obedient to what he is assured is the Master's call, he would do well to give careful attention to the sanctified appraisal and advice of his brethren on the ministerial boards of examination. If their judgment confirms one's inner conviction, he is doubly certain. However, should the consensus of these experienced shepherds indicate serious question as to the basic qualifications of the candidate, this might well be taken as God's voice speaking through His Church.

At best, any shepherd worthy of the name goes to the task with a sense of human inadequacy. His best will leave something still to be desired. Success will be contingent upon a generous supply of supernatural assistance which will compensate for deficiencies of which he is painfully aware. But there is one absolute essential without which none can minister effectively. All other gifts and graces are insufficient without it. In the last analysis it separates true shepherds from hired hands. It is . . .

Compassionate Love for the Sheep

After pastoring for several years with less than satisfactory results, one pastor acknowledged that his moment of truth revealed that while he loved God, he really couldn't stand people! Theologically, Christians must and do love everybody. But practically there are worlds of difference between this kind of "love of people for their souls' sake"

---

11. Mark Gibbs, "They Deserve a First-Class Education," *Theological Education* 4, no. 1 (autumn, 1967): 24.

and shepherd-love. The former comes with grace. The latter takes more than grace. People—all sizes, shapes, and descriptions . . . literally good, bad, and indifferent . . . with their humanity painfully apparent. The only possible common denominator is that they're all members of the flock. Some are obviously happy to be. Others seem almost ashamed that they are. Still others are genuinely wayward sheep. How can you really, sincerely love them—all of them?

The only conceivable answer is found in going back to Jesus. In the sixth chapter of Mark's Gospel we find Him taking a day off with His disciples. Nobody needed it more than He. But when they reached their destination, a quiet desert retreat, they found it no longer private but overrun with people. People who wouldn't let well enough alone. People so rude and inconsiderate that they didn't even apologize for aborting His plans for much-needed rest and relaxation. Certainly He would have been justified in telling them to "get lost"! After all, enough is enough. But He didn't. He couldn't. "And Jesus, when he came out, saw much people, and was moved with compassion toward them, because they were as sheep not having a shepherd: and he began to teach them" (Mark 6:34).

COMPASSIONATE LOVE WAS THEN AND ALWAYS WILL BE THE DISTINGUISHING MARK OF THE BONA FIDE SHEPHERD. The kind of concern that goes beyond the line of duty—even on one's day off. Born in the shepherd-heart, this compassion sees beneath the mask and the veneer. It hears the silent cry for help which is never voiced. Real shepherds know that cows may manage without cowboys, but the most helpless thing in the world is a band of sheep without a shepherd.

Compassion means "to suffer with," and the bruises and raw wounds of the littlest lamb hurt the herder just as much as they do the animal. The shepherd identifies with his sheep. That's why pastors never go on strike for an 8-hour day or a 40-hour week. Here's the reason behind the uncomplaining all-night vigil at the bedside of a critically ill child. Shepherd-love mingles the preacher's tears with those of a wayward teenager. Real pastors die a little every time they conduct a funeral. They can't help getting involved with their people and their problems.

Of course the Saviour was making specific reference to His redemptive mission when He spoke of the Good Shepherd laying down His life for the sheep. But there is more. He was also alluding to the sacrificial spirit which must characterize all true shepherding. This selfless devotion to the flock is the sine qua non of pastoral ministry. Without a compassionate love which renders himself and all personal interests expendable in the service of others, no minister—regardless of his other strengths—can achieve genuine shepherdhood. The possession of this cardinal quality compensates for the lack of almost any other ability. Let none undertake this ministry without it.

Other Important Qualities

The index of qualifications necessary for successful shepherding is almost endless. Some of the most vital of these will be discussed in succeeding chapters in relation to the several areas of specific ministry. But one further consideration in this regard is in order.

Presbyterian Pastor David Redding suggests that the true man of God may be identified by asking the right questions about him, such as:

What angers him?
What makes him laugh?
What is important to him?
How does he take failure or success?
What does he cry about?
Can he take blame?
Can he forgive?
How does he treat those who are at his mercy?
Or (how does he treat) those who have him at their mercy?
What would he die for?[12]

R. E. Thompson proposes this test of attitudes as an indication of leadership capacity:

---

12. Redding, *What Is the Man?* p. 14.

Do other people's failures annoy us or challenge us?
Do we use people or cultivate people?
Do we direct people or develop people?
Do we criticize or encourage?
Do we shun the problem person or seek him out?[13]

Honest answers to these questions provide a strong indication whether or not one possesses the basic temperament and disposition for this calling. While none will have an equally high score in all the characteristics, a failing grade in any might well indicate a personality or character flaw which, unless corrected, will sooner or later jeopardize his effectiveness as a pastor. Shepherds now in service might well secure a progress report on their vocational fitness by asking these questions of themselves. Remedial action at points of weakness can not only upgrade the quality of their ministry but also lengthen the tenure of it. Such self-criticism is in itself one of the most important hallmarks of leadership.

---

13. John O. Sanders, *Spiritual Leadership* (Chicago: Moody Press, 1967), p. 28.

He called them; and they . . . followed
him. And . . . he taught them
(Mark 1:20-22, RSV).

The minister . . . will have a thirst
for knowledge, especially of the
Word of God (Manual, par. 401.4).

CHAPTER 2

The Schooling of Shepherds

The biblical precedent is very clear—first, the call; second, the acceptance of the call; third, training for the ministry. Before these two sets of fishermen-brothers (Simon and Andrew, and James and John) were sent out to shepherd, Jesus exposed them to a period of education and orientation. It is significant that their first recorded activity was a learning experience.

Ministerial recruits traditionally have had understandable impatience to fulfill their calling. There is something suspect about anyone's call if it does not have this element of urgency about it. Men are lost. Their darkness cries for the light of the gospel. Time is of the essence, for the night approaches when none can work. No one was more aware of this than the Master, and yet He deliberately gave first priority to a period of instruction. Dr. P. F. Bresee once declared that if he had only 10 years to minister, he would spend the first 5 in preparation. He went on to explain that with proper training he would accomplish more in 5 years than he would in 10 years without this enrichment. This principle is still a valid one.

Part of this tension between the readying period and active service has developed because of the fallacious but all too commonly held idea that the two are mutually exclusive—either education or ministry. Nothing could be farther from the New Testament pattern. *Christ was the Originator of in-service training.* He built no ivory towers where theory would be separated from practice. It was both/and. Newly-called tax collectors and fishermen could not do everything, but they could do something. And as He taught them, our Lord found sacred employment for them which was commensurate with their abilities. In the strictest sense they were not waiting to enter the ministry—they were already in it.

Contemporary ministerial training might well take this page from His book. College sophomores and even many seminary middlers are not ready for the total responsibilities of the pastorate. But if one is genuinely called to this ministry, he ought not to wait until graduation to get into it. *Service should not be an elective.* It ought to be a requirement! Students must be channeled into ministry-related activities as early as possible. Dr. Paul S. Rees has been recognized as one of the most eloquent voices of Protestantism in this century. A master pulpiteer, he inherited significant natural gifts for this ministry. But it is more than coincidental that he began preaching in pre-college days and attributes much of the credit for his proficiency to this learning by doing. To their credit it should be acknowledged that our theological institutions are placing more and more emphasis upon in-service training. May it be accentuated earlier and earlier in the training process.

Formal Preparation

The continually rising educational level in our world makes it imperative that ministerial training keep pace. The early disciples succeeded with only a short course of instruction. Few modern ministers can. This is increasingly true throughout the world. Once-backward nations are emerging from their deprivation thanks to rapidly expanding school systems. Where national preachers were once capable of doing only very elementary Bible school work, now many have high school diplomas and are eligible for college-level studies. Mission policies on ministerial preparation have adjusted accordingly and have made higher education available in many areas.

How much formal training does a minister need? Gene Moffatt answers this question:

> When lack of education is lauded as a virtue it can only be done out of ignorance. Nowhere is education in the total sense of that word more vital than in the ministry. . . . A *minister needs as much training as he can possibly acquire.* The wider his knowledge the better his opportunity to get understanding. The minister need never fear that he might come to know more than is needful. To the extent that his knowledge is limited so, too, is his ministry. *He can rise above all obstacles other than his own ignorance*[1] (italics added).

This evangelical Baptist pastor states the case well. With more laymen having earned not only baccalaureate but also graduate degrees, it is only natural that they expect their pastors to have reached a level of academic preparation comparable to theirs. Is the care of the soul less important than that of the body? Why then should the candidate for the ministry settle for less than the 7-year, college-seminary training period when the physician is judged incapable of entering practice until he has completed a minimum 9- or 10-year medical education?

College

All things being equal, one who anticipates the ministry should begin his preparation with four years of liberal arts education in one of his denomination's colleges. The advantages of a future minister attending one of his own church's institutions are self-evident. General Motors does not send its trainees to Ford Motor Company. The informal indoctrination and orientation as well as the lifetime friend-

---

1. Moffatt, *Anatomy of the Ministry*, pp. 65, 69.

ships which accrue during these years are invaluable by-products. And what better place to find a shepherdess than here? A divisional major in philosophy and religion with good concentrations in English, the social sciences, and psychology constitutes a basic preseminary curriculum. If one decides on another major, he would be wise to minor in religion so that he will have an adequate background for graduate theological studies. The exposure to the full spectrum of subjects available in the liberal arts curriculum provides the enrichment necessary for effective ministry in the last quarter of the twentieth century.

Two very practical electives should also be included in one's course schedule. The first of these is in the area of *speech*. It is strange that so many prospective preachers find time for athletics and the arts (both good) but cannot seem to make room for more speech training than the minimum requirement. Debate and other forensic activities are invaluable preparation for preaching and the additional speaking demands of the ministry. Pity the congregation that must suffer through years of inept pulpit performance at the hands of a pastor who neglected this vital phase of his training. Then, too, one might well take one or more courses in *basic business practice*. Sooner or later the shepherd will find himself involved in the intricacies of mortgage loans, real estate purchase or sale, and church construction. An understanding of these procedures will stand him in good stead.

Understandably, after four years of college one is prone to agree with Solomon that "of making many books there is no end; and much study is a weariness of the flesh" (Eccles. 12:12). The temptation to accept a pastorate or an associate's position is very inviting. Some have successfully followed this procedure for two or three years before going on to seminary. However, others have become so involved in church and family responsibilities that this detour in effect became a dead-end street, robbing them of the golden opportunity of pursuing graduate study. In spite of mental fatigue, the college graduate is wise to proceed immediately to seminary. There will never be an easier time.

Seminary

Notwithstanding the traditional jibes at theological "cemeteries," these three years of advanced study were never more necessary or valuable. A study of seminary curricula has revealed that the major criticisms have centered in (1) the inflexibility of the program which resulted in the student's being unable to select the major emphasis of his studies, and (2) a serious lack of field education.[2] To meet these needs the seminary has done extensive reevaluation of its philosophy of ministerial training. Without doing violence to a proper proportion of biblical and theological requirements, it has broken away from the traditionally regimented curriculum in favor of a more interest- and need-oriented one. Seminarians now enjoy a variety of practical course offerings and a flexibility in scheduling which have made this final phase of their formal education most fulfilling. Opportunities for actual in-service training have been expanded to include even full-time internships.

In addition to its academic function, seminary also provides a very necessary segment of the maturing process. Few students are sufficiently developed in mind and spirit at the end of their undergraduate career to undertake the demanding responsibilities of the pastorate. In the friendly, intellectual climate of this theological "incubator," the fledgling minister can think his way through to a satisfactory understanding of the faith which he is to proclaim. From personal observation I have come to understand the vital role which the seminary can and must play in the spiritual deepening of the ministerial student. Many have testified that it was at seminary chapel altar where they made the final, full commitment and received the Holy Spirit in His entirely sanctifying fullness. Without this experiential certainty the ministry will lack its most important dimension.

Wise, indeed, is the seminarian who finds it possible to

---

2. Nathan M. Pusey and Charles L. Taylor, *Ministry for Tomorrow* (New York: Seabury Press, 1967), pp. 92-95.

serve a student charge or associate pastorate during his last year or years of preparation. This practical involvement will ready him for full-time ministry like no classroom lecture or textbook can.

Alternate Routes

As stated previously, all things being equal the college-seminary course is the preferred educational itinerary. But all things are not always equal. For reasons of age, academic deficiency, or other valid deterrents, some individuals find it impossible to secure this standard preparation. *The door to ministry and ordination must never be barred to those who have a genuine call but are unable to secure the higher levels of formal training.* Numbers of men and women have made a valuable contribution to the Kingdom enterprise in spite of educational disadvantage. Preparation is important, but the person is all-important!

1. BIBLE COLLEGE

An increasing number of young adults are being called from their "nets" (lathes, tractors, or desks) to become fishers of men. In their twenties or thirties and with family responsibilities, many cannot conceivably undertake the long and costly preparation which the younger, single student can afford. The church has very wisely made provisions for such persons to secure Bible college training. This concentrated three-year program provides the studies necessary to meet ordination requirements. Experience has proved that those who have pursued this course conscientiously have received mental stimulation, spiritual enrichment, and practical skills which have enabled them to render commendable ministerial service.

Denominational growth almost invariably results in a serious shortage of pastors, especially for the smaller churches. The seminary does not produce enough graduates to meet this demand. The Bible college feeds into this stream of supply a significant number of dedicated young ministers who provide shepherdless flocks with much-needed pastoral leadership. While it was never intended to be and should never become the standard method of preparation, the Bible college program serves a very valuable purpose in educating its particular clientele.

2. HOME STUDY

In some extreme cases individuals are unable to avail themselves of even Bible college training. To these the church makes available a course of study which may be pursued at home under the supervision of the district board of ministerial studies and the general Department of Education and the Ministry. At best this method of instruction which must of necessity be carried on largely through correspondence leaves much to be desired. However, diligent application to the prescribed curriculum can provide a basic understanding of the most fundamental areas of ministerial training and make one eligible for ordination.

3. CONTINUING EDUCATION

Regardless of the length and depth of one's academic preparation, the slaking of the "thirst for knowledge" is a never-ending endeavor. Consideration will be given in a later chapter to the absolute necessity of a disciplined, systematic study program after the completion of formal training. Without this any minister will suffer a fatal case of intellect arrest. While this malady produces only a feeling of malaise in its early stages, unless corrected by strong doses of mental stimulation it will inevitably result in a lingering ecclesiastical death which is equally painful to both preacher and congregation.

Out of a growing concern at the point of the number of pastors who drop out of the ministry prematurely, serious consideration is being given to ways in which ministerial manpower may be more effectively conserved. Dr. Donald Super has charted the career of the shepherd in the following way.[3]

---

3. Ross P. Scherer and Theodore O. Wedel, *The Church and Its Manpower Management* (New York: National Council of Churches of Christ in the U.S.A., 1966), pp. 65-74.

Late Formal Education	The Establishment Stage	Midcareer Stage	Pre-retirement	Retirement
Trial Period	Advancement Period			

Entrance into each of these stages is often accompanied by crisis.

The first of these, and perhaps the most critical, comes at the close of the *trial period*. A study of 4,908 ministers revealed that 42 percent identified their major stress period as coming in the first five years of their ministry. One-fourth of them reported that the first or second year was the first of these periods.[4] Contributing to this stress is the shock of reconciling the theoretical idealism of formal training with the practical realism of the first pastorate. Mark Rouch deduces that this trial period will have one of two basic outcomes: *stabilization* or *floundering*.[5] And floundering all too often leads to frustration and sooner than later to vocational failure.

Those who successfully negotiate the *trial period* enter the *advancement period* which is concurrent with the *establishment stage*. This 10- to 15-year segment is usually a rather stable period marked by personal progress and some measure of achievement.

The second major crisis usually comes at the *midcareer stage*—for most ministers in their forties. During "middlescence," "the search for identity and meaning are strikingly similar to adolescence."[6] To many, this stocktaking reveals that young adult years have passed, and goals which were set in the beginning days of their ministry have not been realized. Some of their peers have advanced more rapidly

---

4. Edgar W. Mills and John P. Koral, *Stress in the Ministry* (Washington: Ministry Studies Board, 1971), p. 11.
5. Mark A. Rouch, *Competent Ministry* (Nashville: Abingdon Press, 1974), p. 107.
6. *Ibid.*, p. 122.

than they have. Awareness that more and more strong churches are looking for pastors who are characterized by the magic words *young* and *sharp* brings a growing sense of insecurity to the man who faces a decreasing amount of both of these qualifications.

Ministerial fallout at this period is alarmingly high. At the time when they should be moving into their highest productivity, too many surrender to professional defeat. Others conclude that they are too old to start another vocational career and settle into a virtual *management stage* where they are content to maintain the level of achievement reached in the establishment stage. This lack of productivity results in a sterility in performance which leads to a lack of demand for their services and early, unhappy retirement.

The church is beginning to respond to this need with a purposefully structured program of continuing education. Hopefully it will build a bridge across these periods of potential crisis in the minister's career. By providing courses of instruction in such subjects as pastoral leadership, church management, and biblical preaching, fresh motivation and new methodology are transfused into the vocational bloodstream of those who are floundering. Periodic exposure to these times of mental renewal complement the traditional pastors' retreats where primary emphasis is placed upon spiritual renewal.

Wise indeed is the man of God who avails himself of these opportunities for intellectual stimulation. There is no graduation from the school of learning for the pastor who serves his Lord with maximum effectiveness.

The Lord is my shepherd . . . he leadeth me (Ps. 23:1-2).

The pastor shall *give leadership to the evangelism, education, devotion, and expansion programs of the local church* (*Manual*, par. 109.13).

CHAPTER 3

The Leadership Role of the Shepherd

If the congregation is to enjoy the delights of green pastures and still waters, it must be led there by the pastor-shepherd. This is a sobering responsibility. Like Moses and Gideon, most ministers feel totally incapable of filling this role. But God's call provides the necessary assurance that He sees potential leadership in these whom He has summoned to the shepherding task. Diligent application to the development of effective skills will produce satisfactory proficiency in this area.

Gen. (President) Dwight D. Eisenhower's book *At Ease* should be required reading for every minister. From a very modest beginning he rose to the highest level of both military and political leadership. He gives this profile of the basic qualities of the successful leader:

> Men who can do things are going to be sought out just as surely as the sun rises in the morning. Fake reputations, habits of glib and clever speech, and glittering surface performances are going to be discovered and kicked overboard! Solid, sound leadership with inexhaustible nervous energy to

spur the efforts of lesser men, and ironclad determination to face discouragement, risk, and increasing work without flinching are imperative. Added to this he must have a strong tinge of imagination. . . . Finally, he must be able to forget himself and his personal fortunes.[1]

How interesting that this description of secular leadership should climax with the necessity of self-forgetfulness. If this is true in the army and in the government, how much truer it is in the church. It is the "kiss of death" for a preacher's work to betray any indications of self-serving or political motivation. There is a place for legitimate ministerial aspiration, but it must always be genuinely sanctified ambition. After 50 years of evangelistic ministry, Dr. Vance Havner could write: "No man with God's message need politick, nor pull wires, nor sit hunched over cafeteria tables making contacts, nor wait for some talent scout to find him. He need not chase key men around if he knows the Keeper of the Keys!"[2] This eminent Southern Baptist testifies to the infilling of the Holy Spirit as a second crisis experience and identifies this as the enablement for self-effacing, Christ-exalting service.[3] If the cleansing of the heart means anything, it means a sublime release from carnal concern about personal ministerial fortunes.

Authority—Right and Wrong

A careful reading of the New Testament reveals that authority, in itself, is not wrong. We have allowed some unfortunate connotations of authority as exercised in our world to color our thinking on this subject. Authority in the church is different from that outside it, basically because of *the way the leader exercises his authority*. This begins with his *servant role*. Jesus spelled this out in Matt. 20:25-27: "Ye know that the princes of the Gentiles exercise

---

1. Dwight D. Eisenhower, *At Ease* (New York: Doubleday and Co., 1967), p. 254.
2. Vance Havner, *Living in Kingdom Come* (Westwood, N.J.: Fleming H. Revell Co., 1967), p. 12.
3. *Ibid.*, pp. 28-29.

dominion over them, and they that are great exercise authority upon them. But it shall not be so among you: but whosoever will be great among you, let him be your minister; and whosoever will be chief among you, let him be your servant." This concept is unique and adds a fundamental dimension to the exercise of leadership in the church. No true shepherd should ever forget it.

Then, the minister's authority is *self-authenticating.* As a God-called leader, his life and ministry will document his authority. His "authority rests in his ordination by God and in the faithfulness with which he lives and teaches his message. The authority is intrinsic. Thus the Christian leader has no need to demand or to scheme, to politick or to plot."[4]

Successful leadership is contingent upon the ability to find the median between two equally dangerous aberrations.

1. *The autocratic, dictatorial abuse of authority.* David Redding reminds us that "Joseph's hardest test was power. The life of slavery, the temptations of women were little things compared to the peril of sinning with the scepter."[5] Evidently the Apostle Peter sensed this problem area in the Early Church. In his timeless advices to elders he cautions against "lording it over" your charges (1 Pet. 5:3, NASB). Dag Hammarskjöld was entrusted with one of the most crucial assignments in recent history when he was elected the first secretary-general of the United Nations. His pattern of leadership was exemplary. Out of this experience he wrote, "Position never gives you the right to command. It only imposes the duty of so living that others can receive your orders without being humiliated."[6] The basic difference here is between leading and driving. Tyrants and despots drive. Real leaders lead.

A safeguard against this temptation to autocracy is *seeing the ministerial office not as special privilege but rather as a*

---

4. Lawrence O. Richards, *A New Face for the Church* (Grand Rapids, Mich.: Zondervan Publishing House, 1970), p. 118.

5. Redding, *What Is the Man?* p. 21.

6. Dag Hammarskjöld, *Markings,* trans. Leif Sjöberg and W. H. Auden (New York: Alfred A. Knopf, 1964), p. 105.

particular responsibility. It must be properly related to the scriptural chain of command. Christ is the Head of the Church, and all ecclesiastical authority derives from living under His lordship. Through the ordination commitment the minister places himself under the authority of the church as administered through its duly constituted leadership. In turn the local congregation relates itself to the properly constituted pastoral authority. A lack of respect for and responsibility to the higher level of authority in each case will result in anarchy with its attendant evils. The pastor who disregards the supervision of his denominational superiors creates a climate of disrespect in his church which will ultimately lead to a lack of regard for his leadership on the part of his parishioners. The same is true in the higher echelons of administration.

2. *Failure to assume the proper stance of leadership.* This peril is just as dangerous as the first. It may cloak itself in an honest attempt to display genuine Christian humility. However, if this commendable effort results in a leadership vacuum, dire consequences will inevitably follow. Kyle Haselden points out the inherent peril in letting the pew rule the pulpit until the pastor becomes only a paid special speaker. People will respect our high calling in Jesus Christ only if preachers respect it themselves, he observes.[7] If laymen preempt the leadership role which is clearly designated to the pastor in both Bible and *Manual*, the fault must lie at the parsonage door. Congregational sheep are generally willing to be led if the shepherd is ready to lead.

Creative Leadership

There are no such words as *status quo* in the vocabulary of a truly New Testament church. Therefore, leadership must involve more than just caretaking. In his excellent book *Spiritual Leadership*, J. Oswald Sanders states the

---

7. Kyle Haselden, *The Urgency of Preaching* (New York: Harper and Row, 1963), pp. 106-7.

case in these words: "Some have more gift for conserving gains than for initiating new ventures. . . . The true leader must have venturesomeness as well as vision."[8] Achieving churches are the result of imaginative pastoral direction. Most lay leaders will respond enthusiastically to fresh, creative programs and procedures. This does not mean that every church is ready for extensive overhauling immediately. Dr. A. E. Sanner, veteran district superintendent, wisely counseled that two major changes might be a safe limit in one's first year, or else the third change could be the pastor! However, variety adds spice to church life, and the majority of the flock will welcome variations from their customary practices.

Only a very small percentage of ministers is gifted with the ability to innovate. All too many could spend a week in a "think tank" and come out with nothing more than a headache. But every man can be an imitator. There are very few copyrights in the Kingdom. Wise pastors who sense their limitations in creativity will become successful borrowers. Denominational headquarters and publishing houses make available a continual supply of practical materials on church programming and promotion. Wide-awake boards provide their pastors with travel allowances so that they can visit pace-setting churches, counsel with their ministers, and bring home ideas and plans which can be adapted to their needs.

There may be a variety of excuses but there are no real reasons for churches to exist in a near fatal state of lethargy and sheer boredom. Any pastor can have access to methods and materials which will awaken the sleepiest saints and spark a surge of new vitality in the most lifeless congregation.

Ministerial Motivation

Church growth and achievement begins not with better-laid plans but with better-motivated people. And this starts

---

8. Sanders, *Spiritual Leadership,* p. 116.

with the shepherd-leader. Periodically the man of God should give attention to his own basic motivation.

Because their wage negotiations had broken off, the pilots of one of the major airlines instituted what they termed the W.O.E. program. These letters stood for "Withdrawal Of Enthusiasm." Passengers were met by a sustained silence from the cockpit. There was no "Welcome aboard!" No announcement was made of ground speed, altitude, or projected arrival time. No travelogue was given. Only the basic services were supplied.

When the ministry becomes just a matter of minimums and all enthusiasm has been withdrawn, the matter of incentives should be carefully examined. In Peter's treatise on pastoral practice referred to earlier, he admonishes that care of the flock should not be monetarily motivated—"not for filthy lucre" (1 Pet. 5:2). The minister's support is a legitimate responsibility of the church. Bishop Gerald Kennedy once stated that the poorest bargain in the world is an underpaid preacher. But by the same token, better salaries do not guarantee better ministers. The pay will never be good enough if we are just working for wages. However, men who are properly motivated and see the work of the Kingdom prosper will in turn find that their congregations are better able and more willing to increase their salaries.

It is even more necessary that there be proper and adequate motivation when church operations are not producing visible results. At best there will be some low ebbs in this enterprise. Whitlock describes the successful minister as "the kind of person who can encounter frustration and temporary failure, and be able to rebound rather than capitulate to defeat."[9] Such fortitude is an absolute necessity. But what fuels this ability to bounce back? How can one maintain the dynamic enthusiasm so imperative in effective leadership?

The apostle provides the authoritative answer when he

_____

9. Glenn E. Whitlock, *From Call to Service* (Philadelphia: Westminster Press, 1968), p. 88.

identifies the only adequate motivation in these words: "Because you are eager to serve the Lord" (1 Pet. 5:2, TLB). There is no other expedient. We are not serving the superintendent—either district or general. Our service stewardship is *through* the church, not *to* it. *We do it for Jesus' sake!* And that imparts a kind of glory to even the most mundane tasks. Here is the source of the eagerness to serve that lifts our ministry above minimums. This is the secret of maintaining the necessary romance in our vocation. It was love slavery at the beginning. It must always be so. There is a constancy about this motivation that is impervious to changing circumstances and fluctuating emotions. It will endure when all secondary incentives are exhausted.

The Minister as Motivator

This basic personal motivation equips one in turn to be an effective motivator. Laymen's service must be elevated from *have to* to *want to*. Duty is good but not good enough. If not raised to a higher motivational plane, it will almost invariably devolve into drudgery. No other shepherding skill is more pivotal than that of being able to lift the incentive level of the sheep.

Dr. Richard LeTourneau, in *Management Plus,* writes:

> Motivation cannot be created simply by following a set of rules or conditions. . . . Motivation is a characteristic which develops spontaneously when the proper conditions, circumstances, and attitudes are present. One of the main conditions or attitudes that contributes to this motivation is the enthusiasm and drive of you, the manager.[10]

Essentially, *motivation is a man, not a method.* It can be caught better than taught. And it is more contagious than measles! Don't apologize for asking your people to "follow the leader" in this regard. Paul didn't. In dealing with the problem church at Corinth, which had among its other needs a lack of understanding of proper motivation, he

---

10. Richard LeTourneau, *Management Plus* (Grand Rapids, Mich.: Zondervan Publishing House, 1973), p. 64.

went so far as to say, "Follow my example, as I follow Christ's" (1 Cor. 11:1, NEB). This involved more than just the fact of following. Here was a selfless challenge to emulate the ardor and single-minded devotion with which he served his Lord.

Listen to Eisenhower's words again: "Leadership with *inexhaustible . . . energy to spur the efforts of lesser men*" (italics added). This is the public demonstration of that inner motivation. How do I energize others? By being more energetic myself. How do I get others to work harder? By working harder myself. Don't expect to follow Christ at a snail's pace and expect your people to sprint. Too many ministers find genuine renewal at a convention or retreat and then just come home and talk about it. As soon as the glow wears off, it's "business as usual." Small wonder that congregations don't get excited. They're waiting to see the difference demonstrated. A new evangelistic zeal in the pulpit. A fresh passion for personal soul winning. A driving concern which makes pastoral calling more than perfunctory and sets a pattern for lay visitation.

Another key to effective motivation is the leader's "*credibility.*" There is no way to estimate the amount of good which could be done if no thought were given to who would receive the credit for it. LeTourneau comments,

> The ultimate degree to which you can motivate people to action . . . involves taking an idea . . . and then convincing your co-worker . . . that it is his idea, not yours. He will become very enthusiastic about something he feels is his idea because he has identified with it. . . . You should be more interested in getting the job done than in getting credit for it.[11]

This selfless strategy is another evidence of exemplary leadership motivation.

Like Shepherd, Like Sheep

Someone has wisely observed that every great institution is the lengthening shadow of a great man. This truth has a

---

11. *Ibid.,* pp. 84-85.

universal application. Mr. Eisenhower in his discussion of leadership comments, "You can judge a . . . unit merely by knowing its commander. . . . The exact level of a commander's personality and ability is always reflected in his unit."[12]

What a frightening responsibility rests upon the pastor (commander). His church will be an accurate copy of its leader. No other human influence will be as formative as his. In the words of the plaque which President Harry S. Truman kept on his desk, "The buck stops here!" It cannot be passed on to anyone else.

But what a challenging opportunity! By precept and example the godly shepherd can reproduce an exemplary godliness in his flock. His faithful discipleship will be mirrored in theirs. His ethical patterns will become theirs. Through shared concerns for this common cause they will be welded together in a spiritual union until "the commander and the unit are almost one and the same thing."[13] This battle-ready army is now prepared to wage aggressive warfare for its Commander in Chief.

---

12. Eisenhower, *At Ease*, p. 253.
13. *Ibid.*

*It is only and always the coming
together of believers which constitutes
a church* (Lawrence O. Richards).[1]

CHAPTER 4

Shepherding Through
Church Services

"O day of rest and gladness"—the hymnwriter's tribute
to the Christian sabbath. Gladness, yes. But for the minister—rest, no! It is the "day of all the week the best" (and
busiest) for the shepherd. But honestly now, is all this pastoral activity really necessary? Is it still imperative that the
flock be gathered for feeding, watering, and other spiritual
care? Is Heb. 10:25 still relevant when it advises, "Let us
not give up meeting together, as some are in the habit of
doing" (NIV)? Perhaps it is time to reexamine the rationale
for these Sunday services.

Public Worship

The word *worship* in its most basic form means "worth-
ship." Whatever one attaches the most worth to in his life
becomes the center of his worship. Despite the increasing
commercialization of Sunday, it is still the day for rest and
worship. What a person does with this day is a declaration
of what he worships, whether it is working in his garden,

---

1. Richards, *New Face for the Church*, p. 105.

cheering for his favorite professional football team, going
fishing, or going to church.

But why worship God publicly? Jay Rochelle gives this
answer to those who argue that they worship in the mountains and meadows:

> We also worship because, by so doing, we are saying to
> the world—when we are serious about our worship life—that
> the preliminary things don't count in any final way. . . .
> There is a recognizable danger in the lives of those who
> have "given up" worship in a community experience such as
> the Sunday service. They may wind up worshiping nothing
> at all. . . . They will not receive much in the way of com-
> munication from God in the field. God communicates through
> his community. He speaks to us in the needs and in the
> words of others.[2]

In his book *The Worship of the Early Church*, Ferdinand
Hahn concludes that "the coming together of the faithful is
the significant feature of Christian worship."[3] While there
is both time and place for solitary meditation, Christianity
is dependent upon the body life which derives from regular,
communal worship. Nothing else will compensate for it.
The strength drawn from fellow worshipers is an integral
part of the Christian's spiritual sustenance.

But several guiding principles should be followed to
guarantee that public worship achieves its full potential.

1. *It should be inclusive.* While the major thrust will
naturally be to those of the household of faith, none should
be excluded from the scope of its ministry. There must be
elements which speak to both saint and sinner, member and
visitor, old and young. The "church services" conducted by
Jesus certainly set this pattern. The despised tax collector
was as much a part of this worship experience as was the
pious Pharisee. The Saviour's ministry reached out to both.

---

2. Jay C. Rochelle, *Create and Celebrate* (Philadelphia: Fortress Press,
1971), pp. 5-6.
3. Ferdinand Hahn, *The Worship of the Early Church*, trans. David E.
Green, ed. John Reumann (Philadelphia: Fortress Press, 1973), p. 36.

2. *Form must contribute to communication.* David H. C. Read makes this indictment: "The message of Christ is often sealed off by the wrappings of organization and ritual."[4] What a tragedy! Instead of serving the purpose of exalting and exposing our Lord, some of our traditional worship forms can become an end in themselves and actually obscure the view from the pew. A pastor should periodically take a careful look at each of the components of his services and ask himself, "How effectively does this convey spiritual truth to the first-time worshiper, to the teenager, or to the mature Christian?" No matter how long or widely a form has been used, if it has outgrown its usefulness it should be abandoned in favor of something which will clarify and amplify communication.

But a word of caution is in order at this point. Some congregations are more susceptible to change than others. The shepherd must bring the whole flock along with him. He is wise to test the wind with minor innovations before proposing more radical ones. Explanation of why the new procedure is being used and what it is intended to accomplish will help to secure acceptance of it.

3. *True worship produces response.* It is not a program put on by the pastor and the musicians for the benefit of an audience. It should be a shared experience. Worshiper participation should not be limited to such "knee-jerk" activities as congregational singing and giving in the offering. James F. White makes this pertinent observation:

> The forms of response of recent past have been tied to a tight concept of good taste. The period of 1920-1970 has been a period of respectability for Protestant worship. . . . We got embarrassed out of the fervent "amen" during the sermons or the exclamation of "hallelujah" at any point in the service. . . . Anything spontaneous disappeared and the service became as smooth as butter. Nothing unexpected

---

4. David H. C. Read, *Religion Without Wrappings* (Grand Rapids, Mich.: Wm. B. Eerdmans Publishing Co., 1970), p. 211.

happened. . . . Few of us noticed that the fastest growing churches . . . tended to be [those] with an emphasis on spontaneity in worship. The unexpected could and did happen.[5]

This is certainly not to make a case for unplanned services which work up emotional response with the use of cheap psychological inducements. This is a sacrilegious travesty. But it is a plea for the right kind of freedom in worship which makes it natural for laymen to respond. On occasion it may be in the form of a "fervent amen." Or it may take the form of a silent tear tracing its way down the cheek of one who responds to the message of the preacher or singer. Still again it may be a spontaneous testimony which will be used by the Spirit to charge the atmosphere with warmth and blessing and even change the whole order of the service. Such genuine response is always in order and is a real part of the genius of the New Testament church. It is one of the hallmarks of true worship.

4. *Coming must eventuate in going.* While worship is based upon the premise of coming together, it is not complete until it produces dynamics which propel the worshiping church back into the world to become the working church. Dr. Findley Edge levels the charge that too much of the life and program of the modern church are built around what he terms "come" structures, leaving the impression that "if you don't come to our meetings, then we have no ministry for you."[6] In all honesty this is too true too much of the time. But the very designation "worship service" testifies that there is no real worship without accompanying service. *And laymen do not serve by sitting in the pew!* They are served by the pastor and those who assist him in ministering. Service begins when "the service" ends.

Dr. Kenneth Chafin makes an interesting analogy at this point. He compares church meetings to practice sessions of

5. James F. White, *New Forms of Worship* (Nashville: Abingdon Press, 1971), p. 48.

6. Findley B. Edge, *The Greening of the Church* (Waco, Tex.: Word Books, 1971), p. 163.

a football team. The depth of motivation during practice is directly related to the importance of the game to be played on Saturday. He deduces that it is increasingly difficult to get members out to practice (church services) because we spend all our time practicing and never play the "game on Saturday."[7]

The solution for this problem lies in identifying worship with ministry. A careful study of the Scriptures reveals that while the Old Testament issues a continuous call to worship, the New Testament contains next to none. The reason— worship experiences have ceased to be an end in themselves and are now viewed in the context of ministry. Christians met together to receive spiritual renewal through worship so that they could go out to confront their world with their Christ. This was the total task of the total church. Paul Benjamin rightly insists that in this light "the Sunday morning service of the congregation should be looked upon as a meeting of the ministers of the church."[8] Just as the missionary is dispatched to his assignment from a special sending service, so every worshiping Christian layman should view Sunday's meetings as "sending services" which launch him or her out into a week of witnessing on his personal mission field. One pastor keeps this objective before his congregation by concluding the order of service with this directive following the benediction: "Departing to share and serve March 10-15" (dates of the following week). This is not a revolutionary, new concept. It is simply a rediscovery of the basic principle of New Testament Christianity which the modern church by and large has either forgotten or neglected. May the day soon come in every church when in fact "there is no longer any distinction in principle between assembly for worship and the service of Christians in the world."[9]

---

7. *Ibid.*, p. 165.
8. Paul Benjamin, *How in the World?* (Lincoln, Ill.: Lincoln Christian College Press, 1973), p. 64.
9. Hahn, *Worship of the Early Church*, p. 38.

Planning and Preparing

Effective services do not just happen. They are the result of careful, prayerful preparation. Early in the week planning should begin on one's knees. With the memories of the previous Lord's Day still fresh, the shepherd does well to seek the guidance of the Spirit as to the direction which the next Sunday's services should take. He alone knows who will be present and what their needs will be. The consequences of failing to relate to these people and their problems may be fatal. What a blessed assurance it is to know that you have been sensitive to divine leadership and have drawn on the resources of His omniscience. Then it is not surprising to have parishioners comment as they leave the church, "That service was just what I needed!"

A final prayer check is in order early Sunday morning. Some pastors closet themselves with the Lord privately. I have preferred a time of prayer at the church altar with the select saints who volunteer to keep this tryst. The intercessory lift of their prayers has proved invaluable. The petitions which they voice help to point the way for pulpit prayers which relate to contemporary needs. This atmosphere is conducive to an openness to any last-minute instructions which the Holy Spirit may wish to give concerning the day's activities.

Variety not only adds spice to life—it adds zest to services. Gone forever should be the outdated idea that the format of services must be exactly the same as it has been each Sunday for 40 years! Small wonder that laymen's appetites become jaded when the sabbath's menu is exactly the same every week. Familiarity breeds boredom if not contempt. Why not arouse the sanctified curiosity of parishioners by varying the order and ingredients of the services so that they won't know exactly what to expect when they come to church? While we have traditionally identified the morning service as "worship" and the evening hour as "evangelistic," this order is not sacrosanct. There is wisdom in the strategy of surprising some "Sunday morning only" parishioners with a strong emphasis on evangelism occasionally. And there is certainly nothing wrong with making the theme of a night service one which relates to missions or some phase of Christian living.

This same principle applies to *the hour of the service*. Too frequent change can be confusing, of course. But occasionally it is well to give consideration to whether there would be value in adjusting the times of meeting. For years 11 a.m. and 7:30 p.m. were considered standard service hours. But many churches now begin the Sunday school session at 9:30 a.m. and morning worship at 10:45, giving an additional 15 minutes before noon.

With more and more youth meetings shifting to weeknights or following the evening service, the trend is toward beginning on Sunday night as early as six o'clock. In farming communities, "chore time" would dictate a later hour, of course. There are several definite advantages to the earlier service:

1. *Security.* In metropolitan areas people are increasingly concerned about being out at night because of widespread crime and violence. Starting early allows them to get home before dark much of the year.

2. *Fellowship.* Even if there is an altar service, the evening is still young and affords an excellent opportunity for after-service fellowship. This can be a very convenient time for inviting visitors and new members out for refreshments and a time of getting acquainted. This is a basic New Testament concept, for Acts 2:42 reports that the converts won on the Day of Pentecost not only devoted themselves to the apostles' teaching and prayer but also "to the fellowship [and] to the breaking of bread" (NIV). An added inducement to young couples is the providing of attendants in the nursery for a period of time after the service so that small children can be left there while their parents enjoy a time of fellowship.

First impressions are tremendously important, and careful planning should be made for the greeting of every visitor and member. Some pastors and their wives station themselves at the main entrance to the building to welcome their people. Others prefer to greet them at the close of the service. In any event, a warm, friendly greeter should be assigned to each door to give a handshake and personal welcome to each worshiper. First-time visitors may be directed to the guest book or given cards to sign. Some churches have a registration of all members and friends during the service. But the name and address of every new person should be secured in some way. Ushers should be stationed in each aisle to seat the people. It is a breach of etiquette and poor public relations for visitors to have to find their own seats.

These first contacts may well determine whether a person feels welcome or not and whether he will return.

The Order of Service

Whether an order of service is printed in the bulletin or not, there should be order in each service. God gets no glory out of the disorder that results from poor planning. If an order is printed for the morning service and none is given for the evening (as too many churches have done), one of two inferences can be drawn:

1. The morning service is more important and deserves better preparation; or

2. Sunday morning is more formal and Sunday evening more free. Neither is necessarily true, but if a complete printed program is in order for one service, it should also be for the other. My personal preference is the listing of the musical selections and sermon topics for each service rather than a complete order. It has been my experience that this practice contributes to a spirit of freedom and spontaneity while the printed program tends to encourage rigidity and ritualism. If a complete order is not printed, ministers and musicians should know the sequence in which their participation takes place. Of course all programming is subject to change at any time should the Holy Spirit choose to set aside human plans in favor of a special divine order of the day.

THE SERMON IS THE CENTERPIECE OF THE SUNDAY SERVICE, so all planning starts here. Once the subjects for morning and evening have been selected, the other segments of the service should be fitted together so that they will all point toward the pulpit. The exception to this rule would be on occasions where a special musical presentation would provide the message through song rather than sermon.

MUSIC. The ministry of Christian song is second in importance only to that of the preaching of the Word. As soon as the sermon subjects for the coming Lord's Day have been selected, the pastor should confer with his music director on the choice of the hymns and special music for the services.

It is wise for the pastor to choose at least the congregational songs which will be used in the morning service. If the person who directs the music selects those which will be used in the evening, he/she should be guided by the theme of the pastor's message and should pick hymns and gospel songs which will be contributive. Attention should be given to a good mixture of the great traditional hymns of the church written by the Wesleys, Watts, and others, and the more contemporary gospel songs and choruses. Both have their place in both morning and evening services, and neither should be used to the exclusion of the other. While congregational participation in the ministry of music is important, it is equally important that this portion of the service not consume too much time or energy. Two such selections in the morning and three at night should be sufficient.

The choir plays a most important part in creating the atmosphere and conveying the message of the service. Every church should have one! Many should have more than one. More and more smaller congregations have members who have some musical training or experience and who can direct adult, youth, or children's choirs. The use of such choirs not only provides the opportunity for involvement for those who sing but also results in the attendance of relatives and friends who will come to bring young people and children and stay to hear them sing. Wise is the pastor who employs this strategy of maximum participation.

Choir robes serve a useful purpose in maintaining uniformity and modesty, but they are not an absolute necessity. Some larger churches have discontinued their use and allow choir members to find seats in the congregation while the offering is being taken. This makes them feel more included in the sermon and also results in less distraction during the message than when they remain seated behind the preacher.

Special numbers by the choir, small ensembles, and soloists add to the effectiveness of the service. The evening meeting often allows more latitude for such presentations. Adequate preparation is imperative if the messages in song are to make a spiritual impact upon the listeners. Sufficient rehearsal must be done so that poor execution will not draw attention away from the truth which is being communicated. It must be more than a performance. Musicians should be instructed to prepare their hearts in prayer so that God can speak through their ministry in song.

SCRIPTURE READING. One of the most neglected means of grace in evangelical church services is the reading of the Word. But if the Bible is indeed God's written Revelation, what is more important? If people know that a prominent place in the service will be given to scripture reading, they will be more faithful in bringing the Word with them. Occasionally the reading of a passage in unison by the congregation from their Bibles is a welcome change from the regular responsive readings in the hymnal. Using laymen, staff members, or youth in this segment of the service is also effective. The lesson should complement the theme of the service and may or may not be the passage from which the sermon will be preached.

Until such a time as another version replaces the King James as the most commonly used, it is my opinion that it is wise to use the KJV for public scripture reading. The beauty of its English is timeless, and more people relate to its wordings than to those of any other translation. The use of more contemporary versions for sermonic exegesis is understandable, of course. But for congregational reading the KJV is preferable.

PRAYER. Invocation, offertory, and benediction prayers are important and may be assigned to staff members and laymen on occasion. Visiting ministers may well be invited to offer the main prayer in the evening service. But almost without exception the morning worship prayer should be offered by the pastor. This is one of his most meaningful shepherdly functions. No one else is quite so well equipped to bring the needs of his people to God as he.

One of the most beneficial innovations in public prayer is the use of the *open altar*. As the choir sings an appropriate prayer chorus, the pastor invites those who would like to bring special praise or petition to the Lord to come forward and kneel at the altar, representing the whole congregation. The impact of this spiritual exercise often transforms prayer time into one of the most blessed and meaningful parts of the service. Personal victories have often been won by those gathered at the altar for this tryst with God. The pastor may wish to kneel on the inside of the altar as he leads out in prayer. His spontaneous intercession for the needs of those present, those absent because of illness, those in authority, and those in need around the world is one of his most vital contributions to the life of the congregation. A prayer begun with thanksgiving and concluded with a confident affirmation of faith and victory leads the flock to higher ground.

The congregational posture for prayer may be varied from time to time. Standing, sitting, or kneeling are all in order. However, since some people are physically unable to kneel and are embarrassed to remain seated when others are on their knees, it is not wise to use this posture too frequently.

Another consideration is *prayer language* (not to be confused with glossolalia!). Traditionally we have employed the King James Version form of address to Deity—"Thee" and "Thou." But there is a strong trend to change to contemporary terminology. Daniel Stevick comments:

> If language moves on while that portion of language which is used for worship remains static, no one notices for a long time. The specialness of the language of worship seems to reflect the specialness of worship itself. . . . But the

language of worship must also have a bond with everyday speech and common reality.[10]

No less an authority than William Barclay points out that the name "Abba" which Jesus used repeatedly in addressing His Father and which Paul twice says is our Spirit-given privilege to use is precisely equivalent to our English word *Daddy*. He goes on to comment that it seems a contradiction in terms to address this God whom we know so intimately in Elizabethan English which no one has used for 300 years. He concludes: "I do not talk to my best friend like that. God is my best friend. How can I talk to him like that?"[11]

Another writer observes, "When worship is cast in language which is out of date, the implication is that worship as a whole is out of date."[12] Without reducing the reverence with which God should be approached, the pastor might well give attention to terminology which will make prayer the most meaningful experience possible.

VISITOR GREETING AND ANNOUNCEMENTS. An increasing number of pastors recognize visitors and make their announcements at the very beginning of the worship hour even before the choir comes in. This leaves the service free of all matters which may disrupt the spirit of worship. It also enables the pastor to break down any barriers of strangeness and establish rapport. Whenever verbal announcements are made, they should be at a minimum. Doesn't it seem strange to go to the time and expense of printing the activity calendar in the bulletin and then take the congregation's time to repeat this information? Actually this is an affront to their intelligence and literacy! Just a reminder to check the bulletin for the announcements should be sufficient. Some churches have a "Visitors' Moment" when the congregation stands and greets guests who have been requested to remain seated. Others

---

10. Daniel B. Stevick, *Language in Worship* (New York: Seabury Press, 1970), p. 3.

11. William Barclay, *Daily Celebration*, ed. Denis Duncan (Waco, Tex.: Word Books, 1971), pp. 119-20.

12. Rochelle, *Create and Celebrate*, p. 15.

read the names of visitors and have them stand. The time devoted to making guests feel at home is well spent and should be carefully planned.

OFFERING. A well-trained corps of ushers is a necessity if the offering is to be taken with a minimum of time and confusion. Lengthy exhortations regarding the financial support of the church are completely out of order. In the offertory prayer the pastor may thank the Lord for His goodness, identify some of the Christian causes to which the offering will go, and pronounce a biblical blessing on the faithful stewards who are bringing in their tithes and offerings. Periodically it may be well to vary the order, sometimes praying before and sometimes after the offering is taken.

The importance of carefully weaving these essential components into a well-ordered service is reflected in this statement by William L. Howse:

> If the pastor plans all the worship services of the church in such a way that the members are led to have fellowship with God through the leadership of the Holy Spirit, the worshipers will know more of God through this experience than they can know through other channels. Concepts will develop through worship which cannot be as accurately conveyed in any other way.[13]

Sacraments and Special Services

The administration of the sacraments is one of the pastor's most sacred responsibilities and most blessed privileges. Between the two extremes of sacramentarianism with its baptismal regeneration and transubstantiation; and non-sacramentarianism with its total lack of observance, there is a happy medium of correct emphasis. P. T. Forsyth comments: "Sacraments, and not socialities, make the centre of our church life. . . . Make much of them. Clothe them with

---

13. William L. Howse, *The Church Staff and Its Work* (Nashville: Broadman Press, 1959), p. 12.

great seemliness, great earnestness, great reverence, great, but not formidable solemnity."[14] He comments further, "There can be no doubt whatever that baptism and the Eucharist stood for far more in the Apostolic Church than they do in the estimation of the bulk of the members of the Free Churches today."[15]

The meaning and witness of both are timeless, and rather than being antique and outmoded worship forms, they are most contemporary.

> It has become common in recent years to talk about multimedia worship as if it were something new and exciting. The Christian sacraments have always been multi-media worship. Indeed, this is their most distinctive feature. The sacraments involve a variety of media that stimulate, at one time or another, all our senses.[16]

THE LORD'S SUPPER. This sacrament should be celebrated at least once each quarter. It is well to alternate its observance between the morning and evening services. Holy Week, New Year's Watch Night, and other such occasions are natural times for Communion. In smaller congregations it may be served at the altar with great meaning. Larger churches may find it necessary to distribute the elements to worshipers as they are seated in the pews. In either case the call to the table should make it clear that *all Christians*, regardless of denominational affiliation, are welcome to participate. Following the public observances the sacrament should be taken to members of the congregation who were absent because of age or illness. No one needs or appreciates it more than they.

BAPTISM. This sacrament is the outward witness of the inward work of regeneration. While it may be administered by sprinkling or pouring, immersion has become the most frequently used mode since it graphically portrays the death and resurrection of Christ and the Christian. New

---

14. Peter T. Forsyth, *The Church and the Sacraments* (London: Independent Press, 1917, 1955), p. 244.

15. *Ibid.*, p. 165.

16. White, *New Forms*, p. 149.

converts should be urged to be baptized. Classes should be formed as often as there are candidates. A good time for such a service is during or following an evening service. If the church does not have a baptismal pool, another church's facilities may be borrowed or a service shared with another congregation.

A rehearsal should be held with all candidates including a demonstration of how baptism will be administered. Robes should be provided so that modesty may be maintained. After a brief devotional service consisting of congregational singing, scripture, prayer, and a message, the baptismal charge should be given to the candidates as a group. Then they may be dismissed to the dressing rooms while the congregation engages in a period of singing and testimony. Candidates may be given the opportunity to share their testimonies before they are baptized. This adds a very personal meaning to the sacrament and is often a source of great blessing to the congregation.

INFANT BAPTISM OR DEDICATION. Forsyth declares, "There is no infant baptism in the New Testament. I mean in the practice of the New Testament. It is within the principle of the Gospel, but not in the New Testament use."[17] Hugh Thomson Kerr states, "The Christian home was the first Church, and it was inevitable that infant baptism should become the natural practice of the early Christians."[18] If it is administered, parents should be instructed that this is not synonymous with the baptism of those who have reached the age of accountability and have accepted Christ as Saviour. Because of confusion at this point, unless parents strongly prefer baptism it is the practice of many pastors to dedicate babies. *No water should be used in such dedication services.* It is well for the pastor's wife to assist her husband by holding the flowers and certificates and presenting them to the parents. Such services provide a tremendous opportuni-

---

17. Forsyth, *Church and the Sacraments,* p. 180.
18. Hugh T. Kerr, *The Christian Sacraments* (Philadelphia: Westminster Press, 1944), p. 68.

ty for confronting young parents with their responsibility for Christian nurture and example.

MIDWEEK SERVICE. Rather than being only an adult prayer meeting, this service has evolved more and more into a family night with "something for everybody." Children have Caravan or scouting activities. Many youth groups meet on this night rather than Sunday evening. Adults gather for Bible study and prayer, and often the choir rehearses at the conclusion of the adult hour.

One pastor makes this plea for varying the emphasis of the adult service:

> I firmly believe that our people will go where the fire is. Unless *we* institute reforms, unless *we* innovate, Wednesday night will always remain a flicker instead of a fire. . . . We will waste celestial oratory on the faithful few and wonder why.[19]

He makes a plea for a "people's night" with *no preaching*. Among the possible emphases are visitation (before or after), special music by people who don't get to sing on Sunday, discussions of doctrines, family relationships, attitudes, etc., and inductive Bible study.

Prayer should still be a central emphasis, but the method should be varied. The traditional method of asking for requests and then calling on one or two people to lead in prayer leaves much to be desired. Too often the one praying cannot remember all the requests which have been made and inadvertently fails to mention several. Unless he or she has an unusually strong voice or uses a microphone, it is difficult to hear his prayer. Two variations have proved effective.

1. As each request is made, call on someone to stand and lead the group in praying for that specific need. This not only gives attention to all requests but also involves a larger number of people in the valuable exercise of leading in prayer.

---

19. Mike Norris, "Midweek Innovations," *Preacher's Magazine* 49, no. 10 (October, 1974): 10.

2. Divide the group into small units with one individual being designated as leader for each. Experience has proved that more people will actively participate in prayer in these more intimate groups than will in a congregational setting. It is possible for everyone to voice his prayer audibly and thus to feel a genuine involvement in this vital activity. Such groups serve an especially important function immediately preceding revivals or evangelistic campaigns. Intercession for a maximum number of spiritual needs can be successfully carried out in this setting. Many people who attend the midweek service but who would not be present in other prerevival prayer groups are thus involved in this most important spiritual exercise.

Testimony time is another traditional activity which needs periodic variation. The value of the "redeemed of the Lord" saying so is as great as ever. To deny the layman this opportunity of personal expression robs both him and the congregation of spiritual blessing. But just throwing the service open for testimonies without any guidance too often eventuates in the same old (or young) people saying the same old things! How much better to direct this part of the service in one of the following ways:

1. *Suggested subjects.* Ask each one who testifies to tell specifically about his conversion or sanctification, relate a recent answer to prayer, or quote a scripture which has been especially meaningful.

2. *Restrict those who testify* to those who have led a soul to Christ in the past year or to those who have witnessed to someone since Sunday. This puts the right kind of pressure on evangelistic involvement.

3. *Chain testimonies.* Call on someone to testify and ask him or her in turn to call on someone else whose testimony he would especially like to hear. This invariably involves some who otherwise would not take the initiative themselves.

These and other innovations will serve to make this hour one of the most interesting and effective activities of the week. The midweek service is important. Don't give it up— brighten it up!

Feed the flock of God (1 Pet. 5:2).
*Preach the word; press it home on
all occasions* (2 Tim. 4:2, NEB).

CHAPTER 5

Flock Feeding

1. Preaching—Why and What?

The number one priority in shepherding is preaching.
The scriptural precedents are unmistakable. The Old Testament prophets were primarily preachers. Jeremiah testified,
"And the Lord said unto me, Behold, I have put my words
in thy mouth" (Jer. 1:9). Jesus' first identification with
Isaiah's messianic prophecy was at the point of His preaching ministry—"He hath anointed me to preach" (Luke 4:18).
After He had undertaken this ministry, He commissioned
His disciples to do the same—"He went throughout every
city and village, preaching. . . . Then he called his twelve
disciples together . . . and he sent them to preach" (Luke
8:1 and 9:1-2). Simon Peter got the message. When he
penned his classic chapter on pastoral practice (1 Peter 5),
his first exhortation concerned the feeding ministry. Though
he was not one of the disciples who received the preaching
mandate directly from the Master during His earthly ministry,
Paul clearly felt that he was included as the "thirteenth
apostle." For him nothing ever challenged the primacy of
preaching. His opening admonition to young pastor Timothy
has become the traditional charge to ordinands, "Preach
the word" (2 Tim. 4:2). And this mandate has never been
revoked.

Why Preaching?

This evidence above is sufficient to refute the arguments of those who predict that preaching is a dying art which will be replaced by dialogue and discussion before the end of this century. But there is more than the weight of ancient tradition on the side of preaching. Its relevance is supported by a strong, contemporary affirmation of the Pauline declaration that "it pleased God by . . . preaching to save them that believe" (1 Cor. 1:21). A rising chorus of voices from all sectors of the modern church continues to speak up in support of the importance of the preaching ministry. Representative of these is this forthright statement from the pen of James S. Stewart, the eminent Scottish preacher-scholar:

> Do not listen to the foolish talk which suggests that, for this twentieth century, the preaching of the Word is an anachronism, and that the pulpit, having served its purpose, must now be displaced by press or radio, discussion group or Brains Trust, and finally vanish from the scene. As long as God sets His image on the soul, and men are restless till they rest in Him, so long will the preacher's task persist, and his voice be heard through all the clamor of the world.[1]

Preaching is the timeless, God-given strategy for the proclamation of the Good News. As such it establishes correct relationships in two very crucial areas.

1. *Between preaching and liturgy.* P. T. Forsyth notes that Christian history records the continuing struggle between the apostle (preacher) and the priest. He observes that the first apostles were not priests. Therefore, the real apostolic succession is one of preaching, not priestly function. He further insists that "our churches are not shrines but stone pulpits."[2] This truth needs to be heard today. When preaching is de-emphasized, ritual is inevitably substituted. When the pulpit is pushed back, the liturgical altar is pushed for-

---

1. Stewart, *Heralds of God*, p. 55.
2. Peter T. Forsyth, *Positive Preaching and the Modern Mind* (Grand Rapids, Mich.: Wm. B. Eerdmans Publishing Co., 1964), p. 4.

ward. True, the pastor exercises a certain priestly function as he leads the congregation in worship experiences. There is also a proper congregational involvement in public worship. But all of this must not be at the expense of the preaching ministry. The minister must stubbornly resist any effort to reverse this priority.

2. *Between pulpit and parish.* This tension is revealed in such comments as "He's a wonderful pastor but he's just no preacher," or "He's a great preacher but a poor pastor." Actually, neither statement can be true. Since feeding is the first shepherdly function, *one can't be any kind of pastor if he isn't some kind of a preacher.* A starved flock will need the attention of a mortician rather than a minister! The call to preach is inherent in the ministry of shepherding. Like the fire in the prophet's bones, this burning commission makes it "pulpit or perish."

The other side of the coin bears a matching inscription. An untended flock may stampede over the cliff and be dead before dinnertime! Successful shepherding includes proper emphasis upon both pulpit and parish. Phillips Brooks stated the case in these words:

> The preacher needs to be pastor that he may preach to real men. The pastor must be preacher, that he may keep the dignity of his work alive. *The preacher, who is not a pastor, grows remote. The pastor, who is not a preacher, grows petty*[3] (italics added).

There is a corollary truth here for those who feel a divine call to the ministry of public evangelism. Though theirs is fundamentally a prophetic vocation, a period of service in a pastorate is a valuable prerequisite. The understanding gained by this shepherding experience adds a very necessary dimension to their distinctive service. Bishop Gerald Kennedy advises: "We must always be pastors before we can be prophets. I have scarcely known a single instance in twenty years of a prophet disdaining the role of the

---

3. Phillips Brooks, *Lectures on Preaching* (New York: E. P. Dutton, 1891), p. 77.

pastor, who did not get into serious trouble."[4] Parish ministry will make a good evangelist even better.

Why preaching? Because it is intrinsic in the building of a truly New Testament church. It was true on the Day of Pentecost and has been ever since. In the power of the Spirit, Peter and the other apostles found preaching to be their most natural method of witnessing. Augmented by the private, personal witness of Spirit-filled laymen, they established patterns of church growth. (These will be more fully discussed later.) It was more than coincidental that it all began with the ministry of preaching. It was by divine intent. Church history has substantiated this. When the preaching candle flickered and burned low, the life-signs of the church invariably became dangerously weak. But the powerful preaching of a Savonarola, a Luther, or a Wesley resulted in a new surge of spiritual life which invigorated the body of Christ.

Helmut Thielicke pastored a thriving church in Hamburg during the strenuous days of World War II and afterward. The outstanding pulpit work of this brilliant German divine led to the publication of many of his sermons in the English language. John Doberstein, his translator, aptly comments that wherever we find a vital, living congregation we find at its center vital preaching. This is universally true. In Britain the Spurgeons and Sangsters proved this principle. In the United States the Edwardses and Truetts demonstrated it. Thousands of lesser known preachers in less prestigious pulpits across Christendom continue to build their churches around the central fact of their preaching ministry.

Against the background of the renewed interest in the gifts of the Spirit, A. W. Tozer, the gifted preacher and editor, testifies, "It is my belief that the one gift we need most now is the gift of prophecy."[5] If the Church of Jesus

---

4. Gerald H. Kennedy, *The Seven Worlds of the Minister* (New York: Harper and Row, 1968), p. 90.

5. A. W. Tozer, *Of God and Men* (Harrisburg, Pa.: Christian Publications, 1960), p. 23.

Christ is to wage offensive warfare against the world, the prophet's voice must marshal its forces, prepare them for battle, and call out the command "Forward march!" No less certain sound will penetrate the apathy and spiritual lethargy of sleepy saints. No one else will speak if the man of God does not, for he speaks for God. David Randolph correctly identifies the divine-human equation in preaching in these words: "The preacher should be encouraged by remembering that while he is waiting upon God for his message, God is waiting upon him to be his messenger."[6]

Preach the Word

There is no more sobering responsibility than that of standing before a congregation as God's spokesman. Pious platitudes and moralistic pap are neither the milk nor the meat which will foster and maintain spiritual life. "The minister of a church in *its* pulpit (not his) is not a free lance. He enters into a position of trust which he did not create. He is not free to rend . . . the extravagances of an eccentric individualism, nor the thin heresies of the amateur."[7] In the same breath that he directed Timothy to preach, Paul instructed him that his subject matter was to be the Word of God. Here again he was harking back to the example set by Christ. As God's Son, He could communicate direct revelation from His Father. On occasion He did. But the great majority of the time His preaching was based upon the written Word. Biblical scholars tell us that nearly 90 percent of the teachings of Jesus are directly related to Old Testament scriptures.

Careful study will reveal that He never questioned the veracity of these manuscripts. He did not waste time trying to defend them. He seemed to go out of His way to place the stamp of His authority upon several of the miracle stories which have given some modern theological critics so

---

6. David J. Randolph, *The Renewal of Preaching* (Philadelphia: Fortress Press, 1969), p. 128.

7. Forsyth, *Positive Preaching*, pp. 68-69.

much difficulty. In predicting His crucifixion, He stated, "And as Moses lifted up the serpent in the wilderness, even so must the Son of man be lifted up" (John 3:14). Again, foretelling His entombment, He declared, "For as Jonas was three days and three nights in the whale's belly; so shall the Son of man be three days and three nights in the heart of the earth" (Matt. 12:40). There is no credibility gap here. In identifying himself with the typology of these Old Testament narratives, Jesus affirms that "*all* scripture is given by inspiration of God, and is profitable for doctrine, for reproof, for correction, for instruction in righteousness" (2 Tim. 3:16, italics added).

Not only was the preaching of Jesus and the apostles Bible-based, but throughout history biblical preaching has been the order of the day when Christianity was at its best. In his lectures on preaching, John A. Broadus comments that the Reformation "was a revival of biblical preaching. . . . Instead of passages from Aristotle and Seneca . . . these men preached the Bible. The question was not what the Pope said; and even the Fathers, however highly esteemed, were not decisive authority—it was the Bible."[8] Following the Reformation, the next great spiritual awakening was the Wesleyan Revival. Every student of Wesley would agree that he and his preachers majored in Bible preaching. And if we see genuine revival in our time, it will be characterized by this same emphasis upon the preaching of the Word.

Preaching the Word begins with a foundation of biblical truth. Professor Randolph puts it this way: "Preaching is the event in which the biblical text is interpreted in order that its meaning will come to expression in the concrete situation of the hearers."[9] Congregations do not assemble to hear what men have to say. This they hear every day. These sheep have existed in a spiritual desert all week. The only oases have been times of personal devotion. But

---

8. Faris D. Whitesell, *The Art of Biblical Preaching* (Grand Rapids, Mich.: Zondervan Publishing House, 1950), p. 28.
9. Randolph, *Renewal of Preaching*, p. 1.

now the flock gathers to have its thirst quenched with living water. What high tragedy if the shepherd should lead them to dry wells or elusive mirages. The only satisfying answers to their questions and solutions for their problems spring from the authoritative Word of God.

But preaching from the Bible may not always mean preaching the Word. We would do well to give attention to Karl Barth at this point:

> The purpose of preaching is to explain the Scriptures. . . . When one chooses a text, a decision is made whether to obey or disobey the Word—that is, God. Disobedience consists of imagining that it is possible to approach Scripture with full freedom to exercise one's own unfettered powers. There can be no thought of arbitrarily laying hold of Scripture in order to find a text which will suit oneself, which seems appropriate to what one wishes to say. *The text must be in command—* it is above us and we are its servants[10] (italics added).

The cardinal homiletical sin is eisegesis—taking the text out of its context. One of the perils of topical preaching is that having taken his text, the minister may quickly depart therefrom and go everywhere preaching the gospel! The Apostle Paul recognized this peril, guarded against it, and could testify, "We use no hocus-pocus, no clever tricks, no dishonest manipulation of the Word of God" (2 Cor. 4:1, Phillips). What is it but "dishonest manipulation" to lift a scripture out of its setting and make it say something completely different from its original intent?

Then what right have we to expect our people to bring their Bibles to church services if the only reference to the Scriptures is that made when the text is read (and sometimes even then the reference is not given)? How much better the presentation of a carefully studied exposition of a passage of scripture, liberally documented with other Bible references. Then and only then can the man of God confidently declare, "This is the Word of God."

---

10. Karl Barth, *The Preaching of the Gospel*, trans. B. E. Hooke (Philadelphia: Westminster Press, 1963), pp. 42, 56-57.

Here is the note of assurance which men are waiting to hear. Here are the spiritual nutrients which the sheep desperately need. Well-fed flocks do not fall prey to the biting winds of adversity or sicken and die like those whose spiritual resistance has dropped to a dangerously low level. Such pulpit fare is the most effective preventive medicine for the soul.

Not only is Bible preaching what people need. *It is what an increasing number of people want.* A survey was conducted among visitors at one of our fastest growing churches to determine what impressed them most about the services which they had attended. The results revealed that the three most frequent responses were (in this order):

1. Spirit-anointed, Bible preaching
2. Outstanding musical program
`3. Friendliness of the congregation

There is a deep hunger for the abiding truth of God's Word in these times of rapid and often shattering change. Nothing else relates to men's basic needs so directly. Dr. David H. C. Read, pastor of a great city church, comments: "I am in revolt against the current mania for adjusting the message of the church to the supposed mood of the moment in the name of the blessed word 'relevance.' . . . The Gospel is always relevant."[11] The basically unchanging needs of men are best served by the proclamation of the immutable Word of the Lord.

A Balanced Sermonic Diet

To the Ephesian Christians, Preacher Paul could testify, "I have not shunned to declare unto you all the counsel of God" (Acts 20:27). Not only must we faithfully proclaim God's Word. We must just as faithfully "declare . . . God's *whole* plan" (italics mine), as Weymouth translates it. You can do one without doing the other. It is possible for a preacher consciously to show *theological favoritism* in his pulpit work. Some areas of doctrine lend themselves more

---

11. Read, *Religion Without Wrappings*, p. 170.

easily to homiletical development than others. Each of us has certain favorite Bible authors and books to which we find it natural to return often for subjects and texts. Unless care is exercised, one can develop exclusive friendships with a chosen few of these sacred themes and in so doing rob his congregation of other much-needed truth. Both the lambs and the mature sheep need the nourishment of the "full counsel."

This calls for *definite planning of one's preaching program.* Some pastors set up a full 12-month sermon schedule at the beginning of the year. It is my personal opinion that this is carrying planning too far. Who can anticipate on January 1 the exact congregational needs on October 10? Opportunity must be given for the Holy Spirit to supply leadership in the choice of subject matter to meet particular needs. One might well plan for the period of two or three months ahead, keeping in mind that all such programming is subject to change at the Spirit's behest.

The basic checklist of sermon subjects should be the doctrines contained in the Articles of Faith. William Sangster advises that "doctrines must be preached practically and duties, doctrinally."[12] This is the secret of keeping doctrinal messages both relevant and interesting. What more succulent sermonic fare for a hungry flock than these subjects.

The Triune God

Jesus Christ

The Holy Spirit

The Holy Scriptures

Original Sin, or Depravity

Atonement

Free Agency

Repentance

Justification, Regeneration, and Adoption

Entire Sanctification

---

12. William E. Sangster, *Power in Preaching* (New York: Abingdon Press, 1958), p. 79.

Second Coming of Christ
Resurrection, Judgment, and Destiny
Baptism
The Lord's Supper
Divine Healing

In addition such major scriptural topics as the following should receive regular attention:

The Church
Christian Ethics
Stewardship
Love
Faith
Hope
Marriage and the Home
Christian Patriotism
Prayer
Evangelism
Missions
Commitment
Adversity

Some of these topics deserve more attention than others, of course. Local situations will dictate the proportionate emphasis which should be placed upon others.

The Christian calendar affords an excellent opportunity for developing several of these themes.

Christmas (Jesus Christ)
Lent (The Lord's Supper, Atonement)
Easter (Resurrection)
Pentecost (The Holy Spirit, Entire Sanctification, The
    Church)
Reformation Sunday (Justification)
Universal Bible Sunday (The Holy Scriptures)

Special national observances are appropriate times for dealing with other subjects.

New Year's Day (Commitment)
Mother's Day (Marriage and the Home)

National Birthday (Christian Patriotism)
Thanksgiving (Stewardship, Missions)

Evangelistic services, both of the every-Sunday and revival-meeting variety, lend themselves naturally to treatment of a wide range of subject matter including: Christian Ethics, Love, Faith, Prayer, Original Sin, Free Agency, Repentance, Second Coming of Christ, Judgment and Destiny, Baptism, Regeneration and Adoption, Entire Sanctification, and Divine Healing in addition to Evangelism itself.

Preaching series based on the subject matter of selected books of the Bible constitute another excellent device for covering a broad range of doctrinal emphases. For example, the First Epistle of Peter lends itself to a series of six messages touching on the following themes:
1. Jesus—the Hope (1:3-12)
2. Peter Preaches on Holiness (1:13-25)
3. Who Are the Chosen People? (2:4-12)
4. The Fine Art of Submission (2:13—3:7)
5. When Suffering Comes (3:8-22 and 4:12-19)
6. Living for Jesus (4:1-11 and 5:1-12)

Still another very interesting vehicle for conveying divine truth is the use of *Bible biographies.* Faith comes alive as we see it demonstrated in Abraham's exchanging the security of his hometown for the unknown but God-promised land. And don't overlook the lessons which can be learned from the little people of the Bible. Take Ebed-melech for example. His story is tucked away in Jeremiah 38. He surfaces only briefly but blessedly. A sermon on "Secondhand Rags and Satisfactory Service" based on the attitudes and actions of this member of a minority group could bring encouragement to parishioners who are overawed by the tremendous accomplishments of the great men and women of the Word.

Then, *preach the whole Bible—both Old and New Testaments.* While all scripture is inspired, all of it is not equally inspiring. Therefore, it is only natural that there is a tendency to look to the Gospels and Epistles for the majority of preaching texts, since they contain the vital accounts of Christ's life and ministry and the basic elements of salvation and Christian living.

But to neglect the preaching values of the Old Testament is to rob our people of very necessary biblical truth. A knowledge of such foundational subjects as Creation, the Fall, the system of ceremonial sacrifices, and the Mosaic law is essential to a full understanding of sin (both original and actual), atonement, and Christian liberty. What pulpit ministry is complete without periodic pilgrimages into the Psalms, a veritable motherlode of inspiration?

And then the prophets. We term some major and others minor, but every one has something important to say. Their predictions concerning the coming Messiah are integral to a proper Christology. Their fearless preaching on the necessity of repentance and returning to God sets a standard for the modern pulpit to follow in pointing the church to genuine revival. Micaiah was instructed to "speak that which is good." But his prophetic response was "As the Lord liveth, what the Lord saith unto me, that will I speak" (1 Kings 22:13-14). This means preaching the truth, and sometimes the truth hurts. Dwight Stevenson comments, "Although the Word of God is meant to heal and to build, it wounds before it heals, it roots up before it plants, it wrecks before it builds. . . . The thing that ails us will not be cured by moral poultices. We need surgery. But after surgery there can be healing and restoration to health."[13] Preaching from the prophets adds this vital ingredient to a preaching program.

Preach Christ

An increasing number of pulpits have affixed to them in plain view of the preacher a metal plate inscribed with this scriptural injunction, "Sirs, we would see Jesus." This should be a constant reminder that *the overarching theme of all preaching in the Christian Church is Christ.* Would to

---

13. Dwight E. Stevenson, *In the Biblical Preacher's Workshop* (Nashville: Abingdon Press, 1967), p. 55.

God that every minister might be able to honestly testify with Paul, "I did not come with eloquence or superior wisdom as I proclaimed to you the testimony about God. For I resolved to know nothing while I was with you except Jesus Christ and him crucified" (1 Cor. 2:1-2, NIV).

Every sermon should have something to say about the Saviour. If the Holy Spirit does not speak of Himself but of Jesus, can we do less? Whatever the subject and wherever the text may be found, the message must relate to Christ if it is to be truly Christian. James S. Stewart makes the analogy that just as every English road leads to London, every sermon should lead to Christ.[14]

Commenting on the unusually effective ministry of Dr. John Stott in All Souls Church in England's greatest city, Elton Trueblood reported that the sanctuary was regularly packed on Sunday night with the majority of the congregation under 25 years of age. And this in a nation where church attendance has drastically decreased in recent years. Why? "His . . . appeal, over and over, being not only both biblical and rational, but above all Christ-centered."[15] When faithfully lifted up, He still draws men.

Wise is the pastor who periodically checks the menu of his sermonic fare to be certain that he is offering his people a well-balanced diet of scriptural nourishment.

14. Stewart, *Heralds of God,* p. 61.
15. D. Elton Trueblood, *The Validity of the Christian Mission* (New York: Harper and Row, 1972), p. 104.

*The spirit of the Lord God is upon
me; because the Lord hath anointed
me to preach good tidings unto the
meek* (Isa. 61:1).

CHAPTER 6

Flock Feeding

2. How to Preach

John Ruskin stated the case both wisely and well when he declared that the preacher has just 30 minutes to raise the dead. Not all of the congregation will have expired spiritually, of course, but many are in varying stages of what may well become terminal illness unless strong medicine is administered from the pulpit. Even as the skilled physician gives attention both to the content of the medication and also to the method of its administration, so God's messenger is concerned about both his message and the way in which it is presented.

The experience of Lin Yutang, the famous Chinese Christian, beautifully illustrates the therapy of good preaching. The product of two generations of Christian heritage, he had gone back into paganism when he came to America. Gradually he began to turn back to his parents' faith. As he began to attend church, he confessed that he usually came away discouraged by second-rate sermons and resolved not to go again. One day he and his wife went to a church in New York City. "That was the turning point. The sermon was rich and stimulating, dealing not with 'theological hocus-pocus' but with an essential element of Christian belief . . . in a way that was thoughtful and inspiring."[1] They returned Sunday after Sunday and finally rejoined the Christian faith. Good preaching does make a difference.

A. Preparing the Sermon

Presentation is completely dependent upon preparation. What happens in the sanctuary on Sunday is a direct result of what has happened in the study during the week. One of the most vital ministerial disciplines is strict adherence to a schedule of study. Preferably this should be in the pastor's office at church during the morning. To escape the distractions of telephone calls and other interruptions, some ministers make it a practice to get there as early as five or six o'clock. Others instruct their secretaries to hold all calls except emergencies during study hours. Congregations should be informed of the absolute importance of this period of uninterrupted preparation and be requested to cooperate with it. After all, it is their spiritual meal which is on the sermonic stove, and they certainly don't want it to be served half-baked! Four hours of each of his regular workdays of the week should be a *minimum* allotment of time invested in sermon study and preparation.

William Barclay observes that "some preachers make shoddy preparation under the guise of depending upon the Holy Spirit. William Sangster heard one of these and commented, 'I never knew the Holy Spirit could be so dull!'"[2] Mental laziness may be camouflaged under a number of excuses, but it is unpardonable in a God-called minister. Paul's words in 2 Tim. 2:15 are very explicit. The only workman who is approved of God is the one who studies the Word so that he will rightly "divide" or analyze it.

Failure to devote proper time and attention to preparation may result in the practice of *plagiarism*. Even God takes a dim view of sermon stealing: "Behold, I am against

1. Lin Yutang, "My Steps Back to Christianity," *Reader's Digest,* October, 1959, p. 60.
2. Barclay, *In the Hands of God,* p. 50.

the prophets, says the Lord, who steal my words from one another" (Jer. 23:30, RSV). Dr. Stevenson comments, "A plagiarizing preacher is a reverend robber."[3] He goes on to state that in the sixteenth century, ministers were forbidden to preach original sermons. However, this ban has long since been removed and there is no excuse for plagiarism now. There are actually two kinds. Hard plagiarism is pirating a sermon word for word. Soft plagiarism is lifting outlines and illustrations. With commercial services offering a variety of complete sermons, Stevenson sadly notes that "pulpit plagiarism is big business."[4] Hard or soft, it is still less than proper preparation for real preaching. Phillips Brooks defined preaching as "Truth through Personality. . . . The truth must come really through the person . . . through his character, his affections, his whole intellectual and moral being."[5] A sermon must be one's own if it is to pass this test.

Sermon Resources

Despite the toll that television has taken of good reading, the latter is still the primary source of preaching materials. Five minutes in a pastor's library will reveal whether his flock is grazing in green pastures or eking out its existence in a desert. In addition to a well-rounded collection of "how to" books on pastoral practice, it should contain the following basic sermon resources:

1. *Bibles*—major versions, translations, and paraphrases.

2. *Concordance*—Young's or Strong's Exhaustive.

3. *Commentaries*—at least one classic (Clarke's) and one contemporary (Beacon).

4. *Bible Word Studies*—lexicons, Robertson's.

5. *Theology and Doctrinal Studies*—both classic and contemporary.

6. *Church History*—standard college and seminary texts.

---

3. Dwight E. Stevenson, *The False Prophet* (New York: Abingdon Press, 1965), p. 72.

4. *Ibid.*, p. 82.

5. Brooks, *Lectures on Preaching*, p. 8.

7. *Biography*—historic Christian leaders and missionaries, contemporary Christians, and great world and national leaders, past and present.

8. *Sermons*—the best in classic and contemporary.

9. *Periodicals*—both denominational and nondenominational Christian journals.

This skeleton library will be fleshed out with other subjects according to interest and ability. Some authors will have more appeal than others to the individual pastor, and his book buying will naturally reflect this fact. But caution should be exercised that one's library does not become lopsided with a disproportionate amount of material on certain subjects and from a limited number of writers. Advertisements in religious journals and visits to Christian bookstores will keep one apprised of current offerings. Catalogues from several large concerns dealing in classic reprints and used books provide information about the availability of materials which are out of print.

In addition to one's own library, the public library offers some preaching resources. A periodic check of the religion section may reveal books which a pastor might not buy for himself but which contain usable material. Then, should there be a church-related college or seminary nearby, one may find its library a treasury of books and current periodicals which may be a worthwhile supplement to his own resources.

Another medium of communication which is being used increasingly for religious materials is the cassette tape. In addition to tapes which may be purchased, many seminaries are building resource libraries of them which may be borrowed by pastors. Some of these are available by mail.

Conserving sermonic material is just as important as securing it or reading it. The brilliant author and preacher, Elton Trueblood, revealed that his lifelong custom was never to be without pen and paper for recording ideas which often prove to be elusive to the memory. My own method has been to use 3 x 5 index cards to record material for future use. Sermon texts and topics are jotted down when they come alive in Bible reading and are filed under the appropriate headings for future consideration. The same has been done with materials from other reading. Either a direct quotation or brief description of the data is written on the card along with the source. Filed under the proper subject, the material can be resurrected to add substance to a sermon at some later date.

Regardless of what method is employed, it is imperative that a reservoir of resources be maintained from one's reading program. This is not plagiarism. *All good preachers are good borrowers.* There is a vast difference between pirating an entire outline or sermon and borrowing selected ideas and illustrations for the enrichment of your own original message.

Constructing the Sermon

As early in the week as possible the specific texts and topics for the next Sunday's sermons should be finalized, the subject area having already been determined in prior planning of the preaching program. The conscious leadership of the Holy Spirit should be sought in these important decisions. McCheyne counseled, "Get your texts from God." The assurance that this is His message for this hour is essential to authoritative preaching. The earlier the text is selected, the longer one has to collect appropriate illustrations and build an outline. One pastor felt led on Monday to preach from Eph. 2:19-22 the next Lord's Day. As he left his office, he drove by an apartment which was under construction. He noted how everything fit together just as Paul described the construction of the church in his text. Like a flash his sermon title came to him: "God's Housing Project." With this excellent start the rest of the sermon developed very naturally.

The first approach to the text should be personal—what does it say to me? To understand really means to stand under. One teacher of preachers advises, "No man can speak movingly on any text as long as he is using it solely as a means of revelation to other men. He cannot speak on behalf of God to another until he himself has listened to God. Otherwise, the preacher will use the text not as a key to open lives to God, but as a weapon with which to bludgeon them."[6] This is a demonstration of the shepherd's identification with his sheep. As he hears the Good Shepherd speaking to him personally through His Word, he empathizes with his people's needs. Only then is he prepared to transmit the truth to his flock.

James Cleland gives us the three fundamentals of sermon preparation which constitute *the steps and stages of development:*

1. *Investigation* (exegesis)—The Then
2. *Interpretation* (exposition)—The Always
3. *Application*—The Now[7]

Without exception real Bible preaching must stem from this progression of preparation. The omission of any one of these elements leaves the sermon incomplete. Equal consideration will not always be given to all three in the final message. Their order may be changed. But correct sermon development must invariably deal with the "Then, Always, and Now" of the text.

The actual mechanics of sermon building are as varied as the personalities of the preachers who construct them. Clovis Chappell, the renowned Methodist pulpiteer of the South, shared his method in a pastors' meeting which I attended. His advice was:

1. Get a good text that you believe in.
2. Read the context repeatedly and write down everything that comes to mind.
3. Organize your material by building a simple outline.
4. Preach the outline until you are ready to write down the body of the message.

The traditional structure of introduction, three points, and conclusion is still basically sound. However, some scriptures

---

6. Stevenson, *In the Biblical Preacher's Workshop*, p. 67.
7. James T. Cleland, *Preaching to Be Understood* (New York: Abingdon Press, 1965), p. 77.

can be better expounded with perhaps only two major divisions—or four. This should be the deciding factor rather than a hard and fast homiletical rule.

One of the most crucial concerns is the necessity of *building to a final climax.* "The sermon should start moving fast and keep moving toward its climax or series of climaxes. One of the most unnerving experiences a preacher can have is to preach into the middle of his sermon and suddenly realize that he has reached his only climax in point one!"[8] Biblical passages are like escalators. Some start at the bottom and move up, and others start at the top and go down. But sermons must always climb. There is no law against beginning the message with a less dramatic truth which appears later in the text and then climaxing with the premier portion of the scripture, wherever it may come in the passage.

The climactic conclusion is not just for effect. It is based on the premise that all preaching is pointed toward the *securing of decisive response* from men. H. Grady Davis, whose book *Design for Preaching* has been one of the most popular homiletic texts, states: "The aim of preaching is to win from men a response to the gospel, a response of attitude and impulse and feeling, no less than of thought."[9] This being true, the crowning impact of the sermon must come at its conclusion when a response is called for.

Outline or manuscript? There are two schools of thought regarding the final form of the sermon. Charles H. Spurgeon never prepared a full manuscript. No less a pulpiteer than Charles G. Finney took a strong stand against writing out sermons.

> I am prepared to say . . . that I think I have studied all the more for not having written my sermons. I have been obliged to make the subjects upon which I preached familiar to my thoughts, to fill my mind with them, and then go and

---

8. Randolph, *Renewal of Preaching*, p. 126.
9. H. Grady Davis, *Design for Preaching* (Philadelphia: Fortress Press, 1958), p. 5.

talk them off to the people. . . . I simply jot down the order
of my propositions and the positions which I propose to take;
and in a word, sketch an outline of the remarks and inferences with which I conclude.[10]

On the other hand, other great preachers advise that at least
for the first 10 years sermons should be written out in full.
Dr. James B. Chapman concurs with the latter view:

> No preacher should fail to write one full sermon a week
> during the first ten years of his ministry. . . . The exercise will
> be laborious and the returns will not be immediately apparent,
> but the preacher's regard for accuracy will be promoted, and
> in the later years of his work he will have occasion to be
> thankful for the results of such discipline.[11]

Undoubtedly, writing sermons expands the vocabulary and
contributes to accuracy. However, Dr. Chappell, in the
aforementioned discussion, held that writing the manuscript
and using it for the basis of the message makes the sermon
sound like it has been written.

D. Martyn Lloyd-Jones suggests that a combination of
both methods is best. His practice was to write his evening
evangelistic sermon in full and to preach extempore on
Sunday morning.[12] The final rule is that there is no rule.
Let every man experiment and find the homiletical armor
in which he can fight the most successfully.

The use of illustrations. T. DeWitt Talmadge once said
that no preacher can hold an audience without telling stories
or painting pictures. In all likelihood, the thing which you
remember most vividly about the last sermon which you
heard is not the carefully thought-out divisions of the outline or even the well-chosen words of the preacher. What
most people remember is the appropriate illustration which
made the scriptural truth come alive. The sermon must be

---

10. Charles G. Finney, *Charles G. Finney: an Autobiography* (New York:
Fleming H. Revell Co., 1903), pp. 94-95.
11. James B. Chapman, *The Preaching Ministry* (Kansas City: Beacon
Hill Press, 1947), p. 88.
12. D. Martyn Lloyd-Jones, *Preaching and Preachers* (New York: Hodder
and Stoughton, 1971), p. 215.

more than a string of stories. But *correct doctrine needs the illumination and ventilation which good illustrations provide.* Such pulpit giants as Henry Ward Beecher, Phillips Brooks, Dwight L. Moody, and George Truett were skillful in the use of illustrations. Some used them to begin sermons. Others made it a practice to conclude with one. But all made effective use of them somewhere in their messages.

Some principles for the fine art of employing illustrations should be noted.

1. *Be sure they are true.* There must be no credibility gap in the proclamation of God's truth. Wallace Fisher sounds this note: "Honesty . . . requires accurate statements and truthful illustrations. . . . The preacher who, seeking dramatic effect, claims another's experience as his own may prove untrustworthy in keeping the parochial records. . . . Certainly he will not be effective in the pulpit."[13] Be honest with God and with the people!

2. *Life-situation illustrations are the most effective.* The old, hackneyed stories from books of illustrations might better be left unused. Never apologize for personal illustrations—they relate to people. And the more recent the better.

3. *Don't embarrass or hurt members of the congregation.* Some enjoy hearing illustrations about themselves; others don't. Some can laugh at themselves; others can't. Know your people before using them in illustrations.

4. *Use humorous illustrations in good taste.* God has a sense of humor, and most Christians enjoy a good laugh. Such illustrations are an effective "change of pace" in the message. But don't overdo it. And don't be crude or offensive just to get a laugh.

5. *Give credit where credit is due.* If the illustration is borrowed, acknowledge its owner. There is a difference between this ethical practice and ecclesiastical name-dropping. The latter practice is never in order from the pulpit. The former always is.

---

13. Wallace E. Fisher, *Preaching and Parish Renewal* (Nashville: Abingdon Press, 1966), p. 29.

B. Presenting the Sermon

Finney points up a very important distinction when he declares, "Great sermons lead the people to praise the preacher. Good preaching leads the people to praise the Lord."[14] A well-prepared sermon manuscript or outline is not enough. Truth must be communicated. The message dare not be self-serving. It must be God-exalting. The messenger is just the mouthpiece. He speaks for God. The more transparent his life and lips, the more clearly the congregation will hear God's voice.

Holy Unction

Good preaching begins with Holy Spirit unction. No preparation is complete until the preacher has prepared his heart as well as his mind. To stand in the pulpit equipped only with human weapons is to court frustration and failure in this holy warfare. Every preacher would do well to hear the words of Francis Schaeffer: "In the first chapter of Acts he gives a command not just to preach the Gospel, but to *wait for the Holy Spirit* and then to preach the Gospel. Preaching the Gospel without the Holy Spirit is to miss the entire point of the command of Jesus for our era."[15]

This initial enduement of the Spirit is where unction begins. But it does not stop here. Careful, prayerful waiting in the presence of God as one faces the awesome responsibility of speaking for God will bring a *fresh anointing of the Holy Spirit*. Preaching then becomes more than religious public speaking. With this preparation he can "do this work in a manner that lifts it up beyond the efforts and endeavors of man to a position in which the preacher is being used by the Spirit and becomes the channel through whom the Spirit works."[16] Happy the man of God who settles for nothing less than this holy unction. Fortunate is the congregation

---

14. Finney, *Autobiography*, p. 91.
15. Francis Schaeffer, *True Spirituality* (Wheaton, Ill.: Tyndale House, 1971), pp. 71-72.
16. Lloyd-Jones, *Preaching and Preachers*, p. 305.

which is favored by having this kind of anointed minister and ministry.

Proclamation

Real preaching is proclamation and must have a note of certainty about it. Armed with the Sword of the Spirit, God's servant goes forth *to conquer, not to negotiate.* Dr. H. Orton Wiley, the esteemed Wesleyan theologian and longtime college president, made it his practice on Investiture Day each year to preach from Isaiah 62. As a student I was deeply impressed by the prophetic note sounded by this humble but mighty servant of God as he preached from such texts as "Behold, the Lord hath proclaimed unto the end of the world, Say ye to the daughter of Zion, Behold, thy salvation cometh" (Isa. 62:11). No halfhearted, trial-balloon type of presentation here! The bugle sounded loud and clear.

What a contrast to much of what passes for preaching today. Vance Havner confesses that in the early days of his ministry his preaching was of the "repent as it were and believe in a measure or you'll be lost to some extent variety."[17] All too many mature ministers have never outgrown this youthful uncertainty. With the world dying for the strong assurance of God's Word, too much of the time all it hears is "the mincing aesthetes, the unemphatic voices providing their congregations with a weekly ration of the abstract."[18]

E. Stanley Jones has exerted an unparalleled influence as a preacher of the gospel. His positive declarations of Christian truth have produced spiritual fruit on many continents. He tells of the record of a business meeting in an old New England church in which a resolution was passed "to examine the squeak in the pulpit." He comments

---

17. Vance Havner, *That I May Know Him* (New York: Fleming H. Revell Co., 1948), p. 76.
18. James W. Kennedy, *Minister's Shop-Talk* (New York: Harper and Row, 1965), p. 81.

that there are still lots of "squeaks in the pulpit—weak, ineffective personalities speaking weak, ineffective words."[19] This is far from the biblical ideal of preaching!

Proclamation has a built-in *earnestness and intensity* which are *expressed in a proper demonstration of emotion.* Daniel Webster stated that when he finished preparing his famous address on Adams and Jefferson, his paper was wet with tears. A fatal defect of too many sermons is a lack of moisture on the manuscript. Frederich Temple, archbishop of Canterbury, was described as "granite on fire"; and though far from a sentimentalist, he could not speak of the love of God without tears.[20] What other subject should produce more deep, moving emotion than this? And why should the preacher of this sublime truth be ashamed to display such genuine feelings? Congregations need to be both mentally stimulated and emotionally stabbed.

Maintain Interest

The preacher's task is to make God live in the minds and hearts of his hearers. To do this he must capture and hold their attention. The eleventh commandment for the man of God in the pulpit is "Thou shalt not be dull." Bishop William Quayle put it this strongly: "The sin of being uninteresting is in a preacher an exceedingly mortal sin. It hath no forgiveness."[21] The surest way to lull a congregation to sleep is to speak in a low, lifeless monotone. However, continuous high-decibel shouting may well produce irritation rather than interest. Careful attention to clear articulation of words and a variety of voice inflections helps immeasurably in maintaining effective contact with one's audience. Periodically every pastor should tape-record his message and then listen to it. In this way he can detect speech man-

19. E. Stanley Jones, *Conversion* (New York: Abingdon Press, 1959), p. 175.

20. D. Elton Trueblood, *The Incendiary Fellowship* (New York: Harper and Row, 1967), p. 118.

21. William A. Quayle, *The Pastor Preacher* (Cincinnati: Jennings and Graham, 1910), p. 124.

nerisms which distract rather than contribute to good communication.

Three other characteristics of interesting preaching should
be noted:

1. *Brevity.* Almost without exception the shortest sermons
are the sweetest. *The days when the attention of a congregation could be held for an hour are gone forever.* This is
true in other professions. Law students are now instructed
to make their summations to juries no more than 20 minutes in length. Anything longer than this is ineffective, they
are told. Few preachers can maintain an attention span of
more than 30 minutes. Some have discovered that 20 minutes works even better. If there is too much truth for this
time period, how much better to break it up into a series of
messages rather than trying to force-feed glutted parishioners beyond their capacity.

2. *Simplicity.* Jesus' sermons without exception were
models of simplicity. Where did we get the idea that preaching is supposed to be profound? The biographers of John
Wesley concur that even though he was scholarly in his
sermon preparation, before he preached a message he
deleted every word from his manuscript which could not be
easily understood by the most ignorant person who listened
to him.

Dr. Reuel Howe distributed a questionnaire to a large
group of upper middle-class laymen in several mainline de-
nominations to secure their major criticisms of their pastors'
preaching. Interestingly enough, these business and professional leaders complained that most sermons assumed that
they had greater theological vocabularies than they really
possessed and that what they really wanted were *simple
messages* that *they could understand.* Several confessed
that the sermons they enjoyed most and remembered long-
est were those prepared for their children![22] The minister

---

22. Reuel L. Howe, *Partners in Preaching* (New York: Seabury Press,
1967), p. 27.

should know theological terminology, but the pulpit is not the place to demonstrate this proficiency. "He is the theological and exegetical money changer, as it were; his task is to take the thousand-dollar bills of specialized theology and change them into nickels, dimes, quarters, dollars, and ten-dollar bills, so that his people can do business with these ideas in the workaday world."[23]

3. *Positiveness*. Finally, effective preaching must sound a positive note. Goethe voiced the plea of every worshiper when he counseled, "Tell me of your certainties; I have doubts enough of my own." The flock gathers to hear the Good News, not a review of the sordid details of the week that was. Frederick Speakman aptly comments that "one of the real clerical errors of the immediate past has been the frequency with which the pulpit has been turned into a kind of whining post, where the dominant theme so often amounted to little else than a recitation of what had annoyed the pastor the most during the week preceding."[24]

Real problems faced by real people must be faced. But this can be done in a frame of reference in which the dominant theme is one of positive answers rather than negative questions. Haselden puts it this way: "The good sermon always presents the Promise over against the Peril."[25] Sin must be denounced but only as salvation is announced. The tragedies of this life must find their final solutions in the triumphs of the life to come. Sounding this dominant note, the preacher takes his people from where they are to where God can enable them to be.

Conclusion

No greater remuneration can come to the shepherd than the certainty that he has faithfully fed his flock. After 40

23. Stevenson, *Preacher's Workshop*, pp. 59-60.
24. Frederick B. Speakman, *The Salty Tang* (New York: Fleming H. Revell Co., 1954), pp. 109-10.
25. Haselden, *Urgency of Preaching*, p. 55.

years of pastoral preaching, Dr. D. Martyn Lloyd-Jones, the renowned British divine, could write:

> The romance of preaching! There is nothing like it. It is the greatest work in the world, the most thrilling, the most exciting, the most rewarding, and the most wonderful. I know of nothing comparable to the feeling one has as one walks up the steps on one's pulpit with a fresh sermon on a Sunday morning or a Sunday evening, especially when you feel that you have a message from God and are longing to give it to the people. This is something that one cannot describe.[26]

Thank God for this indescribable privilege.

---

26. Lloyd-Jones, *Preaching and Preachers*, p. 297.

People are the minister's business,
and "pastor" is his other name.
Therefore, he must look after the
flock in the sheepfold, in the grazing
fields, and in the wild, lost places
(James W. Kennedy).[1]

CHAPTER 7

Pastoral Care

1. From the Cradle to the Grave

Sunday shepherding is invaluable. Congregational needs
may be met in a very essential way through the ministries
of preaching and teaching in the congregational context.
But good as this is, it will not suffice without a complemen-
tary ministry of shepherding between Sundays. The parishioner who reported that his pastor was incomprehensible
on Sunday and invisible through the week registered two
valid complaints. A true shepherd cannot be found guilty of
either charge. Neither area of responsibility can be neglected without endangering the spiritual life of the flock.

Dr. Paul Johnson defines pastoral care as "a religious
ministry to individual persons in dynamic relationships,
arising from insights into individual needs and mutual dis-
covery of potentialities for spiritual growth."[2] The key
word is "individual." Even in dealing with family groups,
there must be conscious attention to each person. And

1. Kennedy, *Minister's Shop-Talk,* p. 160.
2. Paul E. Johnson, *Psychology of Pastoral Care* (Nashville: Abingdon
Press, 1953), p. 24.

"dynamic relationships" must mean more than shaking hands and saying, "How are you?" at the church door on Sunday.

In any congregation there are a staggering number of personal needs. These range from the very critical problems which cry out for immediate attention to the "low-grade infection" type of nagging concerns. With twentieth-century sophistication, most people wear their masks very well. But while they are laughing on the outside, all too many are crying on the inside. Others have become almost numbed by the continual pressure of their problems. Silently but desperately they cry out for help. This is why Carroll Wise states that "pastoral care is not an adjunct to the ministry; it is the very core."[3]

James E. Dittes, commenting on the minister who flees the often frustrating demands of this kind of pastoral service in favor of institutional chaplaincy, teaching, or social work, asks, "Is he evading engagement with life as it is actually lived and struggled by the vast majority? Is he reserving his ministry only for those isolated few who meet his prerequisites of psychological and intellectual sophistication?"[4] This is certainly not to infer that there are not other meaningful ministries. But it does establish the fact that for sheer relevancy there is no other form of ministry that meets a wider range of people at their point of real need than pastoral care.

Christ's Example

The model for this kind of shepherding is found in the ministry of Jesus. He eloquently lived out the testimony of John 10:14, "I am the good shepherd, and I know my own sheep and my sheep know me" (NEB). This was more than *name knowledge*—it was *need knowledge* as well. He ministered to the masses, but He also made himself acquainted

---

3. Carroll A. Wise, *The Meaning of Pastoral Care* (New York: Harper and Row, 1966), p. 12.
4. James E. Dittes, *The Church in the Way* (New York: Charles Scribner's Sons, 1967), p. 6.

with His disciples' life situations. His concern for the physical problem of Peter's mother-in-law is just one illustration of this apparent fact.

F. W. Boreham observes:

> One of the self-imposed disciplines of ministry is not to be able to reserve the right to cordially dislike some people. Jesus related to these five types of unlovables:
> 1. Those who know everything.
> 2. Those who are loud.
> 3. Those who enjoy poor health.
> 4. Those who affect the grand manner.
> 5. Those who fawn and gush.[5]

No pastor worthy of the name can limit his care to those who are easy to love. He must pastor the whole flock.

Moreover, Christ exercised concern for the "other sheep . . . which are not of this fold" (John 10:16). While this primarily refers to Gentiles, it also alludes to sinners of every race. Robert Gilmore makes this commentary on the Saviour's clientele:

> Christ still scandalizes the Pharisees by the company He keeps—the Publicans and sinners. He continues to show His old preference for this world's disreputables. The Great Physician is still of the opinion that He can spend His time more usefully with those who are sick than those who are whole.[6]

Following our Lord to the Samaritan well-curb and the sycamore tree where He gave personal attention to the deep needs of an adulterous woman and a notorious tax collector provides documentation for this thesis.

Shepherding must not be confined to the safe and the saved if it is to follow the pattern set by the Good Shepherd. A liberal amount of time and effort must be dedicated to the straying and lost sheep. It is a frightening fact that on the average, a church loses half as many members as it gains. In addition, almost every membership roll contains

---

5. Frank W. Boreham, *A Tuft of Comet's Hair* (New York: Abingdon Press, 1926), pp. 13-14.

6. J. Herbert Gilmore, *When Love Prevails* (Grand Rapids, Mich.: Wm. B. Eerdmans Publishing Co., 1971), pp. 66-67.

the names of a number of individuals who rarely, if ever, attend services and who make no profession of faith. The reclamation of these backsliders is just as much a part of the pastor's responsibility as is the winning of new members. All too often these inactive parishioners are thought to be hopeless, and their names are dropped from the roll. The *Manual* wisely provides that a member may be removed only "after he has been visited and dealt with faithfully, when possible" (par. 105.1). *As long as there is physical life, there is spiritual hope.* Tender, loving pastoral care can make all the difference in this world and the next for many of these wandering sheep.

Dr. Paul Johnson points up another vital contribution which Christ's example of shepherding makes to the modern minister when he notes Jesus' distinction between persuasiveness and permissiveness, between law and gospel, and between confrontation and consolation.[7] The synoptic Gospels provide a timeless textbook in the principles of the interpersonal relationships of pastoral care. The perceptive pastor will relate the Lord's dealings with a representative variety of personalities and problems to his own situations. He can identify with the basic attitudes and responses of the Master.

On occasion Jesus demonstrated that it can be just as wrong to be too easy on people as it is to be too hard on them. As He diagnosed their real needs, He was able to prescribe the right therapy. This came about by His ability to differentiate between symptoms and causes. While He noted the former, He was careful to treat only the latter. *Too many failures in pastoral care are the result of treating symptoms rather than causes.* Careful consideration of Christ's example at this point is invaluable.

So much for the general principles of this phase of shepherding. Now let us give consideration to those at the two extremes of the age spectrum who desperately need the shepherd's attention but who may be neglected as the pas-

---

7. Johnson, *Psychology of Pastoral Care.*

tor gives his attention to the young adults and middle-agers who comprise the core of the working force of the church. The following chapter will speak to the pastoral care of these latter groups in the ministries of calling and counseling.

A. Shepherding the Lambs

Dr. Paul H. Vieth states: "The ability to hold its youth is almost universally accepted as a test of the vitality of a church. . . . When the qualifications of a man for minister of a church are given consideration, his appeal to young people will be given a very high rating."[8]

It all begins at birth. And the shepherd should be there at the hospital to pray that first prayer for the baby and his/her parents. Enrolling the child on the cradle roll and officiating at the dedication or baptismal service forge meaningful links in the chain of pastoral care. As children grow up, they will relate to the man of God whom their parents have informed them took a very personal interest in them as babies.

Call them by name. Jesus set the example. In the shepherd passage He testifies, "He calleth his own sheep by name" (John 10:3). There is something special about this personal identification. No one appreciates it more than the child or teenager. All too often we have alluded to them as "the church of tomorrow," which is only a half-truth. When they are recognized individually, they begin to feel that they are an important part of today's church, which they really are. Except in "super churches" which have memberships and Sunday school enrollments in the thousand bracket, the pastor has no excuse for not cultivating a first-name acquaintance with his children and youth. In larger congregations, staff members with responsibilities in these age areas should assume this as part of their undershepherd role.

---

8. Nevin C. Harner, *Youth Work in the Church* (New York: Abingdon Press, 1942), p. 5.

The wide-awake shepherd will foster friendship with his lambs by becoming visible in their activities, both in and out of the church. Unless it is absolutely necessary for the pastor to teach a class, it is a good practice for him to be free to circulate among the children's and youth classes during the Sunday school hour. At the invitation of supervisors and teachers he should speak to departments and classes. He should plan to conduct evangelistic services in the vacation Bible school regularly. Appearance at Caravan or Scout meetings, class parties, and school functions serves to build bridges to young lives. Attendance at high school athletic events where his boys are participating stamps the pastor as a "great guy" in their minds. One pastor endeared himself to his youth by writing them a note of congratulation when they had achieved in some school activity.

Another area of great opportunity for pastoral care of the young is in a camping setting. Overnight trips may be hard on flabby ministerial muscles, but they afford priceless occasions for making a personal spiritual impact on boys and girls. Summer camps present openings for more in-depth contact. A fellow pastor of mine became concerned about a teenage boy in his church whose parents were contemplating divorce. He was about to become a spiritual casualty. The pastor prevailed on him to attend youth camp and served as his counselor. One night the boy knelt at the campfire altar and gave his heart to Christ. Several days later he asked his pastor if he could talk with him. As they sat on a log, the young fellow said, "I want you to tell me about sanctification. I'm going to need everything I can get to help me be a Christian when I get home, and if being sanctified will do that, I want it." The shepherd explained about the meaning of full commitment and the cleansing and empowering baptism with the Holy Spirit. "Could I be sanctified right here and now?" the lad asked. The log became an altar. In a few minutes full salvation became his personal possession. Less than two months later, the boy lost his life in a tragic automobile accident. How grateful his pastor was that he had invested the time and attention which resulted in the young man's receiving eternal life.

Youth who are attending college also need pastoral care. Of necessity it must be by long distance and remote control with those who go off to school. Receiving the church newsletter and bulletin and an occasional personal letter from the pastor mean much to the student who is away from home for the first time and experiencing periods of homesickness. Some ministers plan to visit the campus periodically and take their students out to dinner so that they can have a chance to talk with them about personal matters. This kind of concern from a pastor's heart is invaluable.

Then there is a growing number of "singles" in our society. These unmarried young people often feel lost in churches whose activities are largely couples-oriented. Pastoral interest and careful programming can result in not only the salvation of their souls but also the enlisting of their lives in Kingdom enterprises. Many missionary nurses and teachers have testified to the vital contribution which a good pastor's counsel and prayers made to their finding and following God's will.

Dennis Benson describes the current conflict between adults and youth not as a generation gap but a "generational war." "The second half of the twentieth century is an age of two generations: the *other* and the *now*," he concludes.[9] The church's task is to promote understanding and acceptance between the two. The pastor's role is a key one. His personal concern is imperative. No one else can be of greater assistance as they make the six "discoveries" which Nevin Harner says all young people between the ages of 12 and 24 must make:

1. They need to find God.
2. They need to find themselves.
3. They need to find a life's work.
4. They need to find a life mate.
5. They need to find society—and their relationship to it.

9. Dennis C. Benson, *The Now Generation* (Richmond, Va.: John Knox Press, 1969), p. 13.

6. They need to find the Christian society, the church—and their relationship to it.[10]

When Wedding Bells Ring

One of the happiest and most rewarding pastoral assignments is the uniting of couples in holy matrimony. Lifelong attachments will be formed with families because of this meaningful association. In addition to young people from the church, others who have no church relationship will seek the services of the pastor for this important function. If this contact happens to be with the unchurched, it may become a means of grace, resulting in their salvation.

When moving into a new pastorate, one of the first considerations should be to acquaint himself with the area's civil regulations for clergymen in the performance of marriages. These vary widely, and embarrassment and even legal problems will be averted by securing this information early. If registration is necessary, this should be attended to promptly.

Divorced Persons

When a couple requests the pastor to marry them, he should *immediately determine whether or not either party has been married before.* With the tragic increase in the number of divorces, both inside and outside the church, the minister is well advised to seek this information from members of the congregation as well as nonmembers. If he finds that there has been a divorce, he should then ask if there were biblical grounds (adultery) for this action. Since it is increasingly difficult to legally prove adultery, many divorces are granted on other grounds. But the individual must testify that this cause did exist. The pastor is under no obligation to play detective and seek evidence to corroborate this statement. The burden of proof rests with the person involved. If he or she states that such grounds did exist, the pastor is free to perform the ceremony. If they do

---

10. Harner, *Youth Work,* pp. 31-32.

not exist, he should courteously excuse himself from this responsibility. The minister need not be apologetic at this point. He should simply explain that the Scriptures clearly state that only sexual unfaithfulness provides grounds for remarriage and that his ordination vows prohibit him from officiating at the marriage of unscripturally divorced persons.

Pre- and Post-marital Counseling

If the couple qualifies for marriage, they should then be requested to make appointments for premarital counseling. Here again the frightening incidence of divorce makes it imperative that young people give themselves this opportunity to be sure that they are prepared to assume the responsibilities of marriage, which is a lifetime contract. The *Manual* stipulates that ministers "shall provide premarital counseling in every instance possible before performing a marriage ceremony" (par. 34.1). Dr. Robert W. Laidlow, psychiatric marriage counselor, urges clergymen to act as "screening agents" to prevent unhappy marriages by rendering this service.[11] The pastor is entitled to refuse to marry couples who will not agree to this counseling, especially when they are very young and there are questions in his mind concerning their readiness for this major event in their lives.

Counseling sessions should begin with a discussion of the biblical ideal of Christian love and marriage as presented in 1 Corinthians 13 and Ephesians 5. The study of a marriage manual such as *This Holy Estate* by John E. Riley (Beacon Hill Press of Kansas City) would be the next step. The couple should read the text and then discuss the spiritual, economic, and psychological aspects with the pastor. If one or both of the parties are not Christians, the hazards of a Christless or divided home should be emphasized, and a diligent effort should be made to see them converted before the marriage takes place. Many ministers refer cou-

---

11. Johnson, *Psychology of Pastoral Care*, p. 137.

ples to a Christian physician for counseling on the sexual aspects of marriage. He is more professionally qualified to discuss these matters than is the average pastor, and there is less embarrassment to all parties concerned.

The counseling period also provides opportunity to discuss *the plans for the wedding.* A ceremony should be agreed upon. It has been my custom to use an attractively printed and covered ceremony which may be signed and presented to the couple after the wedding. The church sanctuary is the most feasible setting for the wedding service. However, on occasion couples who are not acquainted in the community may desire to be married in a smaller facility. More and more churches are providing small chapels which are ideally suited to this purpose. If the wedding is very informal and for just immediate families, the living room of the parsonage might be suggested as a possible location. This still ties the wedding to the church and adds a special sanctity that another setting would not.

When church facilities are used, a careful understanding should be reached concerning regulations, equipment, and costs. It is wise for the church board to draw up a policy relating to these matters and to have copies available for distribution to prospective users. Brides will want to know whether the church can provide such things as flower baskets, candelabra, a kneeling bench, as well as tables, cloths, punch bowls, etc. for the reception. Fees for the organist and custodian should be stipulated as both are involved in extra work beyond their normal duties. It is also fair to include a reasonable charge for the use of the church facilities to cover the cost of utilities, etc. Some churches waive this charge for member families. An honorarium for the minister is optional.

The wedding rehearsal is a very important preparation for a sacred ceremony. It is well for the minister to check with the bride before the rehearsal to be sure that she has acquainted herself with the traditional rules of etiquette for weddings. However, she should feel free to use whatever innovations she wishes so long as they are in good taste.

The minister's wife can be of great assistance by working with the bride at this point. The minister should officiate at the rehearsal and set a tone which will protect against its becoming frivolous or irreverent. A few well-chosen words about the sacredness of the occasion will serve this purpose. Then the bride should be allowed to outline the order of the wedding service including the musical selections, lighting of the candles, seating of the mothers, and the order of the entry of the groom and the groomsmen and the bride and her attendants. Positions for the attendants should be marked on the carpet with chalk. There should be a preliminary "walk through" of the service including instructions to the bride and groom concerning the rudiments of the ceremony. This should be repeated at least once so that all minds will be clear. Announcements of the time for the attendants to gather and other details should be made. Then it is in order for the minister to invoke God's blessing on the wedding in a closing prayer.

Post-marriage pastoral care should include a visit to the new home soon after the honeymoon. Setting up a family altar is most important, and the shepherd should lay the cornerstone by having Bible reading and prayer with the newlyweds. He must also give attention to getting them into the fellowship of the young adult Sunday school class and other church activities. Experience has proved that this is a very critical period in their relationship to the church, and extra care is warranted. Other couples of their age could well be assigned to call on them and take a personal interest in cementing their ties to God and the church. Marital counseling will be discussed in conjunction with the subject of pastoral counseling.

B. Ministry to the Aging

At the other end of the age spectrum is the ever-growing number of senior citizens who need shepherding. Even with the better health and economic expectancy of today, many male retirees face real trauma at the point of giving up active involvement in business and professional life and being

relegated to a place on the shelf. Their wives also face un-
certainties at the prospect of these declining years. Never
have they needed pastoral care more than in this period of
their lives. Happily the church is recognizing this situation
and is providing an increasing amount of activity and meaningful involvement for these golden agers. The Senior Adult
Ministry program, with its fellowship and service opportunities, its retreats, and its devotional emphases, gives the
minister a challenging occasion for close association with
these choice Christians. Extension Sunday school classes in
nursing and retirement homes open doors for ministry to
the unchurched and the often forgotten elderly.

Pastor, don't neglect the aging!

When Death Comes

At no time is the care of the shepherd more necessary
than in the hour of bereavement, whether the deceased is
old or young. Often death will be preceded by terminal illness of some duration which gives opportunity for preparing
the individual and the family for the inevitable. But with
the increasing incidence of heart attacks and automobile
accidents, many will die suddenly. In any event the pastor
must move quickly into this time of critical need. No one
else can substitute for him. As he has laughed with his people in their joys, so he must be prepared to weep with them
in their grief. His ministry to the family in this extremity
will not only shore up the faith of the believers but also
may contribute to the salvation of those who do not know
Christ as Lord. The reading of such comforting scriptures
as Psalm 23 and John 14:1-6 provides the healing balm
that can only come from God's Word. And nowhere will a
pastoral prayer bring more help and assurance than in this
dark hour. The presence of the pastor's wife will be most
appreciated by the ladies in the bereaved family. She can
speak their language and offer sympathy in a way that is
unique to the shepherdess.

The funeral service should be planned in consultation
with the family of the deceased. Often they will depend

upon the pastor for guidance, and so it is well to have suggestions ready to give them. The sanctuary or chapel of the church should be offered as a fitting place for the service to be held. Especially in the case of faithful members, this is the most appropriate site for the memorial service. Morticians and funeral directors often prefer to have the service in their own chapels, but the family's preference should be honored. The service itself should not exceed 20 to 30 minutes in length. At best it will be a strenuous experience for the family, and they should be spared a long, agonizing ordeal. Copies of the order of service should be given to the funeral director so that he can coordinate his activities accordingly. A typical service may include the following:

Invocation
Scripture
Special Song
Obituary
Prayer
Special Song
Message
Benediction

The whole service, and especially the message, should major in Christian comfort and hope. A tribute to the deceased is in order but it should not be overdrawn. Non-Christians should not be "preached into heaven," and believers should not be prematurely canonized. The one inviolable rule is that *the message must not be a hard-sell evangelistic appeal!* This is neither the time nor the place to exploit the already overwrought emotions of the bereaved.

At the close of the service the minister should stand at the head of the casket while the congregation is ushered out. Whether the remains are viewed or not should be the decision of the family. Often when the casket is closed to the congregation, the family will have it opened for their private viewing. Words of assurance and a prayer for the sorrowing loved ones are most appropriate in this moment of farewell. The pastor leads the procession of pallbearers to the hearse and accompanies the body to the cemetery. A brief commital service consisting of a scripture, prayer, and the ritual of commital will conclude the funeral.

A very meaningful, time-honored service which the church can render is to provide meals for the family on the day of the funeral. This relieves them of the necessity of cooking for a large group of out-of-town relatives. Here again the pastor's wife can be of great assistance in planning this activity or seeing that the fellowship committee of the church attends to the details. Pastoral care of the bereaved in the days and weeks following the funeral can be of inestimable value in helping them to make the difficult adjustments which death invariably brings. The rehabilitation of the widow or the widower back into a productive and fulfilling life constitutes one of the pastor's most meaningful and rewarding ministries.

Probably nothing that a pastor does in the round of his duties will bear fruit as much as pastoral calling (Paul E. Johnson).[1]

CHAPTER 8

Pastoral Care

2. Calling and Counseling

A. PASTORAL CALLING

In his classic treatise on *The Pastoral Office,* written in 1923, James Beebe quotes pastors who were saying then, "My business is not ringing doorbells; let people send for me when they need my services."[2] He goes on to comment that this attitude arises from a misunderstanding of the purpose and procedure of pastoral calling. It is not duty, an official inspection, or high pressure salesmanship. Calling finds its motivation in friendship and a desire to serve. In visiting old friends and making new ones, he seeks to bring the church to people where they live.

Calling is a unique privilege of the clergy. No other profession has an open door to call at any time. The physician, the lawyer, and the teacher must await an invitation in order to be ethical. But by the very nature of his vocation, the shepherd need not wait for a summons. All too many modern ministers have failed to see this phase of

---

1. Johnson, *Psychology of Pastoral Care,* p. 24.
2. *Ibid.,* p. 43.

their ministry as a professional privilege and have come to regard it as a necessary vocational evil. They show an embarrassingly small number of calls on their annual reports. It would be well for them to remember that Dr. George Buttrick, renowned author and pulpiteer, said that if he did not make at least *1,000 calls a year,* he could not preach intelligently to his congregation's needs.

Bishop Gerald Kennedy makes this confession:

> As a young minister I could not believe that punching doorbells and stopping by to see folks was worthy of my educational accomplishments. This seemed such a useless waste of my time and energy. . . . Today, however, I know of its importance. I would be a better pastor if I had it to do over again.[3]

Calling does not come naturally or easily for some pastors. Their anxiety about how to properly relate to people and their fear of saying the wrong thing build a reluctance to get out and call. Feeling safe with their books, they stay overtime in their studies, rationalizing that it is too early or too late to go calling. When they do stand at a parishioner's door, they find themselves hoping that no one is at home. The cure for this malady is twofold. *First, the scheduling of calls that are contributive to the spiritual life of the congregation.* Mere social calling does not justify the time and effort of the shepherd. *Second, self-discipline which makes one go to the task whether he feels like it or not.* This is the same kind of compulsion which the extrovert must exercise in order to keep regular study hours when he would rather be contacting people.

Some of the frustration in calling is occasioned by the fact that no specific purpose is envisioned for the calls. It is my judgment that after the initial round of calls on the members of a new pastorate, a regular rotation of visits in these homes is not necessary. The congregation should be informed that their pastor is as near as the telephone when his services are needed but that he must give priority to the

---

3. Kennedy, *Seven Worlds,* p. 55.

known spiritual and physical needs of the church family and cannot call merely on a routine basis. Most members will understand and appreciate his giving priority to these essential calls. The romance of ringing doorbells will be maintained as meaning and purpose are attached to this ministry.

Whether it comes easily and naturally or not, *no pastor can dispatch his shepherding responsibilities and maintain a healthy flock without a program of consistent calling on his sheep.* The number of calls made per week will vary with such factors as the distance to be travelled and the special needs. However, 20 to 25 calls in a normal work week would be a reasonable goal in the average congregation.

A word of caution should be injected at this point concerning *the necessity of exercising care when calling on members of the opposite sex.* Because of a psychological background of loneliness or lack of love, some ministers tend to identify emotionally with those in need and on occasion may become so involved that they lose their objectivity and self-control. Without ever intending to do so, they may find themselves drawn into compromising situations. The pastor's wife should not have to accompany her husband on all his house calls, but wise is the minister who recognizes potentially dangerous situations and takes his wife with him on these visits. Too frequent and too lengthy calls on the opposite sex should be avoided in the interests of good taste.

The Techniques of Calling

Prof. C. W. Brister suggests that there are three major types of calls:

1. *Routine calls*—in which the church's message and fellowship are carried to some persons and families.

2. *Crucial calls*—in which Christian resources are offered to those experiencing crisis or distress.

3. *Casual contacts*—in which the minister encounters per-

sons in unstructured settings, yet seeks to make such contacts vital.[4]

The type of call will determine the format as well as the frequency. Just as each individual is different, so each call must be tailored to meet the specific purpose for which it is intended.

Time was when the pastor planned to make the bulk of his calls between the hours of two and five in the afternoon. But times have changed. With an increasing number of working wives, the evening is often the only time when he will find anyone at home. There is wisdom in confirming the hour of the call by telephone so that a minimum of time will be wasted in visiting empty houses. However, in some cases it is best to call without prior notice, the element of surprise being necessary. Should there be no response, the pastor's card should be left in the door to indicate his attempt to make a call.

The length of time spent in each call will be dependent upon the purpose and type of need. Sometimes five minutes will be sufficient. Others may require an hour or more. Russell Dicks advises, "We cannot say how long a pastoral conference will take, but we are not justified in counting a call that does not permit the parishioner to speak of his soul's condition."[5] In most instances, time should be taken for the reading of a selected scripture and the offering of prayer. The dispensing of this spiritual food supplement is rightfully expected of the shepherd in addition to his pulpit fare.

Planning the day's calling is the first step. Geographical grouping of calls can save a great deal of valuable time. A large map of the community with the location of the homes of the members, Sunday school families, and prospects marked with different colored pins is a very helpful resource. Hospitals and nursing homes should also be marked.

---

4. C. W. Brister, *Pastoral Care in the Church* (New York: Harper and Row, 1964), p. 150.
5. Russell L. Dicks, *Pastoral Work and Personal Counseling* (New York: The Macmillan Co., 1944), p. 24.

A card file of all constituents should be kept with current information about each family on one side and a record of calls on the other. The last Sunday's visitors should be called on immediately and, if they are local residents, should be added to the file. An information card should include the following data:

Front

FAMILY CARD

Date—2/1/75

Name	Member	Age
Father: Paul J. Smith	Yes	47
Mother: Phyllis B. Smith	Yes	45
Children: 1. Betty	Yes	19
2. Don	No	13
3. Michelle	No	10
4. Craig	No	8

ADDRESS: 16840 Red Bridge Road

GENERAL INFORMATION: Joined church 7/6/75

Back

Date	Type of Call	Remarks
1/21/75	Follow up first visit	Warm reception
2/16/75	Absent for two Sundays	Have been out of town
4/2/75	Mrs. Smith in hospital	May need surgery
4/4/75	Hospital	Surgery performed
4/5, 4/6, 4/7	X	Good recovery
4/8, 4/10, 4/13	X	X X
4/15/75	Home after surgery	Talked about soul need
4/18, 4/25	Visit with whole family	Real spiritual interest
5/2/75	Present the gospel	Parents, Betty saved!
5/3/75	Set up family altar	Real victory

Lucas Buttry suggests that a loose-leaf notebook with the day's calls should be carried in the car as a helpful accessory.[6] Such a ledger might contain this information on the left-hand page:

PROSPECTIVE CALLS

Date	Name and Address	Remarks
10/12	Mr. & Mrs. Bill Ross (Kathy, Joan) 1909 S. 12th	Still out of work?
	Wm. Brown—Farley Nursing Home	Daughter a member
	Mr. & Mrs. James Smith—2709 S. 23rd	Son still in Japan?
	Helen Johnson—Memorial Hosp.	Operation successful?
	Mr. & Mrs. John Rodriguez (Joe, Cindy, Pat) 420 Hampton Park Place, Commerce City	Visited Sunday services with the Phillips
	Dan, Sam, and Paula Bates 6674 Johnson Drive	New bus ministry children, saved in children's church

---

Immediately upon the conclusion of each call, a report should be entered on the right-hand page. In turn, this information should be transferred to the office file the next day.

COMPLETED CALLS

Date	Name	Remarks
10/12	Ross Family	Bill found work at Ford garage
	Wm. Brown	Very feeble—should be enrolled in Home Dept.
	James Smiths	Not home
	Helen Johnson	Operation postponed
	John Rodriguez Family	Excellent prospects—send Browns to visit
	Bates children	Family just moved here—promised to attend

---

6. Lucas W. Buttry, *The Calling Program of the Local Church* (Butler, Ind.: Higley Press, 1956), p. 47.

The keeping of accurate records takes time, but it is time well spent. An effective calling program depends heavily on this information.

Sickness Calling

Soul care is the most crucial concern, of course. But spiritual welfare is often directly related to physical or mental need. Andrew Blackwood in his classic *Pastoral Work* puts this high priority on the ministry to the ill:

> Nothing that the clergyman does provides a more search-ing test of his pastoral skill and intellectual acumen than his care of the sick. . . . The pastor enters the room as the phy-sician of the soul. . . . The patient and his loved ones can often prove responsive. They are likewise sensitive. If the minister fails to come, or if he falls short after he arrives, their hearts may wax cold.[7]

Two important principles should be observed in dealing with the sick.

1. *Call as often as the need demands.* In critical and ter-minal situations, the pastor may need to put in an appear-ance several times a day. It may be necessary for him to keep a night-long vigil with the family on occasion. If the patient is not on the critical list, daily calls may be suffi-cient. As recovery progresses, a call every few days will suffice.

2. *Convey a cheerful, positive attitude.* Certainly the sick-room is no place for jocularity and loud laughter. But neither is it a place for funereal conduct. There is enough concern and gloom there already. The patient and family are looking for lift and light. Seize on every indication of progress. Speak the language of hope. Quote such assuring scripture pas-sages as Psalms 23 and 90; Isa. 40:28-31; 41:10; and 43:2. And when it is time to pray, pray the prayer of faith that God's Word promises will save the sick. Don't make rash promises for God, but rest the patient's case with the omni-potent and omnipresent Great Physician.

---

7. Andrew W. Blackwood, *Pastoral Work* (Philadelphia: Westminster Press, 1945), p. 102.

Hospital calling requires attention to institutional rules and regulations. It is wise to make acquaintance with key personnel at the hospitals where one will be visiting and to familiarize oneself with any particular restrictions which are in force. Most hospitals grant a courtesy to clergymen to call outside of visiting hours, but this privilege should not be abused. Dr. Brister gives these advices on hospital calling:

1. Regard signs on doors such as "Isolation" or "No Visitors."
2. Call back when the patient's meal is being served, when his or her physician appears, or when there are several visitors present.
3. Address others in the room but concentrate on a face-to-face ministry to the patient.
4. [The call's] duration will vary according to the level of relationship with the patient . . . and the patient's condition.[8]

A *personal interest in other patients in the room may prove to be most profitable.* At the dedication of his new church building, a pastor related this incident. He and his building committee had been trying desperately to find property on which to build. Time after time they were turned down when owners found out that they proposed to build a church. One day they approached an elderly couple who had a choice property for sale. When they learned that the group represented a church, they asked what denomination it was. To the pastor's surprise, when they heard the name of the church the old couple brightened up. They went on to relate that when their son-in-law was hospitalized in a large city many miles away, a pastor from this same denomination had called on one of his members who shared the room with their relative. For several weeks he came every day and not only showed concern for his member but struck up a friendship with the son-in-law. He prayed for him and demonstrated pastoral care for this man who had no shepherd. As a result, the grateful old couple sold the property to the church at half the price which they had been

---

8. Brister, *Pastoral Care*, p. 244.

asking! When the building was completed, the son-in-law and his family began to attend regularly. In the first revival campaign conducted in the new church the seed so carefully sowed in the hospital brought forth its harvest. The entire family was converted and later united with the church.

As to the matter of exposing himself to the patient's illness, *the pastor should take reasonable precautions and go anywhere the physician goes.* Is not the soul of even more importance than the body? God can be trusted to take care of His servant when he goes where Jesus would go.

On my first Christmas in the pastorate, my brother-in-law, a fellow pastor, gave me a copy of Russell Dicks's *Pastoral Work and Personal Counseling.* I underlined these words which still contain contemporary truth: "Pastoral work consists more of going to the people than it does in their coming to him, for the pastor who goes to his people ultimately will find them coming to him."[9] Thus calling not only serves its distinctive purpose but builds a bridge to the next area of pastoral care to be considered.

B. Pastoral Counseling

This is a very specialized ministry and should be undertaken only after one has made a serious study of the principles and techniques of successful counseling. This discussion is of necessity only cursory and will attempt to point out some general guidelines for its practice.

Possible Perils

At the very outset let us acknowledge that no area of pastoral ministry contains more potential hazards than this one does. A word of warning must be given to those who offer this service. Dr. W. T. Purkiser observes that "one of the most important contributions . . . the pastor makes in his counselling is in the assurance he gives of care and love

---

9. Dicks, *Pastoral Work,* p. 31.

for one in trouble."[10] In itself, this attitude of solicitude makes one liable to the following perils.

1. *Improper involvement.* Perhaps more pastors have forfeited their ministry by falling into this trap than by any other course of action. The extended periods of time spent privately with members of the opposite sex constitute a setting for possible problems. In addition, the subjects discussed are often very emotional in nature, and the counselor may unconsciously be drawn beyond professional concern into undue personal sympathy. This in turn has all too often been followed by unwise and even illegitimate emotional and physical response. *Pastor, don't play the fool at this point!* Exercise reasonable precautions which will safeguard your future ministry.

2. *Unwise advice.* The nondirective theory of counseling may have gone too far in ruling out the giving of advices, but there is some wisdom in this principle. Among other things it prevents the counselee from assigning the responsibility and blame for an unwise course of action to the counselor. In dealing with interpersonal relationships, it is all too easy for the one who has received the counsel to say, "But Rev. _____ advised me to do it." This can open up a veritable Pandora's box of unhappy consequences. How much better for the counselor to limit his decision-making so that the counselee must accept this responsibility.

While counseling is an important facet to pastoral care, it is only one of several very vital areas. Some ministers have become so absorbed in this phase of shepherding that they have neglected other essential duties. This can destroy the necessary balance of one's ministry and if not corrected may prove fatal to his effectiveness.

General Principles

Dr. Paul E. Johnson defines counseling as *"A responsive relationship arising from expressed need to work through*

---

10. W. T. Purkiser, *The New Testament Image of the Ministry* (Kansas City: Beacon Hill Press of Kansas City, 1969), p. 118.

difficulties by means of emotional understanding and grow-
ing responsibility."[11] This definition points up several basic
principles.

1. *Establish a precounseling relationship.* The pastor is in
a unique position to help those who are under stress. He is
trusted as a man who is unselfishly devoted to the welfare
of others. His pulpit ministry should convey this attitude.
His personal interest expressed in informal contacts and
pastoral calls will certify his sincere concern and open the
way for the counselee to take the initiative in seeking help.

2. *Maintain confidence.* Assurance should be given at the
outset that all counseling data will be treated as classified
information. The eleventh commandment for counselors is:
"Thou shalt not break a confidence!" Not even one's spouse
should be informed of the content of counseling sessions.
And this certainly is not sermon illustration material, at
least in the current pastorate.

3. *Instruct the individual to be completely candid.* There
is great value in the process of catharsis which comes from
the expression of pent-up hostilities, fears, frustrations, and
guilt. Many people do not need advice so much as the opportunity to talk freely and get some things off their chests.
The counselee should be urged to be absolutely free to say
anything he or she wishes to say.

4. *Listen carefully and nonjudgmentally.* Just as much as
they need to express themselves, people need the ear of a
sympathetic listener. Good counselors do not interrupt to
condemn or give advice but listen until individuals have
had opportunity to make a complete representation of their
problems and are ready for discussion of them.

5. *Explore several possible solutions.* Many counselees
will already have a good idea of what their options are. But
it is well to take a careful look at all possible courses of

---

11. Johnson, *Psychology of Pastoral Care,* p. 73.

action and their consequences. As stated previously, the counselor is usually better off not to volunteer advice. In instances where spiritual and ethical issues are involved, he may well give the support of the Scriptures and Christian tradition to solutions which warrant them. Without making up the individual's mind, the skillful counselor will guide his/her thinking toward correct choices by employing such questions as: "Does this seem logical?" or "Doesn't this sound like what Jesus would do?"

6. *Major in synthesis rather than analysis.* In analysis the counselor digs into a person's past in the Freudian manner to find the problems which have triggered maladjustments and unhappiness. In synthesis one seeks to help the person to find fulfillment and recognition. When this is accomplished, the disturbances generally evaporate. James Jauncey comments: "Some of us have a sneaking suspicion that the chief value of psychoanalysis was in the interest shown in the patient, making him feel fulfilled and recognized."[12] Most pastors cannot qualify as analysts and are better off to use the synthetic approach.

7. *Set time limits on counseling sessions.* No less an authority than Otto Rank, the renowned German psychologist, insisted on well-defined time limits to his interviews. He held that this motivated the counselee to produce more, come to deeper issues, and reach personal decisions before time ran out.[13] Failure to do this results in unduly long, drawn-out conferences which rob the busy pastor of valuable time. A definite understanding when the appointment is made that the session will last for one hour makes it possible to terminate the interview courteously.

8. *Refer clinical problems to professionals.* The pastor-psychiatrist relationship is similar to that between the general practitioner and the specialist in the medical field. It

---

12. James H. Jauncey, *Psychology for Successful Evangelism* (Chicago: Moody Press, 1972), p. 35.
13. Johnson, *Psychology of Pastoral Care*, p. 84.

is natural to begin with the pastor. But when the problem becomes too complex, he wisely refers it to a specialist who is trained to deal with mental illness. Ideally, the psychiatrist should be a Christian who will not discount the individual's religious needs. Lacking this, the pastor should maintain contact to safeguard the patient's spiritual life in case the psychiatrist proposes treatment which is destructive of these values.

Marital Counseling

No area of pastoral counseling is more fraught with frustration and failure than this one. By the time couples seek help, it is often too late to salvage the home. But with the tragic climb in the divorce rate and the equally tragic number of marriages that have degenerated into not-so-peaceful coexistence, pastors must put forth their best efforts to reconcile the differences that imperil marriages.

Periodic sermonic attention to the subject of marital happiness is imperative. The biblical ideal should be held up as the norm. This may precipitate private conversations and spiritual decisions which will keep situations from becoming critical. Or it may prompt husbands or wives (or both) to seek out the services of pastors as counselors.

Taking the initiative may be a pastoral prerogative in extreme cases. "If the marital crisis is urgent, [the pastor] may decide to step into the middle of it with understanding love. An office counselor will wait for persons to come to him asking for counsel. But a pastor has a different relationship to his people."[14] Shepherds cannot always wait for sheep to come to them with their hurts.

Some pastors insist on seeing couples together. The obvious advantage is that when he talks to one party first, the other may feel that he is prejudiced. Others prefer to see them one at a time and then together. In any event there is little value in seeing them either together or separately

---

14. *Ibid.*, p. 149.

unless they come voluntarily. If either comes against his will, little can be accomplished.

Johnson suggests six ingredients necessary for this specific type of counseling.

1. Responsive listening
2. Catharsis and acceptance
3. A search for cause-effect relations
4. The planning of steps to take
5. Practice in new ways of loving
6. Growth in faithful and forgiving love[15]

In no counseling is the Christian message more practical and relevant than in this area. The great majority of marital problems stem from rigid, self-serving attitudes. Happiness and harmony are the natural consequence when the interests of the other party are placed ahead of personal concerns. Going the extra mile and turning the other cheek make a great deal of domestic sense. Praying together can be the catalyst which brings husband and wife into a satisfying and enduring relationship.

Group Counseling

It has been estimated that 40 percent of the American populace go first to their ministers with a problem. Seldom can problems be solved in one interview. Thus, the busy pastor finds that it is nearly impossible to counsel with everyone who needs him. If he does not have competent paid assistants who can shoulder some of this load, he must look to laymen for help. A rather new innovation is the use of group counseling.

John B. Oman, a pioneer in this field, cites the following advantages from a pastor's viewpoint:

1. It puts people to work solving their own problems . . . and he is thus able to help as many simultaneously as he used to pray that he could when he relied on conference-type pastoral counseling.
2. Intelligent and compassionate lay leadership from the

---

15. *Ibid.*, pp. 156-59.

church can be trained quickly to take over the work of group leaders, so it is the church and not the pastor alone taking responsibility for counselees.

3. Group counseling successfully conducted in a church setting can only lead to new or renewed religious values.[16]

Another possible advantage is that instead of relating to the pastor who becomes an emotional focus, the individual relates to an entire group. Here several personalities are involved, and the process of relating to them is likely to follow the more normal pattern of the family emotional structure. Edgar N. Jackson lists these goals for such group activity:

1. The helping of individuals toward immediate relief from stress;
2. The helping of individuals to attain long-term goals of understanding and self-management;
3. The stimulation of emotional growth toward maturity in interpersonal relationships.[17]

The key to success in this activity is finding the right leaders. They must be carefully screened, given a year's training (including experience in a group), and involved in monthly meetings with other group leaders. The leader must understand that this is not a class where he lectures or a place for advice-giving. Proper assignment of group members to the proper group with the right leader is essential.

Three general rules apply to such groups:

1. Group members may say anything they wish.

2. One does not have to say anything if he doesn't want to.

3. Whatever is said in the group must not be repeated outside.

Problem areas as well as values are present in such an activity. Jackson frankly acknowledges, "We know that

---

16. John B. Oman, *Group Counseling in the Church* (Minneapolis: Augsburg Press, 1972), p. 12.

17. Edgar N. Jackson, *Group Counseling* (Philadelphia: Pilgrim Press, 1969), p. 101.

group dynamics may work to injure persons as well as to help them. . . . The creative use of group dynamics is not easy. Much group activity is inclined toward the release of primitive emotional drives."[18] Sad experience has proved that *such groups can be nearly disastrous when composed of members of the same church*. The airing of personal problems with a peer group of personal acquaintances will often produce destructive results. For these reasons it is my personal conviction that group counseling should be limited to the following:

1. Large metropolitan areas where such activity is more demanded and needed.

2. Individuals who are not identified with the church but who come to the pastor for help.

3. Groups which are periodically monitored by the pastor so that potentially dangerous procedures and practices can be detected and avoided.

With these safeguards, group counseling may become a worthwhile supplement to pastoral counseling, providing therapy for a clientele which the minister would not have time to counsel individually.

---

18. *Ibid.*, p. 10.

Here is a list of some of the parts he has placed in his church, which is his body: . . . Those who can get others to work together (1 Cor. 12:28, TLB).

CHAPTER 9

The Shepherd-Manager

A large aircraft manufacturing company was in dire financial straits. Its products were of high quality and were in great demand with millions of dollars of orders waiting to be filled. Production was at peak capacity. But the corporation was threatened with bankruptcy. A firm of management consultants was hired to find out what was basically wrong with the operation. Their investigation revealed that poor administration was the primary culprit. A merger was arranged with a smaller firm which had superior executive leadership. With this new managerial team in charge, the combined companies began to show increased efficiency within a short period of time, and at the end of the fiscal year the corporation returned a good dividend to its stockholders. *Good management made the difference.*

A private college was perilously close to having to suspend operations. Enrollment was high. The physical plant was first rate. An excellent faculty had been secured. But failure to face a ballooning current operations deficit had nearly brought the institution down. A change in top leadership was effected. New financial procedures were instituted. Within a few years the school had completely erased the large accumulated debt and has continued to operate with a balanced budget. *Strong management made the difference.*

The successful operation of the church will depend in no small measure upon the management skills of its leaders. This is true not only on the general and district levels but also in the local congregation. Churches that show a consistent pattern of growth in finances and facilities as well as membership are invariably well managed. A practical demonstration of the importance of this phase of shepherding was shown in a time study conducted with a large group of pastors. The results showed that 25 percent of the average pastor's week was spent in the preaching-teaching area and 25 percent in pastoral care activities. *But 50 percent of his time was spent in administrative or management responsibilities.*[1]

Seward Hiltner observes that most ministers find genuine fulfillment in studying, calling, and counselling activities which they can carry on by themselves. But where they experience difficulty is in relating to other people in administering the work of the church. The basic reason for this is that such cooperative enterprise involves risk-taking and risks make the "administration-hater" fearful.[2] There is no do-it-yourself kit for successful ministry, but regardless of the size of the congregation the efficient operation of the church depends upon shared responsibility.

The president of one of America's greatest corporations suggests six tests for determining whether an administrator is successful:

1. Is he skillful at sorting the trivial from the important?
2. Does he inspire excellence in others?
3. Does he remain strong under pressure?
4. Is he curious about activities outside his immediate realm?
5. Do new ideas excite him?

---

1. Pusey and Taylor, *Ministry for Tomorrow*, p. 38.
2. Seward Hiltner, *Ferment in the Ministry* (Nashville: Abingdon Press, 1969), p. 82.

6. Does he get along easily and naturally with people?
These questions point up the profile of the pastor-administrator who will achieve results in church management.

Decision-making

One of the key responsibilities of the manager is the making of decisions. This is one of the liabilities of leadership. Not all decisions are going to be popular. But if you are going to lead the band, you must be prepared to face the music! Then, realistically, all decisions are not going to be right. Shepherds are human and their fallibility will be painfully apparent at times. But the smaller the number of incorrect decisions, the greater the achievement level. Attention to the basic principles involved in decision-making is imperative if management is to be effective.

1. *The starting point is the establishing of priorities.* The Kingdom building enterprise is a never-ending one. There are more good things to do than we can ever get done. This necessitates a system for grading the relative importance of programs and activities. One key government official has devised an ingenious method for handling this problem. The telephones in his office are color-coded to denote the seriousness of each call. When the phone rings, he can immediately tell whether it is a critical or less important matter. But someone has to decide which phone to ring! This is a role which the pastor-administrator must assume. He must sort out *the majors and the minors,* the first, second, and third. He must also separate *the "nows" from the "laters."* Everything cannot be done today—or tomorrow. He must decide what can wait and what can't. While the final decision must be his, the wise administrator will pick the brains of his most capable laymen in this regard. The involvement of knowledgeable people in the assessment of priorities relieves the pastor of the responsibility for unilateral decisions. Two (or 20) heads are better than 1!

2. *Decisions should be made at the lowest possible level.* A part of the responsibility which is delegated to staff

members or lay leaders is that of making decisions in their specific areas. Olan Hendrix comments:

> Decisions should always be made as near as possible to where the work is actually performed. Unless a one-man ruler is tremendously goal-oriented, he will make as many decisions as he possibly can. Even a pastor, unless he is tremendously goal-oriented, will grasp for as much decision-making as he can possibly get. Why? To protect himself, and to be more comfortable. . . . Our very nature will cause us to accumulate things at the top. This retards the progress of the whole group by forcing everything to be channeled through one man. . . . We achieve goals best when people are allowed to make as many decisions as possible which affect their work.[3]

By delegating lower-level decisions to the appropriate persons, the pastor-manager frees himself to give consideration to the executive-level decision-making which is his responsibility.

3. *Define the problem objectively.* This means assembling all the facts and facing them squarely. Incomplete data is one of the most common reasons for incorrect decisions. A wise pastor will do his homework carefully. The extra time taken for such research is well spent. While he must make these decisions himself, he will do well to secure information from the most reliable sources in his congregation. This should be authenticated as much as possible, for even as hearsay is not admissible as evidence in court, it is not reliable as the basis for making decisions.

4. *Anticipate the consequences of the alternatives.* This means asking and answering such questions as these. What will happen if decision A is made? Is this better than the consequences of decision B? What are the negative possibilities of each? Weighing the effects of the several possible choices will contribute a vital dimension to the final decision. Sometimes it will actually come down to the lesser of

---

3. Olan Hendrix, *Management and the Christian Worker* (Fort Washington, Pa.: Christian Literature Crusade, 1970), pp. 86-87.

two evils. Hopefully, most of the time it will be a matter of determining the better and the best courses of action.

5. *Face mistakes honestly and constructively.* Risk is implicit whenever decisions must be made. If an individual is afraid of making mistakes, he will develop a timidity toward decision-making which will render his administration ineffective. Even the greatest baseball player does not bat 1.000. The man of God does not possess omniscience. When he errs, he should admit his mistake and profit from the experience. When associates "strike out," tolerance and understanding should be demonstrated toward them and encouragement given to try again. Next time they may hit a home run!

6. *Rely heavily on divine guidance.* Kingdom decisions are the King's business. He has promised to give wisdom to those who sense their need of His direction. And who qualifies for this assistance more than His ministering servant? The certainty of divine guidance enables the shepherd-manager to make the necessary decisions with the poise and assurance which inspire confidence in members of the flock.

Designation of Responsibilities

This begins with the minister himself. Any unwillingness to assume his ex-officio duties will be contagious. In his advices to shepherds Peter counsels, "Lead them by your good example" (1 Pet. 5:3, TLB). It is more than coincidental that thriving churches are invariably led by pastors who set a vigorous pace of service for their people. Never satisfied with personal minimums they go far beyond the line of duty in dispatching their ministerial responsibilities. Small wonder that lay visitation programs prosper where pastoral calling is the order of both day and night in the schedule of the man of God. And this principle obtains in all areas of church activity.

On the foundation of this pastoral example laymen can be challenged to accept the responsibilities of office holding as an opportunity to render dedicated service to God through the channels of the church. Their role must not be limited to mechanical detail work which reduces them to being virtual puppets who jump when the pastor pulls their strings. There must be a dignity attached to their tasks which will call out the best in them.

Careful attention should be given to the selection of *the right people for the right jobs.* Three qualifications are imperative:

1. *Spiritual vitality.* This is basic and primary. No leader can give proper leadership without the help of the Holy Spirit. The *Manual* wisely requires that all elected officials should be clearly in the experience of entire sanctification. It is in order for all nominees to be contacted by mail prior to election and given a job description of the office for which they have been nominated including this spiritual requirement. Each individual should be given the opportunity to privately decline nomination if he or she feels unable to qualify.

2. *Team concept.* There is no place for "loners" in the successful operation of Kingdom enterprises. The Apostle Paul made this clear when he declared that "we . . . [are] workers together with him" (2 Cor. 6:1). This means not only man working cooperatively with God but also men and women laboring harmoniously with each other. The Pauline analogy of the body of Christ being composed of eyes, hands, and other organs and appendages functioning as a unit is the basic model of the New Testament church.

3. *Aptitudes and abilities.* The church is being blessed with a growing group of well-trained, capable lay men and women. Their sanctified skills should be enlisted. Successful business and professional people have a valuable contribution to make in the wise management of the church. The pastor should not feel threatened by such strong lay leadership. If they are spiritually qualified, they will not be interested in becoming "church bosses," but they will want and deserve the opportunity to be actively and constructively involved in the operation of their church. In cases where such qualified individuals are not available for office, the alter-

native is to seek out those who have some natural aptitudes for service. Willingness to accept training and to give diligent application to learning the necessary skills can compensate for a lack of natural endowment.

The Annual Meeting

This gathering of the membership of the church is the official vehicle for the assignment of responsibility and may well determine the progress (or lack of it) the local church will make during the coming year. The same is true regarding the departments of the church, for the principles which obtain for a successful church meeting are also valid for the annual business meetings of the missionary and youth departments. The date should be set as early as possible before the close of the church year. This gives opportunity for the newly elected officers to organize and meet for planning sessions prior to the opening of the new year.

When should it be held? Whenever the largest possible representation of members can be present. Many churches now designate a Sunday for this meeting. All reports are duplicated and put together in a brochure which is presented to everyone present in the morning service. Members are urged to read it carefully during the afternoon. The pastor might well preach a sermon on the doctrinal beliefs or ethical positions of the church. At the conclusion of the message visitors may be excused and a ballot for church officers taken. In the evening service the results of the vote may be reported and the audited treasurer's report adopted. This eliminates a marathon session of oral reports and enlists maximum participation in the elective process. A by-product of this procedure may be the breaking up of "power structures" which have resulted from the same small group of people processing the business of the church on a weeknight year after year. The conducting of this Kingdom business on the Lord's Day should not be a substitute for worship and evangelistic services, but if well planned it can be a meaningful supplement to these important functions.

The nominating process is also vital. Provision is made in the polity of the church for a nominating committee which may be constituted by the church board. The pastor should chair this important committee. It should be composed of representative churchmen who are well acquainted with the personnel of the church. The committee should be instructed to operate with three important guidelines in mind:

1. *The best interests of the church.* Members must endeavor to be completely objective in appraising the qualifications of individuals. Incumbents need not be nominated just because they have served before.

2. *Complete candor.* Discussion of possible nominees should never sink to the level of character assassination. But neither should information be withheld which would throw light on their eligibility to serve. The time to air such matters is while the committee is in session, not after it has adjourned.

3. *Absolute confidentiality.* Discussions of individuals within the committee *must* be treated as privileged communications. No one should be allowed to serve who cannot maintain this confidence. "Leaks" from committee meetings can easily be taken out of context and may prove disastrous.

In larger churches where there is greater leadership potential, *rotation of elected officials* is often a wise policy. The church board may voluntarily limit the tenure of its members to three or four consecutive years. In such cases the nominating committee would not place a designated number of incumbents on the ballot for the coming year. After a year's absence from the board the names of such persons could be placed in nomination again if the committee saw fit. Such a procedure results in wider participation and the infusion of new points of view into the board's perspective.

Church Board Operation

As chairman, the pastor is obligated to perfect the organization of the board as prescribed in the *Manual*. This should include the appointment of committees. Some representative ones are:

Finance
Buildings and Grounds
Personnel and Program
Education (or Church School Board)
Evangelism and Outreach
Fellowship

Often the board will request the pastor to present recommendations for these committees which will then be officially elected by the board itself. *This is one of the most crucial and determinative functions of the pastor.* Staffing these committees with knowledgeable, forward-looking people may well hold the key to the effectiveness of the entire church operation. While the chairmen and main membership of these committees should be board members, some persons outside of the board who have particular skills in these areas may also be included. The pastor is an ex-officio member of each committee and should meet with them frequently. In these sessions he will have opportunity to share his ideals and goals and aid in formulating specific plans.

Planning session. Prior to the opening of the church year, the new officers should meet to set goals and lay preliminary plans. A Friday night and Saturday retreat is ideal for this purpose. This may well serve as a spiritual launching pad as well as a programming time. Objectives should be clearly agreed upon and definite plans made for achieving them. Committees should meet and do preliminary work.

Regular board meetings. Beyond the devotional period and the monthly report of the treasurer, the agenda of the meeting both for old and new business should be based *entirely* upon the reports of the committees. Any matters introduced spontaneously during the meeting should be referred to the appropriate committee for consideration before any general discussion and action is engaged in by the entire board. Full and intelligent attention can be given to all such items by the committees and recommendations reported back to the entire board at its next meeting. Committee reports should be made by the chairmen. This relieves the pastor of the responsibility of selling the program. He may wish to make constructive comments, but experience has proved that a well-thought-out and competently presented committee report will almost always receive the acceptance and support of the church board.

Financing the Flock

There is no more crucial operation in the church than its treasury, and the pastor of necessity must play the key role in its management. Interestingly enough, though we think of Jesus as being above and against materialism, He had more to say about money and the correct stewardship of it than He did about any "spiritual" subject. He talked about both tithes and offerings. His advice on laying up treasures in heaven by Christian generosity is classic. Sermons on stewardship and instruction of new converts in the principles of dollar discipleship are in order. But the preacher who properly organizes and administers the financial program of his church will not have to belabor this subject.

Successful money management begins with careful planning. As soon as possible after appointment, the finance committee should prepare an operating budget for the year. This should include:

> Salaries
> Local operating expenses
> District, educational, and general budgets
> Proposed building expenses and debt service
> Contingent fund

Consideration should be given to the financial experience of the previous year, but the new budget should be predicated in part upon the anticipation of church growth with the accompanying increase in income. The budget should be based primarily upon the income which will be produced by *the tithe from every member-family.* Anything less than this is unscriptural. But allowance should also be made for a reasonable number of special offerings for missions, colleges and seminary, and building projects which will supplement these receipts. Christian generosity begins where tithing ends. No apology should ever be made for presenting opportunities for investing in Kingdom needs.

Oswald J. Smith pioneered the concept of Faith Promise giving for missions. Many churches have adopted this method and have found it to be of great spiritual benefit to the participants as well as a means of raising unprecedented amounts of money for this vital enterprise. The program is launched with a convention featuring missionary speakers. Then the congregation is challenged to pledge an amount over and above its regular giving for this cause. People are encouraged to make this a step of faith, trusting the Lord to supply the means. Payment may be made at periodic intervals or in a lump sum, according to the desires of the individual. Testimonies of the miraculous ways in which God has honored the obedient faith of those who have made pledges are a blessed by-product of this plan.

Another contributing factor to successful church financing is *good communication.* Too often we take for granted that all church members understand where their money goes. The fact is, some lay leaders have only a hazy idea, and the majority of the congregation is completely in the dark. This is particularly true in regard to the *benevolence budgets* which go to causes outside of the local church. *These are not optional,* and any pastor who expects to continue in the ministry must see that they are paid. There is a romance about these responsibilities if they are properly presented. First, the church board should be intelligently apprised of what each budget is for. Then this information should be conveyed to the congregation. Lyle Schaller tells of a Lutheran church which did this in a most effective way. One wall of the narthex was covered with a series of posters. Each depicted a particular budget. One had a large picture of the denominational college supported by the church with the figure $685 written below it (the amount of the education budget). Another had the picture of a retired former pastor on it along with the amount of their pension budget that helped support him. When each budget was paid in full, a big X was marked across the poster.[4] This dramatic method of communication is just one of several which can be usefully employed.

Sunday bulletins and church newsletters are excellent means of keeping the congregation posted on financial progress. The annual budget should be broken down into the amount needed each week to meet it. The comparison of the previous Sunday's receipts and the weekly need speaks for itself. This information is a silent sermon on the necessity of bringing all the tithes into the storehouse. At the end of each month any deficit should be noted and made a subject of prayer at the time of the offering. A fully informed church will more often than not rise to the challenge of meeting its responsibilities in this regard.

While he must be involved in managing the financial affairs of the church, *the pastor should personally handle as little of its money as possible.* Care exercised at this point may well avert any question about his integrity. In the rare instances where he cannot avoid accepting cash donations for the church, receipts should be sent to the donor so that no question can be raised about the reception of these funds by the church treasurer. All offerings should be counted by the committee appointed for this purpose. Bank deposits should be made by designated persons other than the pastor. *An image of scrupulous honesty in money matters is absolutely essential* if the pastor is to enjoy the full confidence of his people. Without this trust, no shepherd can manage his flock.

Then, a word about *treasurers.* Extreme caution should be exercised in the selection of the treasurers of the church and its auxiliaries. Some knowledge of basic accounting and bookkeeping practices is a prime requisite. In addition, a *cooperative attitude* is most important. Treasurers who develop an ownership complex concerning church funds and exercise their own initiative in their disbursement

---

4. Lyle E. Schaller, *The Pastor and the People* (Nashville: Abingdon Press, 1973), p. 125.

should be dealt with kindly but firmly by the church board. For the church's protection, the treasurer should be bonded. For the treasurer's protection, he should have the benefit of a certified audit of his books by professional accountants at the close of the year. As chairman of the board, the pastor should give opportunity at each monthly board meeting for discussion of the current treasurer's report so that all minds will be clear concerning the receipt and expenditure of funds. *These reports should not be adopted by the board.* Rather, the pastor should state that they are *received* and will be filed with the secretary of the board pending the annual audit. Should the audit disclose mishandling of funds, then the church board is not put in the embarrassing and even legally incriminating position of having officially adopted the unaudited monthly reports. At the annual meeting the audited treasurer's report should be adopted.

Administrative Attitudes and Relations

While there are calculated risks involved in giving a measure of freedom to lay leaders in their assignments, this is the only way to encourage innovation and develop initiative. A biographer of one of our great presidents indicates that one of his strengths was a certain detachment from the details of his administration. He did not try to run everything but gave his people their head. Sometimes he was criticized for letting them go off too much on their own, but this was his way of trying people out.[5] Strong churchmen are not born but made. And the opportunity to learn by doing with a loose rein of pastoral confidence in evidence will contribute immeasurably to this process.

Proper orientation and guidance should be given so that the one appointed or elected to office will have an understanding of the scope of the assignment. *Designated checkpoints* should be set up to avoid premature and unwise decisions. Some pastors have found that a regular schedule

---

5. Arthur M. Schlesinger, *A Thousand Days* (Boston: Houghton Mifflin Co., 1965), p. 686.

of breakfast meetings with department heads, committee chairmen, and other key people serves a very effective purpose. Plans and programs can be discussed while they are in the embryonic stage. Constructive criticism and input can be given by the pastor before such planning reaches a place where the only effective deterrent would be a pastoral veto. This latter action should be a last resort and ought to be avoided if at all possible since it almost inevitably produces interpersonal stress and even a breakdown of communication.

Good interpersonal relations between pastoral and lay leadership are imperative in successful administration. The last of the six questions posed earlier in this chapter may well be the most crucial—*Does he get along easily and naturally with people?* If this is important in business where administrators are dealing with individuals who are being paid for their services, how much more essential it is when our workers are all unsalaried.

Nothing is more damaging to effective management than the impression, warranted or not, that people are being used or manipulated to further the personal fortunes of the leader. Any indication of insincerity on the part of the administrator will cancel out the cooperation of those whose efforts are essential to the ongoing of the church.

Sensitivity to attitudes is imperative. Dr. Russell Bowie describes a woman whose interpersonal relationships were outstanding as being extremely perceptive in this regard. She "had her feelers out making contact with people; she seemed to feel mankind."[6] Happy the minister-manager who has developed this ability.

In reality, administrative success or failure may finally be determined by one's *attitude toward opposition*. Few major programs will enlist unanimous support. Even devoted Christians have differing opinions. Any temptation to unchristianize those who do not accept pastoral leadership must be steadfastly resisted. Dr. Samuel Young has wisely observed that God called Moses to deliver His peo-

---

6. Bowie, *Where You Find God*, p. 89.

ple, not drown them! In our more honest moments some of us must confess that on occasion our initial reaction to rejection may have tended more to drowning than deliverance. Opposition may run the entire gamut from sincere difference of judgment to reactionary, power structure response. Several principles obtain in dealing with such resistance.

1. *Identify the source and strength.* Many times the smallest minority is the most vocal. The opportunity of free expression in church board and congregational meetings with the assurance of no reprisals for opposing points of view should help to identify honest opposition. The attitude of nonsupportive fringe people may be discounted much more quickly than that of fully involved lay leaders. Then, too, the size of the negative vote on official proposals will be determinative. *Seldom, if ever, is it judicious to proceed with any program which does not enlist the support of at least two-thirds of the membership.* Lacking this, one is wise to postpone action until clarification and/or modification raises the percentage of support.

2. *Refuse to accept such opposition as a personal affront.* Even in the rare instances where it may be, no good purpose will be served by taking refuge in this rationalization. Keep the spotlight on *principles rather than personalities.* In relating to strong laymen with equally strong ideas, be sure that subconsciously they are not allowed to constitute a threat. Respect opposing points of view as honest attempts to find the most effective solutions to problems.

3. *Make every effort to salvage the opposition.* This must not be done at the cost of compromising principles. However, anything short of this is warranted if it will save people for God and the church. Liddell Hart counsels, "Never corner an opponent; always assist him to save face." While face saving should not be the Christian's prime goal, it is not incompatible with the holy life. Helping the opposition to cooperate with the will of the majority and still maintain personal dignity may not only save the day but also conserve vital human resources for the Kingdom.

As in all interpersonal relationships, the key word is love . . . love that is "not quick to take offence . . . [that] keeps no score of wrongs" (1 Cor. 13:5, NEB) . . . love that "gives us power to endure everything" (1 Cor. 13:7, Williams). The demonstration of such shepherd-love is the most effective lubricant for all management machinery.

Conclusion

Speaking as one who actually served as a professional shepherd in charge of four-legged sheep, Philip Keller states: "When all is said and done, the welfare of any flock is entirely dependent upon the management afforded them by their shepherd."[7] Spiritual shepherds cannot escape this same responsibility. Let every man of God give diligent attention to the development of these managerial skills so that his efforts will result in a harmonious, smoothly functioning flock.

---

7. W. Phillip Keller, *A Shepherd Looks at Psalm 23* (Grand Rapids,. Mich.: Zondervan Publishing House, 1970), p. 28.

*The multiple ministry is composed
of persons under the call of God in
the universal Christian church who
are selected by a congregation . . .
[to direct them] as they assemble
for worship and nurture and are
dispersed for work and service in
the world* (Marvin T. Judy).[1]

CHAPTER 10

Undershepherd Ministries

The basic organizational pattern for the church calls for
one shepherd for each flock. The scarcity of shepherds and
the smallness of the flocks sometimes necessitates a pastor's assuming shepherding responsibilities for several congregations. On the other hand, the growth of some churches
to larger than average size makes it imperative that they
provide professional undershepherds to assist the pastor in
servicing congregational needs.

While the latter situation is more common than the former, it is still not the norm. The large majority of churches
can support only one full-time minister. Yet in even a
moderate-sized congregation, the work load of preaching,
administration, and pastoral care becomes a nearly impossible assignment for one man. Where does the answer lie?

---

1. Marvin T. Judy, *The Multiple Staff Ministry* (Nashville: Abingdon
Press, 1969), p. 39.

Unpaid Assistants

Even if the pastor could do it all, he should not. Jesus taught this precept by His own example. In the narrative of the feeding of the 5,000, it became necessary to organize this scattered multitude into some semblance of order so that bread and fish could be distributed. The Master could have raised His voice and shouted out the necessary commands. But He didn't. Rather, "Jesus directed *them* to have all the people sit down in groups on the green grass" (Mark 6:39, NIV, italics added). Mobilization of volunteer manpower was an integral part of His modus operandi.

Seward Hiltner contends that as early as the second century the multiple-staff concept of ministry was practiced. The bishop was the counterpart of the modern-day pastor. His principal associates were elders and deacons.[2]

Training

The wise pastor also recognizes that *a vital part of his role as shepherd is the training of these lay undershepherds.* We are indebted to Elton Trueblood for reminding us that Paul was referring to this equipping ministry in Eph. 4:12. The apostles, prophets, evangelists, and pastors were "to prepare God's people for works of service, so that the body of Christ may be built up" (NIV). This takes time, but it is one of the most productive investments which the shepherd can make. The value to the Kingdom enterprise of this extension of his ministry is incalculable. Not the least of these is the personal growth and spiritual development which these unpaid assistants make as they fulfill this calling and "become mature, attaining the full measure of perfection found in Christ" (Eph. 4:13, NIV).

Interestingly enough, Lyle Schaller observes that "one of the most significant changes occurring in many churches is a shift in emphasis from professionalism to participation . . .

---

2. Hiltner, *Ferment*, pp. 33-34.

more widespread participation by laymen in functions that once were the responsibility of paid staff members."[3]

Whether lay or professional, undershepherds might well be guided in their service by these objectives formulated by one denomination's Sunday school board for its personnel:

1. To lead each person to a genuine experience of the forgiving and saving grace of God through Jesus Christ.

2. To guide each person into intelligent, active, and devoted membership in a New Testament church.

3. To help each person to make Christian worship a vital and constant part of his expanding experience.

4. To help each person to know the Bible; the great realities of the Christian faith; the history and status of the Christian movement; and the history, distinctive beliefs, and practices of his own denomination; and to develop deep and abiding Christian convictions concerning all these matters.

5. To assist each person in developing such Christian attitudes and appreciations in every area of experience that he will have a Christian approach to all of life.

6. To guide each person in developing habits and in learning techniques which promote spiritual growth, and in accepting and applying Christian standards of personal and social conduct in every area of life.

7. To guide each person to invest his talents and to develop skills in Christian service.

What a dynamic difference this concept of shared ministry in music, Christian education, visitation, youth work, and other vital areas could make if pastors were willing and able to convey it to their people. Latent abilities can be tapped and trained. The flock will prosper under the expanded care provided by these undershepherds. And it becomes a continuing and enlarging program as trainees develop into trainers.

---

3. Schaller, *The Pastor and the People* (Nashville: Abingdon Press, 1973), p. 23.

Visitation

Nowhere is this emphasis more needful and practical than in the ministry of visitation. No pastor can do all the calling that needs to be done. But there are several ways in which his efforts can be supplemented. *First, by Sunday school teachers.* In a very real sense each teacher shepherds his or her class. Teaching is a form of flock feeding. But this is not enough. Personal interest and spiritual care must be invested in class members through home visitation. As these calls are made, information relative to specific problems and needs should be communicated to the pastor for his attention.

Area or community groups, sometimes called "Circles of Concern," are another vital avenue of service for lay under-shepherds. Every constituent of the church is assigned to one of these groups according to the area of his residence. A dedicated layman is placed in charge of each circle. It is his responsibility to maintain communications with each member of the group. Serious problems can be brought to the pastor's attention, and special prayer needs can be shared with others in the circle. A family spirit is developed which removes the impersonal appearance which the church too often tends to project.

Women's calling groups represent still another possibility for meaningful involvement. Lucas Buttry comments: "Women need and desire an outlet for their service to Christ. Many women have time to serve and need direction in how best to use such time. A calling program answers this need and desire."[4] A specific time each week should be designated for this activity. A period of prayer should be engaged in prior to disbursement for calling. The leader should then make assignments from data supplied by the pastor or director of visitation. Two ladies calling together are the ideal number. Too large a group is unwieldy and impractical. Reports of the calls should be channeled to the pastor for his information.

------

4. Buttry, *Calling Program*, p. 85.

The resource of the retired. A growing number of both men and women are taking retirement from their secular vocations in their early sixties and even late fifties. They are not ready for the rocking chair. The potential of this pool of committed churchmen is tremendous. Many can be challenged to donate a generous block of time to church service. Women with secretarial experience can free the pastor from the tyranny of the typewriter and mimeograph so he can train laymen to assist him in various undershepherd ministries. Both men and women can give time to visitation programs. Freed from the necessity of making a living, these retirees will find tremendous fulfillment in these labors of love for their Saviour.

While we speak of these as unpaid assistants, the truth is they will receive generous remuneration for their services. In addition to their heavenly reward, the satisfaction of responding to need and the personal fulfillment and learning which will come provide valuable compensation for their contribution.

Starting a Professional Staff

In most instances, the first paid staff member will be a part-time or full-time secretary. An efficient office manager can spare the pastor innumerable hours of routine work and free him for study, prayer, and pastoral care activity. In turn, the secretary can train and supervise volunteers to do such busywork as running the mimeograph and folding and addressing mail.

The first impression of the church for many people will be the way the secretary answers the telephone in the church office. A cheerful, courteous response to the caller is excellent public relations. In addition to a good disposition, she must also be able to keep a confidence. A compulsive gossiper can do irreparable damage in this position. No amount of vocational skill can compensate for this debilitating weakness.

The Next Step

When is a church ready for additional professional assis-

tance? Plain talk is in order at this point. In recent years a "second-man syndrome" has developed in the church. Paid assistants have become an ecclesiastical status symbol. Some churches have neglected their benevolence budgets in order to pay the salary of one or more associate pastors who were hired before the churches were financially strong enough to carry this additional load.

There is considerable question whether a pastor who is efficiently employing the services of volunteer lay under-shepherds is in real need of a paid staff member until his membership reaches the 250 mark. W. L. Howse, a real professional in this field who has served on the staff of such great churches as First Baptist of Dallas, raises the minimum even higher. "A church with three hundred to four hundred members needs a full-time staff member in addition to the pastor. . . . As the membership of the church increases, a new staff member will be needed for each five to six hundred members."[5]

Premature staffing can be exceedingly costly both from a financial standpoint and also in denying laymen the legitimate opportunity to serve in the ministries of music, Christian education, and youth. *Only when the size and scope of the program becomes so great that it demands professional assistance to supervise and administer the work of these laymen is the addition of paid staff members justified.*

Another factor to be considered is whether the pastor himself is conditioned for the added responsibilities of a staff. While assistants relieve him of some responsibilities, they add others. Adequate supervision is essential, including the initial orientation as well as continuing surveillance with the receiving of reports and periodic staff meetings. All this makes demands upon the pastor's schedule.

There is also the calculated risk of dividing the loyalties of the congregation. If the assistant is a minister, he will want to preach as often as possible. His pulpit abilities may

5. Howse, *Church Staff*, p. 25.

even make the pastor's suffer by comparison. Experience has proved that, on occasion, associates have innocently (or not so innocently) become identified with factions in the church which are in opposition to the pastor. The results of such polarization are disastrous. All this must be considered before a staff member is added.

The personnel committee and church board should be involved in feasibility studies relative to the need for and ability to support a paid assistant. Only when these groups are fully convinced that the church is ready for the addition of a professional staff member should positive action be taken. The *Manual* wisely provides that the approval of the district superintendent is necessary before full-time paid assistants are hired. The pastor and church need the objective judgment of the superintendent both as to the need for staff and the qualifications of the individual under consideration.

Part-time staff members are often the first step. Ministerial students in college and seminary are available for short-term internship service. This arrangement can be mutually beneficial. Schoolteachers with skills in music and education may be secured on a part-time basis to administer these areas in the church. Retired ministers can make a valuable contribution in visitation and the direction of senior adult ministries. By paying them the modest allowable supplement to their Social Security income, the church can receive a very worthwhile ministry.

Securing a Staff

After ascertaining that full-time assistance is both necessary and warranted, *the first step is to identify the area(s) of greatest immediate need.* The securing of a specialist in a particular field is generally more logical than the hiring of an associate minister whose skills parallel those of the pastor. Financial considerations may dictate the necessity of combining several areas which are compatible. For example, the ministries of music and Christian education or youth and Christian education can be administered by individuals with some proficiency in both areas.

The personnel and finance committees should then be

involved in drawing up a detailed job description for final action by the church board. It should include the following essential items:

1. A statement of duties or areas of responsibility.

2. Lines of responsibility for supervision, reporting, and amenability.

3. Schedule of work time, days off, and vacation.

4. Salary, housing allowance, expense account, and fringe benefits.

Here is a sample job description.

MINISTER OF MUSIC AND CHRISTIAN EDUCATION

I. *Regular Duties*
   A. Music:
      1. Lead congregational singing.
      2. Train and direct choir.
      3. Organize and train special music groups—adult, youth, children.
      4. Plan worship services with the pastor.
      5. Keep music equipment in good condition.
      6. Present budget needs for music program.
      7. Participate in meetings of the music committee as a nonvoting member.
   B. Christian Education:
      1. Have general supervision and coordination of the total educational program of the church.
      2. Work cooperatively with the Sunday school superintendent and the education committee.
      3. Develop and recommend prospective workers.
      4. Counsel and train workers.
      5. Make recommendations for education budget including facilities and equipment.
      6. Participate in meetings of the education committee as a nonvoting member.
   C. Attend all meetings of the church staff.
   D. Give serious attention to soul winning both in personal and public evangelism.
   E. Make a minimum of 1,000 calls a year on persons

both within his areas of responsibility and outside of them.

F. Participate in community, district, and general church activities as opportunity and time permit.

II. *Lines of Responsibility*

A. Direct supervision is from the pastor; regular reports should be made to him including the sharing of complaints and requests.

B. Final amenability is to the church board through the pastor.

C. Tenure is for one year, subject to annual review and renewal by the church board upon the recommendation of the pastor. (Resignation is mandatory at the time of the pastor's resignation.)

III. *Work Schedule*

A. A five-day work week is expected.

B. Office hours, evening responsibilities, and field activities should be agreed upon with the pastor.

C. A day off each week should be scheduled with the pastor.

D. An annual vacation of two weeks (including two Sundays) with pay should be scheduled with the pastor.

E. An additional two weeks away from the church is allowed each year for revivals, conferences, and other church-related activities upon approval of the pastor.

IV. *Salary and Benefits*

A. The base salary shall be $7,800° a year, payable weekly.

B. A housing allowance of $2,400° a year will be provided. If so desired, an additional portion of the salary may be designated for housing (in accordance with Internal Revenue regulations).

C. $500° a year will be provided for travel expense.

D. One-half of the Social Security premium will be provided by the church, and hospital insurance will be covered under the district program for ministers.

E. Salary increases will be considered annually on the basis of the cost of living and also of individual merit.

°Amounts stated are hypothetical.

Having formulated a clear job description, *the finding of the right person to fill the position now becomes the pastor's responsibility.* This will become a subject of earnest prayer that the Holy Spirit will provide leadership in this crucial matter. Dr. Howse suggests this profile of qualifications which should be looked for in a prospective undershepherd.

1. Called of God
2. Love for people
3. Physical and nervous energy
4. Sense of purpose and mission
5. Patience and self-control
6. Willingness to study and work
7. Ability to adjust
8. Ability to cooperate
9. Balanced judgment and tact
10. Sense of humor
11. Ability to take criticism
12. Strong in faith
13. Effective in prayer[6]

To these I would add one more:
14. *Loyalty to the pastor!*

All these are basic qualities which a staff member must have to render effective service. In addition to securing information about an individual's professional skills, it would be wise to have professors and pastors who are well acquainted with this person to rate him or her on these 14 qualifications. A serious deficiency in any of them could well negate further consideration.

A personal interview will serve to provide further information about the individual's preparation, experience, and personality. The job description should be discussed very frankly and openly. While no formal contract will be signed, anyone joining the church staff should be willing to give an unqualified verbal acceptance of these conditions of employ-

---

6. *Ibid.*, pp. 102-7.

ment. Any differences should be completely resolved before the recommendation to invite the individual to accept this position is taken to the church board for final consideration. It is easier to hire than to fire, and careful investigation is worth whatever time and expense are involved.

Shepherding Undershepherds

Once the commitment has been made to staff ministry, the pastor must accept the responsibility of maintaining a HAPPY AND PRODUCTIVE RELATIONSHIP with his assistants. At one and the same time he must command the legitimate respect which his office requires, and yet create an atmosphere of openness and receptivity which will make staff members feel at ease in working with him.

Another important factor which contributes to good staff relationships is giving each member PUBLIC VISIBILITY. By the very nature of their assignments, some will be up before the congregation frequently. But others who work primarily behind the scenes should be invited to participate in the leadership of worship services in a meaningful way. Every staff member deserves this courtesy. Commendation of their work from the pulpit and in the weekly newsletter and church bulletin also will build an esprit de corps in the staff.

The families of assistants need the same pastoral care which other members of the congregation receive, and wise pastors see that they are not neglected. A contented, spiritually healthy wife (or husband) and children contribute immeasurably to the effectiveness of the undershepherd's service and have a great deal to do with his or her decision to stay with the present assignment when other tempting calls come.

SKILLFUL SUPERVISION IS A FINE ART. It is indispensable to the successful administration of the church through the staff. Leonard Wedel suggests these important principles:

- *Show a genuine interest in workers* . . . patience, tolerance, and understanding.
- *Communicate clearly.* Nothing is quite so frustrating . . . as garbled instruction.

- *Observe rules of courtesy.* A "please" makes the assignment less like an order or a demand.
- *Criticize in the right way.* No one likes to be criticized openly where others can hear.
- *Give credit where credit is due.* When a supervisor gives credit to another, he gains credit himself.
- *Fulfill promises.* A good supervisor is careful about the promises he makes.
- *Resolve complaints promptly and fairly.* A problem or complaint . . . should be very real and important to the supervisor.
- *Treat workers fairly and impartially.* Perhaps no act of a supervisor breaks down morale more quickly than showing favoritism.[7]

Attention to these eight rules for successful supervision will result in superior interpersonal relationships and subsequently in a smoothly operating staff.

Intelligent supervision is contingent upon current data. The pastor should expect *monthly reports* from each staff member which detail the time spent in his various activities, the number of witnesses given and souls won, and the number of calls made.

STAFF MEETINGS. After the new assistant is oriented to his task, it is necessary that he become involved in regularly scheduled staff meetings. These should take place early in the week. They will provide a profitable clearinghouse for staff interests. While the content of these meetings will vary according to need, they should generally open with a devotional period and close with a time of prayer. No business is more important than this. The time spent praying together may well be the most valuable part of the meeting. Progress reports should be given on projects already underway. Coordination of activities is another important item for consideration.

---

7. Leonard E. Wedel, *Building and Maintaining a Church Staff* (Nashville: Broadman Press, 1966), pp. 119-21.

A high priority on the agenda should be given to group interaction on problems and plans. Eliot Dale Hutchinson summarizes the process by which creative ideas are born as follows:

1. *Preparation centering upon a problem.* Defining the problem is of major importance.
2. A *period of frustration* . . . the problem seems impossible.
3. *The period of insight.* Ideas begin to flow as new thoughts and insights come to mind. There must be choices made.
4. *The period of testing.* Ideas need to be tested for verification, validity, and usefulness.[8]

Brainstorming in staff meetings is one of the most vital functions of the group. Each member contributes a necessary viewpoint and is a valuable part of the problem-solving and decision-making process. Nothing contributes more to the team concept than this type of activity.

SEVERING RELATIONSHIPS. Good associates will always be in demand, and the problem will be how to keep them. However, a very practical but more difficult consideration is what to do when a staff member's work is not satisfactory. The advisable course of action is to sit down with the individual and frankly ask, "What can we do to improve your situation?" Suggestions should be made and a clear understanding reached that if deficiencies are not remedied within a specific period of time, a change must be made. A date should be set for reviewing progress. At that time a final decision should be reached. A reasonable period of time should be given for him or her to relocate if severance becomes necessary.

To the Undershepherd

This discussion would not be complete without a word directed specifically to those who feel called to this particu-

---

8. Eliot D. Hutchinson, *How to Think Creatively* (New York: Abingdon Press, 1949), pp. 38-40.

lar ministry. With the continued increase in the number of larger churches, your vocation will assume even greater importance. Super-churches cannot be operated without knowledgeable, dedicated multiple ministries. The demand for the services of real journeymen will continue to grow. With a shortage of qualified specialists, a "seller's market" has developed, and the bidding for assistants has driven the remuneration level to an unreal height in many places. Seminarians graduating with an M.R.E. degree have been offered positions at higher salaries than some good pastors are receiving after 10 years of service. Hopefully this condition will remedy itself as supply catches up with demand.

Some of you who are ministers (licensed or ordained) will use your staff relationship as a training experience in your progress toward pastoral ministry. Working with a pastor who is a real pro will contribute a very valuable dimension to your preparation. Take full advantage of this learning experience. And *never betray the trust of the senior pastor*. Let it always be known that you are completely loyal to him. Refuse to listen to dissidents in the congregation who would try to make you their Absalom. Your future ministry will be more fruitful because of these years of under-shepherding.

Some of you are laymen who have dedicated yourselves to a career in this area of service. Nowhere will the ministry of laymen be more contributive and satisfying. While most ministers will experience a growing discontent at the lack of preaching opportunities, lay assistants experience none of this constriction. And the very fact that you are a layman will open up channels of communication with the congregation. The members of the church will identify with you in a unique way, feeling that you are "one of them." You will never constitute a threat to the pastor because of your lay status. And yet you have as much of a ministry, in the true New Testament concept, as anyone. Your opportunities for lifetime service in undershepherding are unlimited. May your tribe increase!

As ministers of music, Christian education, youth, children, visitation, administration, or in other areas, you are full-fledged members of the service team in the church—right alongside our pastors, missionaries, church college professors, and denominational leaders. Your contribution is absolutely essential to the success of the Kingdom enterprise.

Conclusion

In his excellent book *The Multiple Staff Ministry,* Dr. Marvin T. Judy states this very sobering conclusion:

> The ancient saying, "like priest, like people," to a large degree can be applied to the church staff—"like staff, like church." . . . The staff, in a sense, is a church within itself . . . a company of believers who are working toward the fulfillment of their own Christian experience of worship, nurture, and work in the world. How well the staff fulfills this ministry within itself will determine to a large degree how well the congregation will realize its fulfillment of worship, nurture, and work in the world.[9]

May God give us an enlarging number of undershepherds who are aware of this sobering responsibility and fully committed to its successful discharge.

---

9. Judy, *Multiple Staff,* p. 236.

Evangelism is one of the many facets in pastoral work, yet it must be ranked as the most important (Harold John Ockenga).[1]

CHAPTER 11

Flock Growth

One of the surest signs of effective shepherding is growth in the size of the flock. Well-fed and carefully tended sheep naturally reproduce. A shepherd who fails to show an increase in the size of his flock will be discharged and replaced by one who can foster growth.

This same principle applies to spiritual shepherding. A New Testament church never settles for the status quo. Christ's urgent command which has come to be known as the Great Commission was "Go and make disciples of all nations" (Matt. 28:19, NIV). Gaines S. Dobbins declares, "Christianity without evangelism is spurious Christianity."[2] The young Church born at Pentecost went immediately to this task. In just one day the little flock of 120 believers increased by nearly 3,000 percent! Soul winning and church growth were the order of *every* day. "The Lord added to their number daily those who were being saved" (Acts 2:47, NIV).

This mandate has not changed for today's church and its

---

1. Ralph G. Turnbull, ed., *Evangelism Now* (Grand Rapids, Mich.: Baker Book House, 1972), p. 48.

2. Gaines S. Dobbins, *Evangelism According to Christ* (Nashville: Broadman Press, 1949), p. 32.

leadership. George W. Truett cautioned that when the church ceases to be evangelistic, she will soon cease to be evangelical. The final responsibility for growth rests upon the shoulders of the shepherd. The charge to every minister is still "Do the work of an evangelist" (2 Tim. 4:5). This is not an option. No matter how well he dispatches his other duties, *failure to produce consistent flock growth is a serious indictment against his pastoral ministry.* Nothing else will compensate for this deficiency. But just as other shepherding skills which are not native may be learned, so evangelistic proficiency may be acquired.

What Is Evangelism?

Before going farther we must establish what is the nature and scope of New Testament evangelism. In the Greek New Testament numerous references are made to this subject through the noun *evangelion* and the verb *evangelizo,* both of which refer to "bringing the good news." The various versions translate the word in different ways. For example, the *Modern Language Bible* (Berkeley Version) translates Paul's response to the Macedonian call in Acts 16:10, *(evangelisesthai)* "to evangelize there" while most use "to preach the gospel" or "to preach the Good News." Whatever the terminology, the concept of evangelism is a recurring theme of the entire New Testament.

Evangelism begins with the communication of the Good News. Some have contended that it is just *a presence;* witness by silent example. This is good but not good enough. It must also be *proclamation.* A good life will tell, but it will not tell everything. Christ is the Word. The Christian message must be verbalized. Preaching, teaching, personal witnessing, communication through the printed page—all these and every other legitimate medium must be employed to get the Good News out.

Then there must be a *conscientious effort to lead individuals to the acceptance of Jesus Christ as Lord and Saviour.* Even proclamation is not enough. John W. Alexander states: "Evangelism is the attempt to perform two services. The first is to make known the message of the gospel. . . . The second service in evangelism is that of seeking to bring about conversions."[3] Any evangelism is suspect which does not result in people being saved. Of course, some fields are more fertile than others and produce a harvest more quickly. But something is radically wrong when good gospel seed is continually sowed and there is never a time of reaping!

The third dimension of genuine evangelism concerns *leading those who have been converted into the fully sanctifying experience with the Holy Spirit*. More and more evangelicals are coming to a biblical emphasis on the "secondness" of the baptism with the Holy Spirit. While a professor at Trinity Evangelical Divinity School, Elmer Towns, the renowned Christian education specialist, wrote:

> Christ also gave Himself for the church "that He might sanctify and cleanse it with the washing of water by the Word" (Eph. 5:26). So it is, that along with cleansing His church from the guilt and power of sin through regeneration or the washing of water, the Word is also the instrument through which the believer is cleansed from inherited sin or made holy.[4]

Any evangelism is incomplete that does not issue a call to holiness and result in Christians being cleansed and empowered by the blood of Christ and the fullness of the Spirit.

Finally, *evangelism must produce church growth by making disciples out of believers*. There is a difference. Arthur C. Archibald differentiates between the two when he defines evangelism as "the effort to bring people one by one to surrender their will to the King and to enter the service of the Kingdom."[5] The evangelistic task has not been completed until new Christians have been inducted into the fellowship of the committed within the church and dedicated to a complete stewardship of life.

---

3. Turnbull, *Evangelism Now*, pp. 30-31.
4. Elmer L. Towns, *Evangelize Through Christian Education* (Wheaton, Ill.: Evangelical Teacher Training Assn., 1970), pp. 22-23.
5. Arthur C. Archibald, *Man to Man* (Nashville: Broadman Press, 1955), p. 70.

And one of the primary conditions of discipleship is a willingness to participate in the evangelistic enterprise. In the power of the Spirit, the newly saved can become the most dynamic evangelists in the church. The circle of influence among their unsaved friends is a veritable mission field. Trained in the basic techniques of personal evangelism, including the use of salvation scriptures, these new Christians may well set the soul-winning pace for the entire church.

Where Evangelism Starts

The recognition of the primacy of evangelism by the shepherd is the first step. Then this concept must be transmitted to the flock. The congregation needs to be convinced that *the church exists for the world.* It is not a self-serving end in itself—it is a God-ordained means to the end of saving the world. Any other standard of success than church growth must be identified as subscriptural. Program priorities must be established on the basis of their relationship to this fundamental task.

Paul Benjamin perceptively identifies a debilitating misconception which characterizes too many churches.

> An emphasis upon quality in the congregation can often lead to a de-emphasis upon quantity. "We should take better care of the people we already have" is the usual rejoinder to a discussion emphasizing congregational outreach. . . . By the same token, however, it could be strongly argued that the early Christians should never have departed from Jerusalem. . . . Congregational concerns are usually on the side of input rather than outreach. . . . Worship has a way of gaining the ascendancy over witness.[6]

Such a philosophy must be exposed as being completely contrary to the teachings of the Bible. In addition it will sooner than later condemn the church to death. Dr. Eugene L. Smith, secretary of the Board of Missions of the United Methodist church, affirms this sobering truth: "Every age

---

6. Benjamin, *How in the World?* pp. 6-7.

is an age for evangelism. God has no grandchildren. No generation can live on the spiritual experience of its parents. Mankind is always just one generation away from the eclipse of the Christian faith. . . . Every generation has to be evangelized anew."[7] Every flock suffers attrition by death. Only as lambs are born is the size of the flock maintained, to say nothing of being increased. It is *evangelize or else!*

Another strong motivation for evangelism is *the conducive climate which now exists.* In a sense, every age is the time for evangelism. But history proves that there are periods when spiritual harvest is unusually productive. The great awakenings in eighteenth-century England under Wesley and in nineteenth-century America under Finney are cases in point. And all signs indicate that this last quarter of the twentieth century is another such season of reaping. Worsening world conditions contribute to a growing unrest and concern in the minds of an increasing number of people. A major periodical calls ours a "cause hungry" society. We have the Good News. Changed men and women can change our culture and our world. Jesus Christ is the last and only Hope. His life-changing power can do more to right the wrongs in our society than the combined efforts of all our social engineers. And the same amount of effort invested in evangelism today will produce a greater harvest than at any time in recent history. *It is the time for truth!*

Last but far from least, *all evangelism originates with the energizing of the Holy Spirit.* He was and is the Agent of evangelism. Post-Pentecost outreach was a direct result of the disciples' Upper Room empowerment. Until the modern-day church tarries for that same promised enduement, evangelism will be little more than a word. The Church of England's Commission on Evangelism has stated: "To evangelize is to so present Christ Jesus *in the power of the Holy Spirit,* that men shall come to . . . accept Him as their

---

7. Paul S. Rees, *Don't Sleep Through the Revolution* (Waco, Tex.: Word Books, 1969), pp. 60-61.

Saviour, and serve Him as their King in the fellowship of the church"[8] (italics added).

Genuine revival which results in fully sanctified, Spirit-filled lives is the most effective preparation for soul winning. Without this solid foundation of spiritual readiness, all the conventions, seminars, and training sessions will accomplish very little. With the dynamic of the Holy Spirit, *evangelism will become a way of life.* Its contagion will spread as more and more people get excited about sharing Christ. Fed by the fuel of pastoral preaching, training, and example, evangelism will be more than a program. It will infiltrate every program of the church. And growth will be inevitable!

Child Evangelism

Statistics prove conclusively that the great preponderance of those who are saved find Christ in their early years. Unless one is converted by the time he reaches his late teens, the possibility of his ever becoming a Christian is alarmingly remote. This means that we must focus increasing attention on the winning of the young. All the evangelistic activity of the church should place a prominent emphasis upon reaching them at this prime time in their lives. At what age should evangelism begin? As soon as the child reaches accountability—when he/she knows right from wrong. With some this comes even in the preschool years. Most reach this level of understanding during the primary or junior ages. Through this period pastoral involvement in child evangelism is imperative.

While the pastor must play a key role in evangelizing the young, he must cultivate the assistance of dedicated laymen in this tremendous task. *Sunday school evangelism* will be the only means of reaching many children from non-Christian homes. Towns indicates the vital service which the teacher may render in this regard: "The teacher-evangelist should be guiding the pupil into learning experiences that

---

8. Samuel Southard, *Pastoral Evangelism* (Nashville: Broadman Press, 1962), p. 7.

prepare him for salvation, lead him to Christ, and establish him in his faith."[9] D. L. Moody started his evangelistic ministry as a teacher-evangelist, winning the boys in his class to the Lord. This should be the norm. Teaching the lesson is just the beginning of a teacher's responsibility. He/she must be trained for this evangelistic function.

Some pastors designate their Sunday school teachers as a de facto membership committee. When children are converted in their classes, they refer them to the pastor's membership class. On Membership Sunday the teacher presents those from his/her class to the pastor as a part of the membership ritual. This gives appropriate public recognition to the evangelistic teacher.

Bus ministry evangelism has come to be one of the most effective outreach methods of the church. This is a far cry from the old philosophy of busing children in for just the Sunday school hour and then taking them home. Bus pastors call in the homes of their riders consistently, cultivating the goodwill and spiritual interests of parents as well as children. Following the Sunday school hour, the children are involved in children's church. Frequently these services conclude with an altar call and result in the salvation of a number of boys and girls from the bus ministry. One pastor plans to conclude each morning service in the sanctuary with an invitation song. If children have been converted in children's church, the director brings them to the sanctuary altar where the pastor prays with them. Then "spiritual parents" are assigned to these children. It is their responsibility to call in their homes and endeavor to foster their faith and also to impress upon their parents their spiritual accountability.

Regardless of its size, any efficiently functioning Sunday school should be feeding a steady stream of new converted children into the membership of the church. If it is not, the pastor should give remedial attention a high priority on his responsibility list.

---

9. Towns, *Evangelize*, p. 30.

Youth Evangelism

The adolescent period, with its accompanying unsettledness physically, mentally, and emotionally, presents a tremendous opportunity for evangelism. Teenagers are reaching out for satisfactory answers to their questions. Alcohol, tobacco, and drugs make their strongest appeal during these formative years. A live youth program which provides the instruction, fellowship activities, and service opportunities is a fertile bed for gospel seed.

Although many adults are not enamored with it, distinctively youth-oriented music conveys Christian truth and offers excellent opportunities for involvement. Wise pastors use teen musical groups in Sunday night services and in outreach activities. Another method for reaching teens is through a church athletic program. This has a real appeal for unchurched boys who might not be interested in any other way.

E. D. and F. F. Sampson, in their consideration of the evangelism of youth, make this statement: "One of the best ways to win youth is through the witness of Christian teens."[10] Young people want the church to provide more than a sanctified baby-sitting service! They want to be involved in sharing their faith. We must provide these opportunities.

Camp and retreat evangelism offer tremendous possibilities for winning both children and youth. They are looking for group activities during school vacations, and summer camps and holiday retreats have special appeal. Unsaved boys and girls who can be gotten into a Christian atmosphere with wholesome fun and fellowship for a period of several days will very often respond to an evangelistic appeal. They are very conscious of peer pressure, and the influence of a group of Christian children and youth is tremendously helpful in bringing them to accept Christ as Saviour.

---

10. Roy G. Irving and Roy B. Zuck, eds., *Youth and the Church* (Chicago: Moody Press, 1968), p. 174.

These gatherings are also conducive to personal commitment. At no age is the call to complete consecration and entire sanctification more effective. And only eternity will reveal the number of teens who have accepted a call to the ministry or missionary service in these settings. Counseling at such activities is not a vacation! But few pastoral involvements are more fruitful. Good shepherds transport their lambs to these gatherings and are ready to play and pray with them. Then they will follow up with pastoral care and will channel the new Christians into church membership.

Public Evangelism

The evident success of the Billy Graham Crusades has demonstrated conclusively that *the day of mass evangelism is not over.* Although there are doctrinal and methodological differences which are involved in such cooperative evangelistic efforts, there are very real benefits which accrue. The impact of such an interdenominational thrust on the community should not be underestimated. Full pastoral participation in the prayer preparation, committee work, and counseling is imperative if his church is to reap a significant share of the harvest. There are people who will never be reached for Christ except in the setting of a stadium or city auditorium. Every effort should be made to get bus ministry parents and other prospects into these services. Converts whose church preference cards are referred to the pastor should be contacted immediately and followed up faithfully.

But valuable as such crusades are, they will supply only a small percentage of the fruit which the church should produce. In addition there should be periodic *revival and evangelistic campaigns* sponsored by the local church. The format of such special meetings has changed drastically in recent years. Instead of two or three weeks, most are now of one-week duration. But there are still basic values which make such campaigns worth the effort and expense. The concentrated spiritual emphasis, the impact of a new voice in the pulpit, as well as the flock growth are all important.

In planning such a series of services, the following considerations should be faced:

1. *Determine whether the basic purpose of the meeting is in-church revival or outreach evangelism.* There is a basic difference, although there is some overlapping of function. If the main objective is the revival and renewal of the church, emphasis should be placed on getting board members, Sunday school teachers and officers, and all members to attend. One or more special "Sunday School Nights" in which the attendance of classes is stressed may present a golden opportunity for child and youth evangelism. Advertising can be kept to a minimum.

But if the campaign is intended to reach outsiders, special attention must be given to getting visitors in. Findley Edge states the case with embarrassing candor:

> What is the weakness in our present approach? We have tried to win the world by holding meetings within our church buildings. There is one tragic flaw in this approach—the "world" does not attend the meetings. Annually or twice annually the church has a "special series of services" . . . [and] we simply talk to each other. The "world" is untouched.[11]

Does this mean that special evangelistic series should be abandoned as a means of reaching the unsaved? No. But it does mean that just announcing such meetings and circulating a few handbills will not get outsiders in. Special musical attractions must be arranged, extra advertising must be planned, and the congregation must be mobilized to bring their unchurched friends and neighbors.

2. *Secure the services of the right evangelist.* Generally speaking, it is best to call an evangelist with whom the pastor is personally acquainted and with whom he can work effectively. When the call is extended, the amount of his offering should be stated. This should be a minimum of twice the amount of the pastor's weekly salary. If possible, additional amounts for travel and Social Security should be

---

11. Edge, *Greening of the Church*, pp. 44-45.

included. Keeping him in a motel where he can have privacy is a good investment. It should be clearly understood what the major objective of the meeting is (revival or outreach).

In either case *the evangelist should be assured that his effectiveness will not be judged by the number of seekers at the altar.* Pressure at this point has led to unwise and even unethical methods of getting people to come forward. Evangelist C. William Fisher observes:

> In perhaps no other part of the evangelistic service is the temptation to think that the end justifies the means as strong as in the altar call. It is open to all sorts of professionalism, to trickery, to manipulation, and outright deceit. It is no wonder that there is such widespread disillusionment, or outright disgust with this part of an evangelistic service.[12]

The evangelists who are in greatest demand are often those who not only preach at night but are equipped to call in homes during the day with the pastor and do personal evangelism. Often the greatest number of new people are brought to the Lord in their homes rather than in the public services.

3. *Nothing is more important than prayer preparation.* John Wesley White, an associate evangelist with the Billy Graham Association, declares, "A mass evangelistic crusade which is not born and borne in prayer is as unyielding as a crop which is planted, only to die because of all sunshine and no rain. Pour out the tears of concerned intercession on any community and it will ripen for spiritual harvest."[13] If it is necessary to prepare for a Graham Crusade with at least a year of special prayer meetings, how can we expect to adequately ready the local church for spiritual warfare with just a few weeks of halfhearted intercession? Three months of well-organized prayer preparation should be a minimum!

---

12. C. William Fisher, *Evangelistic Moods, Methods, and Messages* (Kansas City: Beacon Hill Press of Kansas City, 1967), pp. 40-41.
13. Turnbull, *Evangelism Now*, p. 83.

4. *The altar service.* What happens in the first few minutes after an individual comes forward is crucial. He/she should not be left alone until the invitation is concluded. Trained counselors should be ready to move in immediately. After ascertaining the area of spiritual need, the counselor should pray with the seeker until he or she either finds victory or shows the need of counseling. The altar worker should be well versed in the Scriptures so that he can quote or read passages on repentance, faith, consecration, and assurance. Those seeking should not be pressured into premature profession but should be encouraged to expect the witness of the Spirit when they have been completely obedient in meeting biblical conditions.

5. *Discipling new converts* is of vital importance. Pastoral calls in the home should be made frequently until the new Christian has established a satisfactory devotional life and has weathered the first storms which Satan will initiate. These lambs must be given a great deal of tender, loving shepherd's care if they are to survive the first critical days of their new spiritual life. Frequently too much is taken for granted and a tragically high mortality rate among those converted is the consequence. The assignment of seasoned Christians as sponsors of these young Christians is an excellent follow-up method. The personal interest and concern of these mature saints is invaluable. New converts should also be given basic Bible study materials which will lay a foundation concerning the fundamentals of discipleship.

In addition they should be enrolled in the pastor's membership class where they can receive indoctrination in both the theology and ethical ideals of the church. Wide-awake pastors keep these classes going continuously, either during the Sunday school hour or on a weeknight. Every effort should be made to get new converts into the strengthening fellowship of *church membership,* but *only when they understand and accept the disciplines of this affiliation.* Even after they have joined the church, they should receive periodic attention.

The assigning of too heavy responsibility in the church too soon may prove to be more of a bane than a blessing. Babes in Christ need a reasonable period of time to feed on the milk of the Word and to learn the basic rudiments of discipleship before they are pressed into service. By the same token, group activities such as singing in the choir, ushering, and the like will help them to feel that they are a functioning part of the family of God.

Pastoral Evangelistic Preaching

No consideration of public evangelism is complete without mention of the pastor's pulpit evangelism. The spiritual harvest cannot all be gained in two special meetings each year. If a church is carrying on a live, attractive program, there should be candidates for salvation in many of the regular Sunday services. The norm should be to emphasize some phase of evangelism in at least one service each week. This is in keeping with what Seward Hiltner describes as the historic evangelical concept of the ministry:

> The history of the ministry in America up to the present century is a movement toward evangelicalism. ' The church and the ministry were to save souls above all else. It is functional in its estimate of the ministry. Not, "What is your status?" but, "How many souls have you saved? Don't tell me your position. Tell me what you have done."[14]

Following this tradition, a young pastor preached evangelistically and gave an invitation in his first service in the new charge. As people were converted, the church began to grow. One of the older members was heard to complain that it used to be that he could come late and get a good seat; but now if he weren't early, he had to stand! May this complaint be registered in more churches. All this does not mean that an evangelistic pastor will not encounter nonproductive periods. Even John Wesley confessed to times of ineffectiveness. His journal records this entry after the

---

14. Hiltner, *Ferment*, p. 39.

great revival of 1766: "May 23—I spoke as plain as I possibly could, but very few appeared to be at all affected."

Dr. James Jauncey speaks to the important matter of establishing rapport with those he is going to attempt to bring to a spiritual decision:

> The biggest problem in gaining rapport with an audience is the initial ego resistance. They recognize that here is a speaker who is aiming to persuade them and thus win a personality victory over them. . . . Unless the speaker succeeds in neutralizing this [ego war] he has had it. . . . Humor and especially laughter are most effective in getting an audience into a receptive mood. . . . Quite apart from laughter, a speaker can lessen ego resistance by readily admitting his own limitations. . . . On the other hand, the evangelist can cut his own throat rapportwise by talking favorably about himself.[15]

Once rapport has been established, attention should be given to the progression in which truth is presented. John Randolph Taylor advises: "The minister or the evangelist who seeks to preach the good news must, by the very nature of his theology . . . first preach the bad news. . . . He must tell us that we ourselves are a part of the world that is going to hell."[16] But he must not dwell there too long. The Holy Spirit has already convicted of sin. Most people who are in spiritual need know full well about their personal "hell on earth." Too many are under the impression that the Christian faith is basically negative and deprives one of joy.

Preacher, tell them the truth! Christ came to provide *abundant* life. There is *joy* and *peace* in believing. If we can convince them that according to God's Word life in Christ brings deep, abiding satisfaction, inner pressure to become a Christian will begin to build. The same is true concerning the Spirit-filled life. The sinful nature must be identified. But then the glorious possibility of having carnality crucified should be heralded. The fruits of the Spirit should

---

15. Jauncey, *Psychology for Successful Evangelism*, p. 79.
16. Turnbull, *Evangelism Now*, p. 23.

be described in all their delicate beauty. Accentuate the positive!

Bishop Gerald Kennedy defines the final ingredient of effective pastoral pulpit evangelism: "Personal witnessing is the power and strength of evangelistic preaching. I never cease to marvel at the power a preacher has when he can say that it happened to him and that his proclamation is not an abstraction but a concrete report."[17] Few preachers have been better schooled in Christian theology than the Apostle Paul. His Old Testament credentials were unsurpassed, and his Christology second to none. But the capstone of his preaching was invariably a positive, personal witness of the transforming power of the death and resurrection of Christ in his own life. This is still the most telling argument and the most persuasive logic.

Personal Evangelism

Henry Sloane Coffin, the renowned pastor of Madison Avenue Presbyterian Church in New York, stated this as the basic premise of shepherding: "As ministers of Christ, we deem personal evangelism our primary duty."[18] Pulpit evangelism must be supplemented by parish evangelism. Neither is sufficient without the other. Archibald is correct that "men won't come—they must be sought after. If the local church is determined not to seek, then both the sinner and the church will die together."[19] Nowhere is pastoral example more imperative. Laymen will catch the vision and contagion when they see their shepherd actively engaged in "one-on-one" soul winning. Then they will be responsive to training and involvement themselves.

The starting point is the compiling of an inventory of prospects. There are at least five sources available:

1. Community survey.

---

17. Kennedy, *Seven Worlds,* pp. 143-44.
18. Morgan P. Noyes, *This Ministry: the Contribution of Henry Sloane Coffin* (New York: Charles Scribner's Sons, 1946), p. 11.
19. Archibald, *Man to Man,* p. 71.

2. Sunday school enrollment.

3. "Friendship in Worship" enrollment of visitors in church services.

4. Names submitted by members of the congregation.

5. Pastoral contacts from weddings, funerals, civic affairs, and casual contacts.

George E. Sweazey classifies prospects into three general categories:

1. *Cold*—those who are disinterested or casually interested, unchurched, and whose confidence must be won.

2. *Lukewarm*—backslider or one who may have had an unfortunate experience with the church.

3. *Warm*—one who attends church and who shows interest in spiritual matters.[20]

The method of approach will vary according to the level of interest, keeping in mind that further cultivation may prove that the individual has much more interest and concern than was originally apparent. Two methods have proven effective in reaching the *cold* and *lukewarm:*

First—the *"Four Spiritual Laws"* or *"Life Can Have Meaning"* type of approach with the leading question, "Do you know that God loves you and has a plan for your life?" Then it moves to the scriptural description of sin and salvation.[21]

Second—the *Home Bible Study* plan such as that developed by Ira Shanafelt.[22] A host home is designated in an area which needs to be evangelized. Neighbors and friends are invited in for fellowship and Bible study. Women's groups meet in the daytime and couples or working singles in the evening. A carefully chosen teacher presents a one-hour Bible lesson which is followed by a fellowship time with

---

20. George E. Sweazey, *Effective Evangelism* (New York: Harper and Brothers, 1953), p. 106.

21. Campus Crusade for Christ, *Four Spiritual Laws* (Arrowhead Springs, Calif.).

22. Ira L. Shanafelt, *The Evangelical Home Bible Class* (Kansas City: Beacon Hill Press of Kansas City, 1969).

refreshments. After several preparatory lessons, a study of 1 John leads to the presentation of the "Five Steps to Spiritual Victory" and the invitation to accept Christ as Saviour.

The *Coral Ridge Plan* of Dr. James Kennedy has proved very effective in the winning of *warm* prospects to Christ and the church.[23] In this approach, the biblical method of going out two by two is employed. After rapport has been established, one of two questions is asked: "Have you come to a place in your spiritual life where you know for certain that if you were to die today, you would go to heaven?" Or, "Suppose you were to die tonight and stand before God and He were to say to you, 'Why should I let you into My heaven?' what would you say?" On the basis of the individual's answer, the subject of his/her personal salvation is pursued with the intent of leading him/her into a right relationship with the Lord. Under this plan the pastor trains and calls with selected prospective personal evangelists from the congregation. Then, after they have become proficient in these soul-winning techniques, they in turn train and call with other prospective lay evangelists.

Whatever method is employed, *pastoral leadership is the key!* Like shepherd, like sheep. There is no remote control in this vital enterprise. But where the pastor becomes personally involved, laymen will follow his example.

Growth Goals

Flocks do not increase by accident. They do so by intentional design and planning. Every alert shepherd should set *specific goals for congregational growth* at the beginning of each church year. These should include Sunday school enrollment and average attendance, youth group membership, church service attendance, and church membership. They should represent a minimum of 10 percent increase over the previous year and in many instances should go well

23. Dennis J. Kennedy, *Evangelism Explosion* (Wheaton, Ill.: Tyndale House, 1970).

beyond this percentage. Such goals must be arrived at in consultation with the lay leadership of the church and should be well publicized. The congregation should be informed periodically of the progress being made toward these goals and the full cooperation of the entire church family enlisted in the enterprise.

Any discussion of church growth would be incomplete without a consideration of *new church planting*. The flock concept includes not only the local congregation but also the entire body of Christ. Growth must not be limited to the individual church but must encompass the larger concept of building God's kingdom everywhere. *One of the periodic growth goals of a dynamic New Testament church should be the establishing of a new congregation.* Just as Priscilla and Aquila became the nucleus of the Corinthian flock, so church members who relocate in an unchurched area should be encouraged to share their faith and start a new flock. A bus route which reaches a clientele in another part of the city can also become the basis for a new congregation. The logical beginning may well be a branch Sunday school in temporary quarters. Then, in consultation with the district superintendent and the home missions board, property may be secured and a church building erected.

This is just as much a sign of ecclesiastical maturity as the bearing of children indicates physical maturity. Members given to the charter of a new church are not lost. They will contribute to the growth of the larger flock (and baby churches generally have a more accelerated growth rate than middle-aged ones!). Funds selflessly donated for the purchase of a location and facilities for the new flock will trigger a spirit of generosity which will result in increased benevolence for the "mother" church.

Another church planting opportunity arises when a congregation finds itself confronted with the necessity of relocating its facilities. The migration of the flock to another residential area may make this imperative. Economic or racial changes in the neighborhood may contribute to this necessity. But to leave an area unchurched by such relocation is less than ideal. Pastors and church boards should face the moral obligation of maintaining a continuing witness in the vacated building. Parishioners still living in the area may well respond to this challenge. District home missions funds may be made available to purchase the facilities. Thus the net effect of the move will be the starting of another congregation rather than the deserting of an area which still needs the redemptive influence of the church. *Shepherd, the founding of other flocks is as much a part of your responsibility as promoting growth in your own flock.*

Then there is also the larger concept of *world evangelism*. Dr. Ockenga, who not only promoted a strong evangelistic program in historic Park Street Church in Boston but also an equally strong emphasis on missions, advises: "Evangelism will carry the whole program of the church when it is emphasized. World missions is evangelism carried on abroad and should not be distinguished from evangelism at home."[24] To promote flock growth at home at the expense of going into all the world with the Good News is less than obedience to the Great Commission which is colorblind and multinational. Contrariwise, to neglect the mission field across town while being completely absorbed in long-distance world evangelism is equally wrong. It is not either/or—it is both/and.

Conclusion

Against the background of his experience in building a great soul-winning, missionary-minded church, Dr. James Kennedy proposes these five basic principles of New Testament emphasis.

1. The church is a body under orders by Christ to share the gospel with the whole world.

2. Laymen as well as ministers must be trained to evangelize.

3. As ministers we need to see ourselves not as the star

---

24. Turnbull, *Evangelism Now*, p. 56.

performer or virtuoso but rather as the coach of a well-trained and well-coordinated team.

4. Evangelism is more caught than taught.

5. It is more important to train a soul winner than to win a soul.[25]

Flock growth will be the inevitable consequence when modern shepherds are controlled by the Pauline determination "that I might by *all means* save some" (1 Cor. 9:22, italics added).

---

25. Kennedy, *Evangelism Explosion*, pp. 2-6.

CHAPTER 12

Bigger and Better Folds

Shepherds are not primarily carpenters. Their first responsibility is to the flock, not to the fold. But one of the many facets of shepherding is a correct understanding of and concern for the housing of the sheep. The reader is invited to give attention to the contents of this chapter even though he does not anticipate a building program in the near future. One's attitude toward the church edifice is more determinative in other areas of his ministry than he may realize. The general principles advanced here are basic and foundational in pastoral service. The "nuts and bolts" of the mechanics of church building speak especially to those contemplating construction.

The Theology of Church Buildings

The New Testament attitude toward God's house is vastly different from that of the Old Testament. An almost idolatrous attitude developed toward the magnificently ornate Temple of Solomon. Paul makes it clear that Christ's Church is a *body*, not *a building*. Today we speak of the church at

---

1. John E. Morse, *To Build a Church* (New York: Holt, Rinehart, and Winston, 1969), p. 66.

Tenth and Walnut, but that building becomes a church only when a body of believers gathers there to worship. The history of Christianity reveals the fact that in its earliest years when it was making its most dramatic growth, the Church operated entirely without physical buildings. Subsequently it has also been apparent that it has sometimes been at its best when its facilities were at their worst. Contrariwise, magnificent cathedrals have too often housed pitifully small and weak congregations. An improper emphasis upon the physical housing of the body of Christ is as unscriptural as lavishing attention upon the human body to the neglect of the soul. The National Conference on Church Architecture correctly states the fundamental function of the church building as "a shell wrapped around the actions of the people called forth by their common faith."[2]

But an adequate fold does contribute to the maximum efficiency of flock functioning. Without reasonably comfortable and functional facilities its growth and effectiveness will be limited. Buildings need not be elaborate or ornate. They should be means, not ends. The underlying purpose is correctly stated by John E. Morse: "To build a church is to create a place for worship . . . where people can be equipped, through teaching, for their tasks as participants in the community of faith."[3] C. W. Brister properly relates the aesthetic and functional aspects in this graphic statement:

> From a pastoral perspective, the place of a church's meeting and the symbols of its sacred life should bring order to man's chaotic existence. The elevated ceiling of its sanctuary should symbolize the majesty of God and man's highest aspirations of faith. The materials—glass, wood, tapestry, and stone—should convey the tenderness of God, reassure man of his presence, and inspire each worshiper to reach beyond his own narrow limits. A church's doors should extend an abiding invitation to passers-by to move from life's chill routine into a house of wondrous miracles. From its sturdy steps

---

2. James L. Doon, in *Journal of the National Conference on Church Architecture*, April, 1965, p. 22.
3. Morse, *To Build a Church*, pp. 7, 10.

departing worshipers should go to persons in need of God in the world, who are to be ministered unto even at great cost.[4]

Serving the needs of people is the primary function of the building. Whether it is traditional or contemporary in its architecture, there should be features which identify it as a house of God where spiritual ministries are available. Bizarre designs which leave one guessing whether the building houses a theater or art gallery rather than a church negate the very purpose for which the edifice has been constructed. In this regard Martin Anderson comments:

> A properly designed church edifice is distinctive. It is different, even as the purpose of its erection is different. By its exterior design, its interior furnishings, and its arrangement it is at once recognizable as a church . . . not just a hall (or) an auditorium. . . . It is a symbol. In architectural language it testifies to the presence in the community of a part of the family of God.[5]

When to Build

Construction of new facilities is costly in many ways. Its financial demands impose an extra load on the congregation. Other important programs will suffer as the pastor and key laymen of the church devote the necessary time and attention to the building program. Then almost invariably interpersonal tensions arise over differences of opinion relative to the plans and procedures of the project. These costs should be counted realistically before embarking on such a program. Any illusions that a new building will solve all the problems of the church should be discounted. While there is an initial curiosity and attraction about new facilities, this wears off soon after dedication day; and it will take the same expenditure of effort to get people to attend that it did in the old building.

The alternatives to new construction should be fully explored before undertaking a building program.

---

4. Brister, *Pastoral Care*, p. 125.
5. Martin Anderson, *A Guide to Church Building and Fund Raising* (Minneapolis: Augsburg Press, 1959), p. 7.

1. *Remodeling* is often a viable option if the basic structure is sound. A new entrance, platform, windows, light fixtures, carpet, and pews can do wonders for an old sanctuary. The expert advice of a Christian education specialist may produce a totally new space use concept for existing Sunday school facilities which can be accomplished at a fraction of the cost of a new unit. Attractive new drop ceiling treatment, modern-fold doors, colorful carpets, and new tables and chairs can produce a dramatic change.

2. *Double Sunday school sessions*. It is almost criminal to build expensive structures which will be used only once a week, perhaps for as little as one hour. Sunday school classrooms are the chief "offenders" in this regard. Before undertaking the construction of a new educational unit, serious consideration should be given to the possibility of going to two Sunday school sessions so that existing facilities will be used twice. Having the first one at 9 a.m. and the second at 11 a.m. with the worship service at 10 o'clock has proved to be a workable plan for many congregations. This approach allows for up to 100 percent attendance increase and forestalls for an extended period of time the necessity of expanding Christian education facilities.

A valuable by-product of the double-session Sunday school program is the involvement of additional personnel. Dr. W. T. Purkiser observes, "The church at large today is afflicted with a serious unemployment problem: not of people looking for work but of work looking for people. Wherever this condition is found, both the church and its individual members are impoverished and growth is stunted."[6] The recruitment of additional officers and teachers to staff the second session will result in the spiritual development of many who have previously been spectators rather than participants.

3. *Duplicate services* are another option. When the seat-

_____

6. W. T. Purkiser, *The Gifts of the Spirit* (Kansas City: Beacon Hill Press of Kansas City, 1975), p. 21.

ing capacity of the sanctuary is taxed to capacity, two morning services can take the pressure off until larger accommodations can be provided. Admittedly this is a temporary expedient. The dividing of a congregation is less than ideal. The preaching of a third sermon will tax the resources of the shepherd whose Sunday schedule is already an exhausting one. Associates or visiting preachers may need to be pressed into service periodically to give the pastor relief from this unnatural load. But rather than plunge the church into an unreal amount of indebtedness through a premature building program, it would be well to consider the use of duplicate services for a period of time.

4. *Purchase of another church plant.* Occasionally, for one reason or another, a congregation finds it necessary to dispose of its facilities. Perhaps it has outgrown them and must realize an equity from the sale of the building to help finance the new church. Or the group may have overextended itself in building its new unit and must trade down to a more modest edifice to avoid going into bankruptcy. Church properties are not generally the most saleable commodities on the real estate market and can often be purchased at prices which are much less than those involved in the construction of comparable facilities. A thorough search for such properties through competent realtors should be carried out preliminary to the inauguration of a building program.

5. *Sponsoring a new church organization.* Not every church should aspire to "superchurch" status. Rather than endeavoring to provide facilities to house one extralarge congregation, it may be the part of wisdom to give members and money to the beginning of a new congregation in a nearby community. The space vacated by these home missionaries will provide a challenge for evangelistic effort to win new people to take their places. One pastor in a metropolitan area has followed this practice in the same church over a period of 30 years. Under his leadership this congregation has spawned a new church every 7 years. In this period of time the "mother" church has repeatedly built

back its numerical and financial strength without having to expend effort and money on expanding its physical plant. The net result is a number of thriving congregations which are making a maximum impact on their communities. If this pattern could become the norm, the evangelistic outreach of older, established churches would be multiplied immeasurably.

These possible alternatives to new construction should be thoroughly investigated by a study committee appointed by the church board. After their report has been analyzed and discussed, a firm decision should be reached as to the best course of action to follow. An integral part of the data contributing to that decision should be the counsel of the district superintendent. From his unique perspective he is in a position to introduce factors and value judgments which deserve careful consideration. *No major building program should be undertaken without his approval.* Frequent checkpoints should be set up to keep him informed of developments and for securing the approval of the appropriate district boards. The surveillance of these official groups is a logical safeguard against unwise building, and the pastor should consult them as the denomination requires. The following is a sample of the type of information which the Board of Church Properties may request preliminarily.

REQUEST FOR PERMISSION TO BUILD OR REMODEL

1. Date of this request _____ .
2. The _____ church requests permission from the District Board of Church Properties to:
   a. [ ] Build a new edifice
   b. [ ] Remodel an existing edifice
3. Briefly describe type of building or remodeling. _____
   _____
   _____

4. How will this new construction or remodeling be used?
   _____
   _____

5. Have you secured the services of an architect? [ ] Yes
   [ ] No. If "yes," who? _____

6. If new construction, where will it be built? _____
   _____

7. What are the exterior dimensions? _____
   a. How many floors or levels? _____
   b. What is the total space in square feet? _____
   c. What type of construction? _____

8. Have you checked and do you know that your proposed building or remodeling is within the limits of the
   building and zoning codes for your city or town?
   [ ] Yes [ ] No.

9. Who is the proposed contractor? _____
   a. Will any of the work be done by volunteer labor?
      [ ] Yes [ ] No.
   b. If "yes," explain. _____
      _____
      _____

10. What is the proposed cost? _____

11. Will it be necessary to borrow money? [ ] Yes [ ] No.
    If so, how much? _____

12. How do you plan to furnish the building? _____
    _____
    _____

13. Has your church board voted to recommend this build-
    ing or remodeling? _____ If so, give the date of
    the action. _____ Total number of
    board members _____. Total board members
    present _____. Total ballots cast _____.
    Yes votes _____. No votes _____. Blank
    ballots _____.

14. When is the earliest date that you could set to have the
    District Board of Church Properties meet with you to
    review building plans, cost proposals, and finance plans?
    _____ (The board will wish to visit the
    premises for any new construction or major remodeling.)

Please return this application to the district superintendent.

The Building Committee

Once the decision has been made to construct a new building, the appointment of a building committee is the first consideration. The vital importance of this committee cannot be overemphasized. From a background of considerable experience, Edward C. Frey comments, "Every crucial element in essential planning pivots upon the building committee's vision of its task and upon its competence. . . . In every church building program failure that I remember, the one constant factor has been the building committee's failure to see its proper role."[7] While the church board should be regularly informed of the progress of the program and should be involved in major decisions relative to it, this committee must assume the major responsibility for the planning and execution of the project. Therefore, careful consideration should be given by the church board to its composition.

Every attempt should be made to secure the services of individuals who have some understanding of the basics of building. Previous experience on a building committee is of tremendous value. The ability to accept the ideas of others is also an absolute imperative. One prima donna on the committee who stubbornly insists on everything being done his or her way can compromise the effectiveness of the entire operation. Every committee member should have the right to make suggestions and state personal preferences. But when the will of the majority has been determined, individual differences must be sublimated to the group's decision. *This ground rule applies to the pastor as well as the layman!*

The size of the committee will depend upon the size of the program and the availability of qualified personnel. The ideal is to have a large enough committee so that it can be divided into subcommittees which will function in such areas as:

---

7. Edward S. Frey, *This Before Architecture* (Jenkintown, Pa.: Religious Publication Co., 1963), p. 108.

1. Site selection
2. Architect selection and building design
3. Finance
4. Publicity
5. Decorating
6. Furnishings and equipment

This division of responsibility will expedite the work of the committee by relieving the total group of the necessity of being involved in all the details of each area. If necessary, committee members may serve on more than one subcommittee. The chairmen of these subcommittees may function as an executive committee in the interim between meetings of the entire committee.

Site Selection

If the program involves the building of a completely new plant, the first step will generally be the choosing of a location. Several factors should be taken into consideration in the feasibility study.

1. *Location of church families.* From the map on which the residences of member families are located, the general areas which are nearest to the largest number of members can be quickly determined. The search for sites should be narrowed down to these general areas. To locate the new building too far from too many families is to court disaster.

2. *Proximity to other churches.* To move too close to another congregation of the same denomination, is to say the least, unethical. Two to three miles is a minimum "safety zone." If possible a site should be secured in a community which is not being served by an unusually large number of churches. If the growth potential is limited by too great a concentration of congregations, a severe handicap is immediately imposed.

3. *Accessibility.* While penetration into the immediate area is envisioned, the largest percentage of constituents will come by car. The distance is not so great a factor as ease of access. Proximity to cross-town freeways is of vital importance in metropolitan areas. The time consumed in

traveling 10 miles on a freeway at 50 miles an hour may not be as much as that of going half the distance in stop-and-go traffic on city streets.

4. *Visibility.* There is advertising value in being located on well-traveled streets where the passengers in hundreds or thousands of cars will be confronted with the name of the church every day. A site with some elevation has an additional bonus. It is false economy to save a few dollars by locating on a little-known or dead-end street where one would nearly have to have both a map and guide to find the church!

5. *Size.* The days when a church could be located on two residential lots are gone forever. Two acres is a bare minimum for even the smallest church, and five is even better. Not only must there be adequate space for the sanctuary, educational, and multipurpose buildings, there *must be space for parking.* On the average, at least 80 percent of the congregation come by automobile. Then, more and more churches are using more and more buses to transport Sunday school pupils. Most communities now require adequate off-street parking when new churches are built. Even where this is not mandatory, the preempting of parking spaces in front of neighboring homes is poor public relations. One stall for each three or four sanctuary seats and a minimum of 300 square feet per car are a necessity.

6. *Zoning regulations.* This matter should be checked carefully. If the property is not zoned for churches, the possibility of a change of zoning should be investigated thoroughly. In the latter case any purchase should be contingent upon securing proper zoning.

7. *Availability of utilities, proper drainage,* and *suitable soil* are other important factors to be considered. Core tests to determine whether there are rocky strata or problem soils which would make building unusually costly are a wise investment.

After a site has been located, the pastor should be prepared to furnish the following information to the district organization.

Request to Purchase Land

1. Date _____

2. The _____ church requests permission from the District Board of Church Properties to purchase land at (address) _____ in (city/town) _____ (county) _____.

3. The total acreage of the land is _____. Has the land been surveyed to assure the church of the exact acreage? [ ] Yes [ ] No.

4. The land is to be used for _____.

5. Have you checked the zoning regulations to assure your desired use? [ ] Yes [ ] No. What is the present zoning? _____. Is a zoning change necessary to complete your intended program? [ ] Yes [ ] No.

6. Is the deed free of all encumbrances? _____
   a. Are there any easements? [ ] Yes [ ] No. If "yes," explain: _____
   b. A competent attorney [ ] has searched [ ] will search the title to this land.

7. Has the land passed a percolation test? [ ] Yes [ ] No.

8. Are the following public utilities available? City water? _____ Sewer? _____ Electricity? _____ Telephone service? _____ Gas? _____

9. If public utilities are not available, what provisions can be made for water, sewage, electricity, gas, and telephone? _____
   _____

10. Is there safe and convenient access to the land from the road? [ ] Yes [ ] No. If questionable, explain. _____
    _____

11. Describe the topography (i.e., level, rolling hills, steep grade, how high or low from the road, rocky ledge obvious or underground, heavily wooded, existing structures).
    _____
    _____
    _____

12. Is there evidence of standing water or poor drainage? [ ] Yes [ ] No. Is there evidence of .substantial deposits of clay? [ ] Yes [ ] No.
13. Has the church made a long-range study of its future ministry and the population trends of the community sufficient to warrant the purchase of this land? [ ] Yes [ ] No.
14. What is the asking price? $ _____ What is the offered price? $_____
15. How does this price compare with similar land in the area? _____
16. What is a professional appraisal of the land? $ _____
17. How much cash can the church place down on this land? $ _____ How much money will have to be borrowed? _____

Architectural Planning

Seven or eight percent of the cost of the building may seem like a large amount for architectural services, but it is money well spent. Not only does the architect serve as designer, he is also coordinator and business administrator, seeing that the contractor fulfills his contractual commitments. Several architects should be interviewed. If possible the committee should visit churches designed by them. The ideal situation is to secure the services of one who has designed churches for other congregations of the denomination and is aware of distinctive needs. In any event *the architect must be open-minded to ideals and ideas of the church*. Of course he must be creative, but not at the expense of the basic desires of the building committee. His services should include these basics:

1. Preliminary design
2. Working drawings and specifications
3. Bidding and letting the contract
4. Supervision during construction

The following basic concepts should be fully discussed with an architect before he begins to draw plans.

1. *The centrality of preaching.* Pulpit placement is indicative of the emphasis placed upon this ministry. It *must* be located in the middle of the platform where it is at the center of the focus of the entire sanctuary. The floor of the auditorium should be pitched enough that the platform will not need to be excessively high to make the pulpit easily visible from all parts of the sanctuary.

2. *An adequate platform.* The pulpit is primary but the platform will be used for other important functions. It should be large enough to accommodate large groups of youth and children on special occasions. On either the back or side should be a *choir loft* which will seat a maximum number of singers. Space should be dedicated adjacent to the choir for the musical instruments. The *organ and piano* should be close enough together so that the musicians can synchronize their playing effectively. The architect should not be allowed to compromise this concept by having an instrument on each side of the platform just to balance the arrangement. A *baptistry* is a "must" in every evangelical church and should be located so that it is not conspicuous but still is functional. A large *projection screen* should be mounted in the ceiling or some other way so that it is not noticeable but can be lowered or positioned easily for the showing of pictures.

3. *Plan for evangelism.* This begins with attention to the *altar.* Adequate space must be dedicated to this vital area. At least four feet of work space should be reserved between the platform and the altar and no less than six feet between the altar and the front pew. Less area than this is self-defeating in doing thorough altar work. Ideally the seeker and the counselor should be able to look directly into each other's face. Therefore, if the space back of the altar is raised one step above floor level, it would be well to have an elevated step in front of the altar on which the seeker can kneel. The *width* of the altar should be no less than *six inches* so that an open Bible can lie on it. Since people of all ages will be kneeling there, the height should be designed to serve everyone. *Twenty to twenty-four inches*

seems to be a good standard height. The length will be determined by the width of the sanctuary. It should extend across the major portion of this area. Too short an altar is both a psychological and practical limitation on evangelism.

The primacy of evangelism also speaks to the *dimensions and floor plan* of the sanctuary. The traditional cathedral-type architecture with a long, narrow, "gun barrel" sanctuary militates against good preacher-people communication and thus limits evangelistic effectiveness. More and more churches are going to a more square or fan-shaped building which allows for *curved seating. This brings a maximum number of worshipers relatively close to the pulpit.* Crowding pews or seats too close together so that it is difficult for those who respond to the invitation to move out is also false economy. *Allow plenty of space for easy entrance and exit.* The same principle applies to aisles.

An adequate foyer or narthex is also an aid to evangelism. Not only is it important to have a place for people to congregate and visit before and after the service, it is essential that those who do not come forward to counsel with seekers have a place to gather while the altar service is in progress. Failure to provide this facility invariably results in talking and laughter in the sanctuary which disrupt altar work.

4. *Careful attention to lighting and sound.* Since more than half of the services in evangelical churches take place in the evening, good lighting is important. Whether chandeliers or indirect lighting are used, enough candlepower should be produced so that there is adequate, uniform light throughout the sanctuary. Care should be exercised that the pulpit area is provided with extra light so that the minister is clearly visible to the congregation. Outside lighting is inexpensive advertising. Floodlights on the front of the church and the steeple and backlighting of stained-glass windows keeps the church before the community in an effective way. These lights can be controlled by a time clock which turns them out at midnight and saves electricity during the hours when there is little or no traffic passing by.

Good acoustics are absolutely imperative. The Roman question "How shall they hear without a preacher?" has very contemporary application at this point. If the people cannot hear, they might as well not have a preacher. *Skimping on the sound system is the most expensive economy in church building!* The architect should employ the services of a professional acoustical engineer to insure that the sanctuary is evenly blanketed with sound. This means giving attention to the acoustical properties of the ceiling, walls, and floor. While an excessive ring is undesirable, it is possible for carpets, padded pews, and ceiling treatments to absorb too much sound. Both the music program and the preaching are more effective if there is the proper amount of ring. And since people absorb sound, too, the engineer must allow for this difference when the auditorium is vacant and when it is occupied.

5. *Don't neglect the lambs.* While the sanctuary will serve the children and youth as well as adults, the planning of new facilities must include attention to their special educational and fellowship needs. Representative of these is the necessity of an adequate nursery. This should include crib and activity areas and toilet facilities. A cheerful, commodious nursery staffed by competent people is a vital factor in attracting and holding young couples.

Christian education experts Widber and Ritenour suggest that those anticipating building educational units should determine their needs by:

1. Defining the purpose of the educational program.

2. Analyzing the program's objectives and goals for persons at each age level.

3. Shaping the educational program that is based on the above to meet the needs of the many involved organizations.

4. Conceiving space as shaped by the total program.

5. Planning facilities and equipment as tools to implement the education program.[8]

---

8. Mildred C. Widber and Scott T. Ritenour, *Focus: Building for Christian Education* (Philadelphia: Pilgrim Press, 1969), p. 16.

This kind of careful planning with advice from Christian education professionals will result in units which can be efficiently used for a maximum number of people and activities.

Selecting a Contractor

After the plans have been completed and a cost estimate is given by the architect, the services of a contractor should be secured unless the church is capable of serving as its own contractor. If the project is a modest one and a capable superintendent of construction can be secured, the building committee can let subcontracts. All donated labor should serve under the direction of the superintendent. However, on a major building program it is the part of wisdom to hire a licensed contractor. Bids should not be sought indiscriminately. The reputation of contractors should be carefully checked and work which they have done examined. Once the reliability of those who are allowed to bid has been verified, usually the low bidder is awarded the contract.

Financial Arrangements

When the contract bid has been selected, the search for a mortgage loan can be consummated. Long before this time a building fund should have been started and considerable assets accumulated. With the sale of the old property and the building fund receipts, a considerable portion of the total cost should already be in hand. Current pledges should be sought from the entire church constituency in public services and by private solicitation. The *debt limit* commonly accepted by the district organization is *no more than three times the annual income of the church.* If the gap between assets and the cost estimate is more than this, either the architect must cut the plans back so the cost will be smaller, or else construction must be delayed until more money is on hand.

Possible sources of mortgage money are banks, savings and loan associations, mortgage brokers, pension funds, insurance companies, and private individuals. Some companies underwrite bonds, but generally on the condition that the congregation buy a major portion of them. Before going into such a program, the reliability of the company and the "fine print" in the agreement should be carefully examined. Loaning agencies will naturally listen with extra care to requests made by men of financial substance who are identified with the building program. A committee of three, the pastor and two such laymen who are customers or potential customers of the lending institution, is an ideal group for approaching loaning agencies. The committee should have in hand the following data:

1. Date of organization and copy of the articles of incorporation of the church.

2. A copy of the church *Manual*.

3. Name and address of district organization with documents of approval from the superintendent and district boards.

4. Description of properties presently owned including parsonage.

5. Title report on new property.

6. Balance sheet of church's financial position showing net worth.

7. Statement of average income for past three years.

8. Copy of current operational budget.

9. Report on building fund account with names of those making current pledges.

10. Statistics on membership and Sunday school enrollment.

11. Set of building plans.

12. Copy of contract and cost of furnishings.

13. Projections of expenditures and schedule of repayment.

Any loan agreement entered into should be with the written provision that permission be secured from the District Board of Church Properties and the district superintendent. The following information should be supplied:

1. Amount of the loan.

2. Purpose for which the loan is being made.

3. From whom the loan will be made.

4. The rate of interest.

5. The term of the loan.

6. How the loan is to be repaid.

7. How the payments of interest and principal will affect your present church budget. (Can the payments be absorbed by your present income and with your present commitments?)

8. How the payments will affect your denominational budgets. (Can you assure the Board of Church Properties that this loan will not place them in jeopardy?)

After the church board has voted on the details of borrowing this money and has made application for the loan, the following details of their vote should be forwarded to the district superintendent:

    a. Date of the vote   _____

    b. Total number of board members   _____

    c. Total board members present   _____

    d. Ballots cast   _____

    e. Number of yes votes   _____

    f. Number of no votes   _____

    g. Number of blank ballots   _____

The next step is to present the proposal to the congregation at an officially called meeting. The following record of the vote should be sent to the district superintendent:

    a. Date of the vote   _____

    b. Total number of church members   _____

    c. Number of members present   _____

    d. Total ballots cast   _____

    e. Number of yes votes   _____

    f. Number of no votes   _____

    g. Number of blank ballots   _____

Disposing of the Old Property

The erection of a new building is to some degree contingent upon the sale of the old facilities. If the old property is reasonably well located and in fair condition, negotiations may be made with the District Home Mission Board to purchase the building to house a continuing congregation. By offering to sell at a reduced price and supply a nucleus of members, the relocating church may perform a tremendous service to the total cause of Kingdom building. If this is not feasible, the property may be offered for sale to other churches or other interested parties. Ideally, occupancy will not be given until the new building is completed. But since an old church is not the most marketable commodity, if a sale must be consummated earlier, temporary facilities may be secured in school buildings, community buildings, or perhaps Seventh Day Adventist churches.

Request for permission to sell church property must be secured from the district organization. A majority vote of the members of the congregation is also necessary before any property can be disposed of. Details of the vote should be forwarded to the district superintendent.

Filling the New Fold

The first Sunday in the new church building and dedication day provide excellent opportunities for inviting residents of the community to inspect the facilities and attend the services. A full-scale, door-to-door visitation effort prior to these events should be carried out to realize the maximum potential for community penetration. New buildings will not automatically guarantee new people. But diligent effort will result in new Sunday school pupils, new church attendants, new Christians, and new members. All of this makes all of the months and years of hard work and sacrifice entailed in building worthwhile and eternally rewarding.

An overseer, then, must be temperate,
prudent, respectable, hospitable . . .
one who manages his own household
well (1 Tim. 3:2, 4, NASB).

CHAPTER 13

The Life-style of the Shepherd

T. Harwood Pattison, in his classic text on pastoral theology, *For the Work of the Ministry,* discusses at length the
qualities which comprise what he calls "ministerial manliness."

This quality of manliness should run through all our
nature: through our moral nature, saving us from the petty
insolence of office and from slavish fear of others; through
our intellectual nature, delivering us from undue subservience
either to tradition or to current opinion; through our social
nature, making us superior to fashion and class distinction;
through our physical nature, teaching us self-denial, bravery,
and endurance.[1]

He quotes an old Scottish parishioner who reported: "Our
first minister was a man, but not a minister; our second was
a minister, but he was not a man; and the one we have at
present is neither a man nor a minister!"[2]

Public and Personal

Paul echoes this basic emphasis upon the character and resulting characteristics of the shepherd-overseer in the First

---

1. T. Harwood Pattison, *For the Work of the Ministry* (Philadelphia:
American Baptist Publication Society, 1907), p. 26.
2. *Ibid.,* p. 27.

Timothy passage quoted above. The personal and private aspects of the parson's life become every bit as determinative of his success in shepherding as his public ministry, for it is in this setting that his fundamental life-style will be molded. What he is and does behind the closed doors and drawn blinds of the study and parsonage and in his social and recreational activities primarily conditions his "ministerial manliness."

Since by the very nature of his vocation he is a public person, serious attention must be given to the cultivation of this private sector of his life, or else it will be victimized by the never-ending official demands upon his time. To ascertain whether there is a proper balance, it would be wise for one to keep a record of the time involved in the various activities which make up his life for a three-month or even better a six-month period. The day's record should be entered in a ledger either the last thing at night or the first thing the next morning. At the end of the recording period the totals will give an accurate reading on whether there is a significant imbalance in one's schedule.

The basic categories of such a study should be:

1. *Official Public* _____ hrs. (total of the following)
   a. Preaching and teaching _____ hrs.
   b. Calling and personal evangelism _____ hrs.
   c. Counseling _____ hrs.
   d. Administration (office work, board and committee mtgs.) _____ hrs.
   e. Denominational (assemblies, boards, camps) _____ hrs.
   f. Community _____ hrs.

2. *Official Private* _____ hrs. total.
   a. Sermon study and preparation _____ hrs.
   b. College or graduate study _____ hrs.
   c. Other study and preparation _____ hrs.

3. *Personal* _____ hrs. total
   a. Private devotions _____ hrs.
   b. Business (banking, shopping) _____ hrs.

c. Maintenance (parsonage, car) _____ hrs.
d. Recreation (alone or with associates) _____ hrs.
e. Recreation and social with wife _____ hrs.
f. Recreation and social with family _____ hrs.
g. Time at home with family _____ hrs.

Pastor, disciplining yourself to make this time study is the first step. The next is honestly to face the results. The schedule should be a servant, not a master. If it needs to be changed, change it! This could make all the difference in your world. Speaking of the minister who has lost the romance of his service, Dr. Stevenson comments:

> He is uninspired because he is undisciplined. . . . The key to the problem, then, seems to lie in setting up priorities and "redeeming the time." In practical terms this means "chaptering" each month and each week and plotting the course of each day. . . . What we need is an appointment book which will include not only public commitments but a number of private appointments.[3]

If one's *devotional life* has been neglected, it should be inserted in the schedule ahead of other responsibilities. In her autobiography of her renowned minister-husband, Mrs. Samuel Shoemaker recalls: "He believed that all clergy should really begin with a rule of life that included at least a half hour of personal devotion at the beginning of the day, and he felt that all discipline started there and succeeded or failed there."[4]

If there are indications that administration or calling have crowded in on one's *study schedule,* remedial action must be taken. Just as deadly is the practice of frittering away time in the study in casual reading or on the telephone. Dr. J. H. Jowett in his Yale Lectures on "The Preacher: His Life and Work" makes this pertinent observation: "If the study is a lounge, the pulpit will be an impertinence. It is,

---

3. Dwight E. Stevenson, *The False Prophet* (New York: Abingdon Press, 1965), p. 91.
4. Helen (Smith) Shoemaker, *I Stand by the Door: the Life of Sam Shoemaker* (New York: Harper and Row, 1967), p. 117.

therefore, imperative that the preacher go into his study to do hard work."[5] Even the most eloquent preacher cannot consistently minister to the spiritual needs of his congregation without a carefully structured study program. Laymen who work hard to be productive in their various vocations have a right to expect their pastor to do the same, even though there is no time clock to punch at the church or no daily production accounting to give. Lacking these mechanical motivators, ministers must be self-starters who rely on a strong sense of commitment to these serious responsibilities of shepherding to keep them consistent in their study habits.

After one has reserved an adequate block of time for study, he must arrange a schedule for *administrative work and counseling.* Since the morning is prime time for sermon preparation, some afternoon periods should be scheduled for these other duties as well as calling. These words which grace many pastors' studies beautifully define the scope of service which the shepherd renders from his study:

> *The pastor's study is a symbol of the calling of the Christian minister to be the shepherd of a flock of God. Here sermons are prepared to feed the congregation on God's Word. Here, the work of the church is planned so that the congregation may grow in grace and bear fruit in service, fellowship, teaching, and witnessing. Here you will always find a friend and counselor in time of need. He will not be surprised at your sins, nor will he judge you in them, but he always invites you to share with him the wisdom and love of God, the knowledge of forgiveness of sins, and the saving grace of God in Christ Jesus, our Lord.*

Recreation and Family Life

Four centuries ago Miguel de Cervantes observed that "the bow cannot always stay bent, nor can human frailty

---

5. John H. Jowett, *The Preacher, His Life and Work* (New York: George H. Doran Co., 1912), p. 114.

subsist without some lawful recreation." The demands of pastoral ministry are never-ending. The conscientious shepherd can work 16 hours a day 7 days a week and never get everything done. But the commandment of God is very clear: "Six days shalt thou labour and do all thy work." While the Sabbath is a day of worship for both minister and layman, it is not a day of rest for the pastor. Failure to take a day off each week compromises the divine provision for the re-creation of one's physical, mental, and emotional being just as failure to observe the Sabbath robs one of spiritual renewal. Dr. Daniel Blain, psychiatrist and minister's son, advises: "The minister will seek to establish an adequate program of recreation, refreshment, and replenishment which will serve to restore his energies and nourish his mind and spirit. . . . High creativity seems to depend upon these fallow periods."[6]

Outdoor exercise, such as tennis, golf, hunting, and fishing, or regular workouts at the YMCA should have a place on the pastor's weekly calendar just as much as any other ministerial activity. *It is not an option!* The rest of the week's work will not be done at full efficiency without it. And the length of one's ministry will be prolonged because of it.

Often such recreation can be made to serve a dual purpose by engaging in these activities with those whom you are seeking to win to the Lord. Cultivation of these contacts in this way is an invaluable aid to evangelism. Also, new converts can be strengthened by this fellowship. Many new Christians face a real adjustment in breaking the old patterns of sinful associations and activities, and these hours spent in wholesome recreation with their pastor will help immeasurably in this process.

Some pastors find Monday to be the best day to take off. Winding down from the strenuous schedule of Sunday and getting wound up for the week's work come naturally on this day. Others prefer to immediately follow up Sunday's

_____

6. Purkiser, *NT Image*, p. 132.

visitors and take the flowers from the church to the sick, waiting until Tuesday for their own relaxation. Still others take a half day early in the week and then a half day on Saturday. But in this last case caution must be exercised that this privilege is not abused and the end result is two days off instead of one!

Pastors' wives need recreation too. Perhaps the parsonage pressures have taken as much toll of their resources as the pulpit pressures have of their husbands'. They need to get away too. There is no law against including them in the plans for the day off. Baby-sitters can be secured. Some of these parsonettes can still swing a tennis racket. Others could learn how to catch a fish. If they are not athletically inclined, maybe the wives of the preachers who are golfing together would enjoy meeting for lunch and a shopping spree. Or, why not dedicate half of the day off to doing things with them? These elect ladies deserve this consideration, and the therapy of shared relaxation will do wonders for them.

Then, *what about the kids?* Too many of us try to salve our consciences by planning one or two weeks of vacation together. This is good, but it isn't good enough. Between Dad's church activities and their school schedules it isn't easy to plan regular times together. But *daily family devotions are a must!* Breakfast time is probably the most practical time for most parsonage families. When the children are small, the reading of Bible stories will make the family altar interesting and contributive to their young lives. As they grow older, a varied menu of Bible readings from modern translations interspersed with selections from good devotional books will provide the spiritual strength which teenagers will sorely need as they go out to face the pressures of an unchristian society.

Charles M. Sheldon, the author of the Christian classic *In His Steps,* testifies that when he went away to university as an 18-year-old freshman, he was invited to join a card game in the dormitory. Peer pressure was strong. He was about to yield when the Lord brought to his memory the sound of his father's voice praying for him at the family altar. He excused himself, went to his room, and made vows to God which were never broken. If we are too busy for family devotions, we are too busy!

In addition to this spiritual sharing, time should be taken for *social and recreational activities which can be enjoyed together.* The recommendation from general church leaders is to set apart Monday night as "Family Night at Home." It should be on the printed calendar of the week in the church bulletin. No board meetings or other activities are to be scheduled on that night. Families are urged to spend the evening together. Children (as well as wives) enjoy eating out. If it's nothing more than hamburgers and milk shakes, it's an event. Then come home and play games or engage in some other activities the family enjoys doing together.

Preacher-dads should not be too busy to attend musical or athletic events at school when their boys and girls are participating. And at least some Saturdays should be dedicated to hunting or fishing trips or other outings which the whole family can enjoy. All too quickly these youngsters are grown and gone, and pastors who have been too busy to take time for family fun and fellowship can never reclaim these priceless opportunities. In the final analysis, what shall it profit a minister if he gain the whole ecclesiastical world and lose his own children? Parsonages may not be palaces, but happy memories of good times shared there will endow preachers' kids with a treasure far greater than a king's bounty. There bonds of affection will be forged which will tie them to God and the church.

The *social life of the shepherd* may be classified somewhere between his business and his pleasure. A large part of it will be spent in the company of his parishioners. An invitation to dinner in a member's home provides an excellent opportunity for both recreation and shepherding. Attendance at Sunday school class and youth group socials should be accepted as both privilege and responsibility.

If such socializing does not come naturally, it should be cultivated. Both the shepherd and the sheep need this informal, relaxed social contact. Then, on occasion the doors of the parsonage should be opened for fellowship. Jay Adams declares: "Every minister and his wife must be 'given to hospitality' (Titus 1:8). . . . Hospitality in the Christian community is so important that two New Testament books were written to discuss the subject (2 and 3 John)."[7] Some pastors' wives entertain the members of the church board and their spouses each year. Others plan to have a reception for new members in the manse following the Sunday night service on the day they are received.

These social occasions weld the lives of pastor and people together as nothing else can. Caution should be exercised that they encompass the largest segment of the congregation possible. Nothing will destroy a shepherd's effectiveness more quickly than social favoritism. While it is only natural that there are certain people whom we enjoy being with more than others, *exclusive friendships must be conscientiously avoided!*

These activities also present an opportunity for the shepherd to be an exemplar of the social graces for the flock. Little things do matter. Such things as opening the car door for his wife and seating her at the table are important. These little courtesies speak volumes both to the pastor's wife (who deserves and appreciates them) and to the members of the congregation who look to their leader for a pattern of deportment. Many laymen do not have the benefit of training in these amenities. If they ever learn the rudiments of gracious living, it will be as they observe the example of their minister. On the other hand, failure to perform these little niceties will be interpreted as a lack of respect for one's spouse by those who know the essentials of social decorum. Carelessness at this point may lead to an erosion of the confidence of such flock members in their shepherd.

---

7. Jay C. Adams, *Shepherding God's Flock* (Philadelphia: Presbyterian and Reformed Publishing Co., 1975), p. 35.

The Shepherd's Support

Ministers' salaries being what they are (the lowest of all professions) and living costs being what they are (higher than ever), making ends meet takes some doing. While Protestant ministers are not required to take a formal vow of poverty, in effect when one enters the ministry this is part of his commitment. Relatively few churches can pay salaries equivalent to what plumbers or bricklayers make, to say nothing of physicians or bankers. And construction workers don't invest the high cost of up to seven years of higher education in preparation for their trade. Neither do they have to wear dress clothes to work, or drive their cars as much as 30,000 miles a year to serve their clientele. At the same time, ministers will not be organizing group pressure to better themselves financially.

The only possible answer is a *selfless commitment to live within one's ministerial means.* This means steadfastly refusing to dabble in "get rich quick" schemes which all too often leave both shepherd and sheep sadder, wiser, and poorer. Secular employment to supplement one's salary is not a viable option except in extreme cases where small churches cannot provide livable support. And as a rule this proves self-defeating, for only the services of pastors who can devote their full time to the ministry will produce congregations which are strong enough to pay respectable salaries. The other side of the coin is that experience has proved repeatedly that *shepherds who are willing to live sacrificially on the church's salary and devote their energies to pastoral endeavors will be more adequately supported as the congregation grows and income increases.* God honors the faith of His servants who will dare to put this principle to the test. And the same God will honor the efforts of district superintendents who evidence concern for their pastors' welfare by systematically reminding church boards that their (shepherd) laborers are worthy of their (best possible) hire.

Ministerial ethics plus good common sense make it impossible for a pastor to broach the subject of his support to the church board. However, more and more districts are recommending that *this matter be considered as a routine item at least annually and preferably semiannually.* The chairman of the finance committee should be reminded by the district superintendent or the church secretary to put this subject on the agenda. By all means it should be discussed at the time the budget for the coming church year is being prepared. Then, cost-of-living and merit increases may well be considered halfway through the year.

A few churches have experimented with incentive salary increases based upon such indicators as membership, Sunday school, and financial growth. This system has some obvious pitfalls, but it does highlight the principle that nonproducing pastors should not expect the same salary raises which their achieving brethren receive. It is hard to convince a church board composed of businessmen who compete in the marketplace for their income that their pastor should be given a substantial increase in his remuneration when there are few if any new members to help provide this additional revenue. And if the financial report indicates that receipts are not up significantly, how can a budget justify a sizable salary raise?

The parable of the talents teaches two timeless lessons. First, that *increase deserves reward,* and second, that *it is possible to be good, but good for nothing!* The one-talent servant was not accused of being crooked. His wickedness was directly linked to his slothfulness. Certainly good shepherds have higher motivation than the monetary; but in the divine economy as in the human, diligence and exceptional service will not go unrewarded.

Dr. W. T. Purkiser makes this wise comment on the minister's money matters: "The pastor's own finances are of utmost importance. He may find himself faced with the necessity of living and looking like a professional man on less than the income of a day laborer. But unless his income equals his outgo, his upkeep will be his downfall!"[8]

---

8. Purkiser, *NT Image,* p. 130.

The Family Budget

Since the pastor's support will always be limited, serious attention must be given to the management of his personal finances. This begins with careful record-keeping. Part of the necessity for this is related to accurate tax reporting. In his excellent book *Money Management for Ministers,* Manfred Holck advises:

> The clergyman who fails to keep adequate records to support his income tax calculations is asking for trouble. . . . You should keep a running record of car expenses, contributions to your church and other charitable organizations, taxes, interest you pay on loans and mortgages, all medical expenses and drugs, and professional expenses (books, supplies, entertainment).[9]

However, even these records are not sufficient. Just as the church must have a budget which anticipates both income and expenditure, so must the parsonage. Without it fiscal chaos can easily result.

Budget items for a pastor in a utilities-furnished parsonage should include the following:

Taxes
Food
Furnishings and equipment
Operations (sundry supplies and repairs)
Clothing (and cleaning)
Medical care
Personal care (hair care, cosmetics)
Tithes, offerings, and other contributions
Reading and recreation
Education
Transportation (car payments, official and personal travel)
Insurance
Interest
Savings
Miscellaneous

---

9. Manfred Holck, *Money Management for Ministers* (Minneapolis: Augsburg Press, 1966), pp. 32-33.

Some of these are fixed items—taxes, tithe, insurance, etc. Others such as food, clothing, and medical care must be estimated. The total should be balanced against one's anticipated income. Then the budget should be checked monthly to see if it is being kept in balance; and, if necessary, certain restrictions should be imposed in areas which are getting out of hand.

One of the mortal enemies of a balanced budget is credit buying. More than one pastor has finally come to the place where he has burned his credit cards and reverted to paying cash for all purchases. There is really no such thing as "easy payments"! How much wiser to institute a plan of *enforced savings* where up to 10 percent of one's income is deposited in a savings account. Then when sales on clothing, furniture, or appliances are advertised, paying cash will not only result in the benefit of the reduced price but also in saving the interest charged on installment payments. Some pastors follow this procedure in purchasing their cars and find that this results in hundreds of dollars of savings. This discipline pays big dividends.

But even the best-kept budget will get out of balance occasionally and necessitate the borrowing of money. A reasonable line of credit at a local bank can be a very present help in time of need. The acquaintance of an officer in the bank where you do business should be cultivated so that a loan can be secured when necessary. Prompt repayment and, if possible, prepayment will insure that your credit is good when you need it. *Finance companies should be studiously avoided.* Their exorbitant interest rates do not constitute even a last resort.

The Parsonage

Traditionally churches have provided housing for their pastors. Too often this amenity is taken for granted by ministers. While it does not show on his income, the financial benefit of a utilities-furnished parsonage is considerable. In most cases it is tantamount to from $2,500 to $4,500 in tax-free cash income annually. In addition, the church supplies maintenance of the parsonage, including painting and re-pairs, and often puts in carpeting and even some items of furnishings. This can quickly add up to several hundred dollars a year. The other side of the coin is that there are also advantages for the church in owning a parsonage. It builds an equity in the house which provides a valuable asset on its balance sheet. Then, too, many states exempt churches from paying property taxes on parsonages, so this rather sizable amount of money is saved.

In recent years a growing number of pastors have indi-cated an interest in purchasing their own housing as a means of building equity toward retirement. There is some merit in this plan. Without the necessity of owning a home, too many ministers spend their total income and face their retired years without housing or funds with which to pur-chase it. Some of the ADVANTAGES of owning one's own home are:

1. The peace of mind in knowing that the preacher's kids are not abusing the church's property.

2. The building up of financial equity which is further enhanced when a rising economy appreciates the value of the property.

3. Property taxes and mortgage interest may be taken as tax deductions and are therefore not total losses.

4. Owning property is an inducement for longer tenure. Unless one stays at least 10 years, most of his payments have gone toward interest and very little equity is built up.

On the other hand there are some definite DISADVANTAGES to this policy.

1. Few pastors have accumulated enough savings for a down payment and consequently must face the added fi-nancial load of a second mortgage.

2. Too many churches cannot or will not pay a housing allowance sufficient to enable a pastor to buy a house adequate for pastoral entertaining responsibilities.

3. The pastor must pay property taxes which the church often need not pay, and many church boards are reluctant to add this amount to a housing allowance.

4. The pastor must bear the total cost of furnishing and maintaining the house.

5. In a depressed economy the pastor may have difficulty selling the property when he moves and may take a sizable financial loss on the transaction.

6. Owning property may tend to make a pastor stay longer than he should.

Among those who have had experience with both procedures the consensus seems to be that *in most cases the church-owned parsonage proves to be of greater advantage to all concerned.*

Providing for the Future

Certainly it is the part of wisdom to make reasonable provision for the tomorrows. This should begin with an *adequate insurance program.* With the extremely high cost of medical care it is imperative that the pastor and his family be covered with *health insurance.* Many churches have written this into their budgets, but if necessary the pastor should pay the premiums. One major hospital bill can bring financial disaster to the parsonage if there is no insurance coverage. Then, very early in his ministry every pastor should begin investing in *life insurance.* John C. Banker counsels, "Along with a savings account there should be a sound scheme of insurance equal to at least two or three years' salary to protect the family in the event of the death of the breadwinner."[10] A good insurance agent can design a program of both decreasing term and endowment insurance which will provide maximum security for the family during the years when the children are at home.

During the period beginning at age 50 and continuing up to retirement, the pastor should give maximum attention to laying aside funds for the time when his ministerial income will cease. *Social Security* benefits coupled with the basic *pension program* of the church should provide "bread

---

10. John C. Banker, *Personal Finances for Ministers* (Philadelphia: Westminster Press, 1968), p. 10.

and butter" support. Additional *money-purchase pension* and *tax-sheltered annuities* will lift this minimum to a more livable level. With the children educated, more money should be available for these supplemental programs. *Savings* invested in government securities, banks, savings and loan institutions, and credit unions are generally very safe.

Investments in *real estate* can pose problems. Unless one has a competent agent to manage rentals, they can take a great deal of time and attention which no pastor has to spare. However, if a pastor is certain where he wishes to retire, the purchase of a home which can be rented in the meantime to make the payments has some merit. There is a question whether many ministers should invest in the *stock market.* Two safeguards should be employed if one invests in equities.

1. Don't buy stocks and bonds with funds you cannot afford to lose; *never with borrowed money.*

2. Seek qualified professional counsel before purchasing equities.

Last but not least, *make a will!* Young pastors and their wives as well as older ones dare not neglect this matter. Even if one does not have sizable assets, a will is absolutely necessary so that in case of a tragedy the legal guardians for minor children will be officially appointed. Without this the court may assign them to unchristian homes which stand for the exact opposite of what their parents believed. The services of a well-recommended attorney in the state where you are presently residing should be secured. Since the statutes of states differ widely, it is wise to have wills redrawn when you move to a new state. And both husband and wife should have wills. These should be kept in a safe deposit box with other important papers. It is well to have the signature of a close relative authorized for entry to the box so that insurance policies and other documents can be secured in case of emergency.

CHAPTER 14

The Shepherdess

Author's note: No study of shepherding would be complete without a chapter on the shepherdess. The importance of her contribution to her husband's effectiveness cannot be over-estimated. It is my hope that every pastor or prospective pastor will make this material required reading for his help-mate. For very obvious reasons I am putting the pen into the hand of my wife, Faye, who for 20 years served as the queen of our parsonages.—*Eugene L. Stowe.*

Who Is a Minister's Wife?

She's a woman who fell in love and married a man called "Reverend," a church leader, a pulpiteer, a minister. She's referred to as a woman, yet often she's a young girl fresh out of college.

A few short months ago she was thinking of a nursing, teaching, or secretarial profession. Now she's embarking upon her new career as a clergyman's wife. She's not at all sure what this entails. Is she adequately prepared? No seminary has witnessed her feminine figure walking its corridors. Theology, public speaking, ethics, and psychology are subjects quite foreign to her.

She feels excitement and enthusiasm, yet a real sense of apprehension too. Yesterday she was simply Jane, Bette, Esther. Today she's Mrs. Long, Mrs. Wilson, Mrs. Sharp.

Why? Because now she's the minister's wife. That makes her someone set apart.

She suddenly finds herself performing from a pedestal with a stained-glass window for a backdrop. She's expected to play a part in a script she's never read. Public communication in prayer is something brand-new for her. Social entertainment in the home is supposed to be an easy, happy experience for her. But in the past her mother had assumed full responsibility for this, leaving her uninitiated.

But she will learn. Since the Lord led her down this particular path, He will just as surely take care of the details. Discipline now becomes a way of life for her. She's careful not to destroy but to preserve her own identity, her individuality. She strives hard, not for mimicry but for a Master. Not to create a copy but by God's help to develop her own authentic character.

Her life is not an easy one, but it will always be a good one. Her mental attitude will make it so. She enjoys a sense of fulfillment, but she knows frustration as well. Her days are exhaustingly busy, but they are as changeable and colorful as a newly formed rainbow.

She's the woman who pledged to walk hand-in-hand with God's anointed. "Whither thou goest, I will go." Small congregations or large ones, it really doesn't matter. It's wherever God directs that they go. Each move means a different parsonage—some perhaps extremely lovely, some unbelievably plain. But she manages to make it more than just another house. It is their home.

She views with discernment and compassion the people who make up her parade of life . . .

. . . the conscientious and spiritual—the irresponsible and callous;

. . . the extrovert—the introvert;

. . . the generous—the greedy;

. . . the haughty—the harassed;

. . . the weak—the strong;

. . . the poor—the proud.

They are all there—looking to her for spiritual guidance, an expression of love, a word of encouragement. But she isn't the only one who gives. She is probably the recipient of more love, attention, and kindness than any other woman in her congregation. *God's people are so good!*

She may not be a woman of unusual beauty or possess the charm of brilliancy, but she can know the charm and beauty of sincerity, goodness, and purity. She can realize the true meaning of loveliness as the reflection from her life of holy living gives new meaning, hope, and purpose to others. She can so practice the presence of Christ in her life that her husband, her children, her parishioners may say of her, "Behold the handmaiden of the Lord."

A minister's wife? Yes, indeed! One of the highest privileges and rarest opportunities ever afforded any woman.

The Successful Shepherdess

In observing ministers it has been interesting to note that hard work, true dedication, and deep spiritual insight often lift the "less likely to succeed" far above those possessing every outward advantage for accomplishing the most for Christ. Now the question comes, "Where do I fit into this picture? I'm only the minister's wife." Being *only* the minister's wife makes you a very unique and important part of your husband's whole world. Although it's true that a wife will be limited in exercising her influence in some areas, I sincerely believe that under God she can be his greatest asset in many ways. We are assuming, of course, that your dedication to Christ eliminates any unworthy motives, attempts at self-glorification, or self-centered ambitions. Such would be disastrous.

As we walk together through these next pages, let's examine some of the ways in which our service may be made effective and contributive to the success of our shepherd-husbands. I have tried to avoid the trite and traditional in favor of the practical, personal concepts which I have learned by both experience and observation. It is my prayer that they may prove to be helpful to shepherdesses young and older who are studying to show themselves approved unto God.

1. BE YOURSELF

God created you as an "original" with a personality, potential, and natural abilities that are unique to you only. Your husband married you for who you are and what you represent to him through Christ. Yes, and for what he may be because of you.

This does not mean that you should ever come to a stagnation point in the development of your total being. Under God a continual improvement and growth pattern should be realized in every area of your life. Your mental attitude toward life in general is of vital importance. Especially significant is how you react to your responsibilities as a minister's wife.

Although it's possible to profit from observing the good qualities in another person's character, you should never allow yourself to get under bondage to anyone, either inside or outside the church. To do so will only hinder the effectiveness of your service for Christ and the church. .

I like to picture a Christian character as not built on the foundation of a single quality but rather on a three-dimensional base made up of *decision, direction,* and *dedication.* When we make a decision to go Christ's way, we cultivate a communication with the Lord in which He not only becomes very real to us but He is in essence the true meaning of life itself. It's only as He becomes the Master of our life that He can then direct us. Since none of us can do everything well, we must necessarily narrow the scope of our activities in order for the forces of our lives to reach the maximum in usefulness. Being selective in our priorities is a must.

Decision, under His *direction,* now becomes complete *dedication*—delighting to do His will. Our souls can now claim the Lord as our Inheritance. We can hope in Him. In no life is this more apparent than in that of a minister's wife who through her own personality serves Christ.

So, *be yourself*—that self that is shaping its entity by her every action, thought, and word. Who knows, you may even symbolize someone's dream by just BEING YOURSELF!

2. MAKE THE MINISTRY A SHARED SERVICE

From the pulpit to the parsonage there must be a caliber of leadership that is willing to pay the price of mental fatigue and physical exhaustion in order to seize the swiftly passing opportunities of the day. The ministry of our Lord was a classic example that no lasting good can be accomplished without the expenditure of nervous energy and bodily strength. One day in the midst of His wearisome schedule He found it necessary to rest by the well. On another occasion a little woman troubled by her physical ailment reached out and touched the hem of His garment, so great was her faith in His healing power. Jesus sensed immediately that power had gone out of Him.

Does this encourage you, my dear friends of the parsonage . . .

> . . . when the man of your life finds the fields white unto harvest and too few laborers to help shoulder the load;

> . . . when his hours are too full and the days too short to fulfill the demands that are made of him;

> . . . when he feels a bit guilty because the best hours of the day are spent away from you and the family that he loves?

Are you able to accept the fact that he, too, may be paying the ultimate price of leadership in order that he "might by all means save some"?

But he cannot do it by himself. You must share in this vital service. Paul might well have been speaking of pastors' wives when he wrote, "Help these women for they have labored side by side with me in the gospel" (Phil. 4:3, RSV). When Jesus gave His life to atone for our sins that we might have eternal life, He became the Fountain of Life for you and me.

Yet, though the waters are flowing and the Fountain is free, millions are dying today of soul thirst. Could some of the blame be placed on our shoulders as ministers' wives? Have we really been committed to the task of soul winning? Have we been sensitive to the leadership of the Holy Spirit in letting Him loosen our tongues? Have we failed to hear the cry of "I thirst" from the needy round about us?

Studying, praying, sharing, witnessing—they all become a vital part of your life. Your minister-husband has a mission to accomplish, but so do you. Not because you're a minister's wife, but because you are a Christian; saved from sin, but saved to a life of service. What a high privilege! What a tremendous responsibility.

3. LEND YOUR INFLUENCE PSYCHOLOGICALLY

Perhaps your first step of helpfulness will fall in the realm of your psychological influence on your husband. This is the ground level from which he will get his basic bearings for carrying out his God-given call to the ministry. From here he will venture to climb those steep mountains of life, to cross its tumultuous rivers, to go down into the dark valleys, or to excel to the highest heights.

Although any man of God must stand on the biblical promises from which he draws strength for each day, there will be times when he will draw strength from you. The daily demonstration of your love, understanding, sympathy, and trust should make even your presence a symbol of helpfulness and inspiration.

If you're optimistic, it will be contagious. If you think big, believe big, and imagine big, beautiful dreams that lie in the realm of the possible, it should automatically enlarge your husband's own aspiration for his work through Christ. It should not only give him added confidence in himself but should increase his faith to believe that God can move a mighty mountain—that He "is able to do exceeding abundantly above all that . . . [he can] ask or think" (Eph. 3:20).

Without indiscriminate flattery any man should be heartened by the intelligent appreciation of his wife. Don't ever hesitate to say, "I love you" or "I'm proud of you!" With the proper support, respect, affection, and attention, any minister should be prepared psychologically for wherever God chooses to lead in His design for his life.

4. ENCOURAGE YOUR HUSBAND'S SPIRITUAL DEEPENING BY YOUR PRAYER SUPPORT

Praying together as a family, praying together as a couple, praying alone in the inner sanctum of your own heart—each is important to any successful Christian. But this is especially true of the minister and his wife. No one is exempted from the tricks of the enemy, and the pastor's wife should be mindful of this fact. Being an example of prayer before her husband and family will make an indelible impression upon those in her household. Sending your husband from the parsonage every morning with the pledge of your love and prayers will lay the best possible foundation for a successful, victorious day for him.

Then it is essential that we inspire our husbands to spend much time in prayer! Let me give you an illustration. We had been in college with this young man. He possessed a dynamic personality, a good mind, and more than average talent. One of his special gifts was the ability to preach in such a way that people responded readily to his call to repentance and holiness. Then one day we heard that he was no longer in the ministry. I saw his mother-in-law at a district assembly. In answer to my expression of sympathy she said, "Faye, keep your husband on his knees in a spirit of humility and dependence upon God. If our son-in-law had not possessed so much natural ability, perhaps he would still be in the ministry today. He was too confident. He felt that he could accomplish everything in his own strength. Consequently, he became drained in his own spiritual life and allowed Satan to creep in, ruining his own life as well as the happiness of our daughter."

Yes, prayer *is* important. Prayer *will* make the difference in our obedience, in our victorious living, in our successful service.

5. HELP TO LIFT HIS SIGHTS TO GOALS HIGHER THAN HIS OWN HUMAN ABILITIES

When we lift our sights so high that our goals are only attainable through the power of the Holy Spirit, then we have to recognize God at work in our midst. Some wives have actually moved in the opposite direction. Instead of encouraging their husbands in their outreach and faith, they have limited their ministry because of a possessive attitude.

"I don't want my husband to pastor a larger church. I hardly see him now," she said. You know what? She's gotten her wish. He's gone from a medium-size church to a smaller and then a still smaller congregation. Shepherdess, God wants your pastor-husband to have the largest sphere of influence possible. Ours is not to hinder but to help!

Although you dare not be selfish in limiting your husband's ministry, neither should you be guilty of pressuring your husband into position seeking. Never being quite satisfied with your husband's status can be very deflating to his confidence and self-assurance. Yes, and to his normal masculine ego!

I have heard church leaders say, "A minister must create a demand for his services." You, pastor's wife, constitute a vital part of that demand. If you are desiring to further the demands for your services, you will refrain from ever being the dominant, opinionated woman who has to have the last word about matters in the church. One member of a particular church board felt that his pastor had difficulty in finalizing any major decision during board meetings for fear his wife might express a different opinion when he arrived home. Only one captain can be in command on the Good Ship Zion, and *that individual must be the pastor,* never the pastor's wife. You can, however, play a significant role by keeping the communication channels open for the exchanging of ideas and the sharing of creative concepts.

Without being either too timid or too aggressive, you can encourage and challenge your husband to step out in faith to accomplish things that will multiply the effectiveness of his ministry.

6. STAND BESIDE YOUR HUSBAND IN TIMES OF CRISIS INVOLVING THE MEMBERS OF YOUR CONGREGATION

James Barrie says that those who bring sunshine to the

lives of others cannot keep it from themselves. So dare to be happy! Give joy to others and watch your own personality blossom. If praise is the spirit that edifies and worry is of the flesh and destroys, then let us sing our songs in the night and glorify the Lord.

However, for some, songs will not come easily. Are you willing, minister's wife, to become involved with the needs as well as the joys of those around you? Jesus was. He socialized with the happy, empathized with the sorrowful, and gave of himself to the sick. Would you dare to pray this impressive prayer penned by an unknown author?

Lord, help me to show toward my fellowmen that kindness which I have so often craved from them. May I think of my neighbor not as my rival who would undo me, but as my brother who needs me. Give me the compassion of Jesus that I may never be able to turn coldly from any man who needs me. Make me quick to hear the cry of the suffering. Turn my feet toward the house of sorrow. May I know the joy of carrying hope to hearts that have long been strangers to hope. I remember how lonely I have been in sickness; help me to relieve the loneliness of the sick. I remember how often I have longed for the touch of a friendly hand; help me to relieve the heart hunger of the neglected. For Jesus' sake. Amen.

Your place of service may necessitate a special kind of dedication—one that far exceeds the basic requirement and duty of a pastor's wife. This is why it's imperative that you channel your strength, physically and emotionally, into the areas of service which are peculiarly yours as a pastor's wife. Since your zeal and interest may often excel your strength, allow the Holy Spirit (not people) to guide and direct what you do, how you do it, and how much you do. This immediately discourages any conformity to a particular model sometimes associated with those in your position. God created you. He has the original mold in which you and you alone will fit. He knows your potential. He knows your limitations. So live to please Christ, and He will take care of the humanity in people that might make it impossible for them to always understand.

A kind, thoughtful heart is not only one of the greatest virtues, it is the parent of many others. As you demonstrate these virtues, there will be something special about the influence you can lend through your feminine, gentle touch.

This special gift of service as a woman was beautifully demonstrated during the Crimean War. A soldier was desperately in need of surgery, but the dispensary had exhausted its supply of anesthetics. When the surgeon informed the young man of their predicament, he said, "If Miss Nightingale will stand by my side and hold my hand, it will be all the anesthesia I'll need."

The British troops were this devoted to Florence Nightingale and she to them. Her love and concern had crossed the barriers of generations, race, and economic standing. Many of these soldiers reported that their hearts had not only been won by this gracious lady but their souls had been edified through her influence. Her sensitivity, gentle smile, and tender touch were God-inspired.

Lady of the parsonage, you too can be a Florence Nightingale as you allow your motives and actions to be governed by Jesus. For instance, a loving caress given to a woman in distress will sometimes say more than a volume of words spoken by your husband. This is not to underestimate the effectiveness of a minister. But a compassionate wife has a very special contribution to make in implementing her husband's ministry in this way.

Dr. Samuel M. Zwemer recalls that the only thing Jesus took pains to show after His resurrection were His scars—scars that were the authentic marks of His redemptive ministry. May we be able to say with Paul, "From henceforth let no man trouble me: for I bear in my body the marks of the Lord Jesus" (Gal. 6:17). Why the marks? Because all too often learning comes from tears and grief and pain. It may sometimes come from your own, or sometimes from sharing the grief of others. It's surprising how an understanding heart can lift the heavy burden of another, just as sharing their joy can add to their happiness. How very favored we are to be in a situation where we can lend our support and love in both extremes.

7. Be Trustworthy with Your Tongue

Kindness in Words creates confidence.
Kindness in Thinking creates profoundness.
Kindness in Giving creates love.

—Lao-tse

What we talk about reveals a great deal about ourselves. Jesus recognized this when He said, "Out of the abundance of the heart the mouth speaketh" (Matt. 12:34). The Apostle James, who was keenly aware of the power of the spoken word, especially when spoken without love for his fellowman, said, "If any man offend not in word, the same is a perfect man" (Jas. 3:2).

Confidentiality is a very sacred trust. When a parishioner shares a personal matter, he or she has a right to know that it will *never* be revealed to anyone under any circumstances. An outstanding theologian and teacher of young ministers was very emphatic at this point. He said, "You are not at liberty to err in this area. If a lawyer and physician observe this principle on their most sacred honor, how much more should a minister and wife follow such a practice." He continued by saying that it is an inexcusable breach of ethics in any profession where counseling is given.

If this be true, as I sincerely feel it is, any betrayal of confidence places such an individual in a questionable light as a spiritual leader representing Christ. If you prove yourself trustworthy as a minister's wife, it's quite possible that you will be told things that you cannot even discuss with your husband. If you have been trusted with such a confidence, don't ever be guilty of disappointing that friend. Not now, not ever. Hold her faith, her trust in you.

Then there is the matter of loose, careless talk. We all realize that the staple of most gossip is rumor, half-truth, and exaggeration. The unspoken mood of the gossiper is expressed in the words of one who said to another, "There's something I must tell you before I find out it isn't true." One man said of his pastor's wife, "She's a termite. She's termination wherever she goes with her unruly tongue."

Nothing will destroy a man's ministry more completely than this.

A church leader was once asked if he weren't going to do something about a piece of gossip that had been started about him. He answered, "I don't have the time. I'm too busy serving the Lord. You've seen a large dog running along with pups nipping at his heels. Well, that's the way I feel about busy tongues that bite away at people. You simply keep moving fast enough to leave them behind. As long as God's encircling presence surrounds you, no one can do or say anything that will *really* touch you."

8. HAVE A SENSE OF HUMOR

I believe God added a spice of humor to the nature of man that he might more fully enjoy the whole universe. If it were possible to hear the inflection of God's voice and to see His facial expressions as He speaks to us, I'm sure we would find that He possesses this capacity too.

A good sense of humor is the best possible therapy for releasing those tensions and frustrations that often come to the minister and his partner. If you don't enjoy the luxury of laughter with your husband and your family, work at it. Let your home be a fun place in which to live.

I heard a world missions executive say that one of the most important prerequisites for being a successful missionary is to possess a sense of humor. A hearty laugh, telling a joke on oneself, or seeing the funny side of a situation, he said, has saved many an ulcer from forming or tears from flowing. His comment concerning a pastor's wife was very similar. "There is a time to weep and a time to laugh. May the good Lord help and protect the lady of the parsonage without humor enough to laugh, for great will be her weeping."

The wife of any minister must, of course, have enough dignity of character to shun and turn off anything that's unchristlike. It isn't the shape of a woman's mouth that makes it beautiful; it's what comes out of that mouth. So she should be true to herself and to her Lord in all manner of conversation.

Have fun, yes! Laugh, yes! But be a Christian lady in every sense of the word.

9. Support and, if Necessary, Stimulate Your Husband in Setting Up a Systematic Study and Calling Schedule

Unfortunately, some men have never developed a love for books or for studying. If your husband falls into this category, you may find it profitable to work with him building his library. Surround him with books. It's so very important that he read, read, read! How else can he possibly please the Lord in feeding his flock?

Of necessity a pastor's schedule will be more flexible than that of many professional men. However, his wife should not take advantage of the fact that he does not punch a time clock and thoughtlessly keep him from his post of duty. Running errands, baby-sitting, even housework has kept some pastors at the parsonage long after they should have been in the church office. Such a practice could easily rob them of valuable study, promotional, or visitation time. This should not be! If you are at fault, discipline yourself. If he is careless about keeping a prompt, regular schedule at the church, then he may need some guidance and encouragement from a conscientious wife.

You may feel that your responsibilities should not include the planning of your husband's schedule. True. No minister should need the prodding of his wife to motivate him in fulfilling his God-given call. However, there are a few men who will never make it unless someone close to them gives a slight shove occasionally.

A true helpmate in every way. *That's a minister's wife!*

10. Let Love for Your Husband Protect Him Against Anybody or Anything That Would Threaten His Reputation or Damage His Influence for Christ

Some women will be especially attracted to ministers. There's often a reason for this. Where there's a conflict in the home or a serious domestic problem between a husband and wife, it's very possible that the woman involved may see in her minister qualities that she secretly desires in her own mate—tenderness, kindness, understanding, sympathy. A pastor is usually oblivious to such an attraction since his only interest lies in helping and developing the spiritual lives of his congregation.

Counseling is known to be one of the danger areas. One pastor's wife related this incident to me in confidence. Then she said, "Please feel free to use this as an example of caution if you can do so without revealing my name." This was her story:

A young lady had separated from her husband and was suffering from emotional and mental strain. She took the liberty of asking often for my husband's counsel. Her contacts became too frequent. It became a concern to me. When I cautioned my husband about it, he laughed and innocently remarked, "Honey, I do believe you're jealous."

My response was "Yes, I suppose I am. But it's not for the reason you suspect. I'm jealous for your reputation, your influence, your ministry. I love you too much to allow anyone to take advantage of you."

The wise minister's wife accompanied her husband to the next two counseling sessions. Suddenly the young woman no longer needed her pastor's attention. This minister expressed his genuine appreciation to his wife for her sensitivity and her loving concern for him.

May I insert here that no wife possessing a genuine love and respect for her husband, will ever be guilty of expressing any hint of distrust or lack of confidence in her husband to anyone, at any time. She is to protect him—not destroy him! And she always approaches him from an attitude of caution, never from one of suspicion.

Your love, loyalty, respect, and complete trust should be a steadying force in the busy routine of your husband's daily pastoral reponsibilities.

11. Demonstrate Kindness and Courtesy to Your Husband

Let us imagine every couple in the church patterning their relationship after you and your husband. Would they reflect a strong, healthy relationship of mutual love, understanding, and respect? Would your members detect something very special in your desire to exemplify every courtesy and kindness to your mate? They do watch you, you know.

Good manners show good breeding. This is desperately needed in our homes. Thoughtfulness is contagious, whether it be in our actions or our spoken words. What greater joy is there than to give of ourselves in loving kindness to those within our own family circle.

Again, may I emphasize the importance of nourishing the love relationship between the man and woman who have been set apart by God to be an example in ministering His Word. Love is kept strong and lasting only when we protect it from being hurt and bruised by neglect, by carelessness, by lack of communication. This God-given beauty of deep affection between two individuals was never meant to diminish, but to mature and grow until their lives become a beautiful duet of Christlikeness.

12. Be Your Husband's Loving and Constructive Critic

First of all, may I emphasize the *loving* portion of this suggestion. This will eliminate any possibility of nagging or harping, both of which destroy the effectiveness of one's efforts to help anyone. The timing of making suggestions is also very important. For instance, you will never want to offer criticism to your husband immediately following any service when he may be tired and possibly discouraged. Approach the subject when he's rested and in a frame of mind to listen. Then, *always* approach him in a positive way. Perhaps complimenting his good points would be a good opening.

One of the areas in which you can probably be of the most assistance is in the correction of pulpit mannerisms which he has unconsciously developed. Laymen will be hesitant to mention such habits, so you must. Some wives, however, have called attention to such distractions and received a negative reaction from their mate. In fact, one husband refused to believe that he spoke more to the empty seats in the balcony than to the people on the main floor. So one Sunday his wife decided to sit in the balcony—alone.

Every time he raised his eyes to the balcony during his message, she smiled and gently waved to him. Was he convinced? So much so that he could hardly complete his sermon!

Besides mannerisms there are sometimes grammatical errors in speaking. Perhaps this is the most delicate and difficult area in which one person should correct another. If either of you recognizes a need here, may I recommend visiting a library or bookstore where an abundance of authoritative material can be found. Obtaining assistance from someone who teaches or tutors in English is another possibility.

Constructive criticism or corrections must stay within the family unit. They are never expressed publicly to *anyone* at *any time*. This would definitely reflect an act of disloyalty to your married partner. "Correction through love" is God's way. May each of us follow this pattern.

The Parsonage and Entertaining

Have you ever heard a minister's wife say, "We're not accepting a call to this church because they have an inadequate parsonage"? I surely hope not! You *may* say to yourself, "I wonder what creative power will need to be exercised in decorating this one?" Sometimes it gets to be quite a challenge.

Parsonages come in all sizes and ages—from small "dollhouses" to spacious, four-bedroom homes. There may have been a time when pastoral housing was a problem, but today many parsonages are far better than the average home of the congregation and are a delight to see.

However, if yours is less than it should be, you might try doing what one clever shepherdess did. Their floors were bare and the splinters were a trial to their crawling baby. The pastor spoke of making the necessary arrangement for borrowing money in order to take care of their immediate need. But his wife had another plan. She suggested that the next monthly board meeting be held at the parsonage. "Be sure," she said, "that you have them kneel as they pray!"

Her plan couldn't have worked better. When one board member rose from his knees, he said, "I have a splinter in the knee of my slacks. These floors need some attention! They should be carpeted." From there they took a tour through the parsonage and were amazed at the poor conditions under which their pastor's family had been living.

Churches really shouldn't function without a committee to look after such needs, but sometimes they do. Consequently, if the doors of the parsonage are never opened to the people of the congregation, they may never be aware of the need for redecorating or a possible change of houses.

The parsonage may be owned by the church, but it must have the privacy of a regular home—your home. First of all, it should be a laboratory of love and offer spiritual therapy for your own family. No church activity or outside entertaining is important enough to warrant the possibility of causing your children to feel that they are being neglected or taking second place to the people of your congregation. I say this after having been in a church with a large congregation while our three children were still very small. No matter how heavy the responsibility, *your own family must always come first in your priorities of love, attention, and spiritual guidance.*

Don't let your two-year-old child have cause to say to you what a preacher's son said to him one day. They had gone through a very busy time in their church and had decided to get away for a day's rest in the mountains. The father and his small son were seated on the embankment of a river, watching the water run very swiftly over a large rock. The little fellow looked up into the face of his father and said, *"Daddy, is the ribber going to a meeting?"* The swiftness of the water brought to his mind the motion and actions of his parents as they rushed about going from one meeting to another.

"The Lord surely forgot me when He handed out the ability to do anything artistically. Interior decorating is not one of my skills, and my cooking is certainly below par. How much entertaining will I have to do in the parsonage?

This is the phase of pastoring that frightens me." This statement was made to me by a young pastor's wife when my husband was president of the seminary. My suggestion to her was that she invest in a few choice magazines and a cookbook. And she did. It was surprising how quickly she mastered the mechanics of cooking. Today, people thoroughly enjoy coming to her home, not only because she's a good cook and her home is charming, but because of the warmth of her personality. There's no greater tribute that anyone can pay a hostess than this: "She puts everyone at ease. Each person is equally important to her." So much depends on our attitude toward entertaining. You can make it a chore or a game. There is endless worry in the one and endless joy in the other.

Perhaps we should ask ourselves, first of all, what is our motive for entertaining? Are we extending hospitality in love to those who are in need of Christian friendship and encouragement? While they're in our homes, are we more concerned about their comfort and needs or about displaying our ability as a hostess? It's important that we season even our food with love, for you see, good fellowship is far more important than good food. People are more important than materials. Remember that Jesus said, "Inasmuch as ye have done it unto one of the least of these my brethren, ye have done it unto me" (Matt. 25:40).

The furnishings in our homes should be for our convenience and use more than looks. If something is spilled on your carpet or your furniture scratched, accept it. No one enjoys looking at an unused home! I'm not, however, advocating inefficiency or untidiness. It takes organization, discipline, and patience, as well as a large portion of love and understanding to run a home smoothly. It's work, whether you have a family of four or eight. Is it an art? Yes, if you do it successfully.

To me there are two keys to all successful entertaining in the home, whether it be for a large group or a small dinner party.

First, proper preparation. Everything possible should be

gotten out of the way the day before. Silver, dishes, and linens should be checked. Many salads and desserts can easily be made the previous day.

Second, allow time for emergencies. In planning for any gathering in your home, allow time for interruptions and delays. This will eliminate any need for pushing a panic button if unexpected emergencies present themselves during the day.

As far as the people of your congregation are concerned, you will find it more advantageous and advisable to entertain by groups rather than by couples. A buffet table is an excellent way of serving groups such as the church board, Sunday school classes, missionary groups, showers, etc. The ladies of the church will want to help you. Let them. It's an excellent way of becoming acquainted, and you'll have fun doing it.

How much you entertain in the parsonage will depend on several factors, such as the size of your home, the facilities with which you have to work, the age of your children, the amount of money available for entertaining, your physical condition, and how much you enjoy having people in your home. It does take time and work, but everything does that's worthwhile.

Weddings

The time has come for that most important and significant occasion when a young couple starts making plans for their wedding. Most brides know exactly what they want and are well informed as to the proper procedures of a wedding. However, there will be some who lean very heavily on the pastor's wife for inspiration, information, and a helping hand. If you have been asked to assist and do not have the necessary information at your fingertips (or in your head), pick up a handbook on this subject from a bookstore or wedding shop. It will outline everything for you.

Often the bride will request that you cut the wedding cake. This is always an honor, and you will want to accept it with joy. If this is your first experience and you lack confidence, consult a cateress. She will be happy to show you exactly how to do it. The bride *is* pleased if the front of the cake is left pretty as long as possible. It's surprising how many pieces you can cut before disturbing the part that the guests see as they pass by the table.

Perhaps the most valuable and lasting contribution that you make to that little bride will be to pray with her and for her—emphasizing the sacredness of her wedding and the new responsibilities that will soon be hers as a wife. What a joy and satisfaction there is in serving the Lord in this very special capacity as a minister's wife.

Funerals

Madame de Stael observed that we understand death for the first time when he puts his hand upon one whom we love.

When one of your parishioners loses a loved one, you and your husband will want to go as a couple to express your sympathy and offer your services to the family. It will also be an open door of opportunity for the church to communicate its love and concern by relieving the bereaved family of food preparation. This may be sponsored through the social committee of the church, or you may prefer working through a Sunday school class or missionary group. How much food is taken to the family during the intervening days before the funeral should be left to the discretion of the committee. However, it is customary for the church to provide the entire meal on the day of the funeral.

You will want to comply with the wishes of the family in every way possible by consulting with them as to the most convenient time and place for serving the meal. Some will prefer eating in their own home rather than going to a fellowship hall in the church.

Some people have been brought to a personal knowledge of Christ within their own hearts because God's people extended kindness to them during a crisis or period of loneliness. May each one of us take time to *"give a cup of cold water in His name."*

Conclusion

We started with the question; now we close with the same question: "*Who is the minister's wife?*"

She's many things to many people. She cares for her husband's needs, gives guidance to her children, keeps her house in order, and yet reserves time to give of herself to others. She wouldn't exchange her way of life for anyone else's because the remunerations of joy and fulfillment far exceed any fleeting moments of discouragement and frustration. She relies constantly on the power of the Holy Spirit to give her wisdom, direction, and strength for each day's walk with Him.

May the beautiful words of the song "Submission" be the heartfelt expression of every minister's wife who today serves with her husband in the ministry.

> *The path that I have trod Has bro't me nearer God,*
> *Tho' oft it led thro' sorrow's gates.*
> *Tho' not the way I'd choose, In my way I might lose*
> *The joy that yet for me awaits.*
>
> *Submission to the will Of Him who guides me still*
> *Is surety of His love revealed;*
> *My soul shall rise above This world in which I move;*
> *I conquer only where I yield.*
>
> *Not what I wish to be, Nor where I wish to go,*
> *For who am I that I should choose my way?*
> *The Lord shall choose for me; 'Tis better far, I know.*
> *So let Him bid me go, or stay.*
>
> —C. AUSTIN MILES

*[The pastor] must have a good
reputation with the non-Christian
public (1 Tim. 3:7, NEB) to prove
ourselves allies of the Truth
(3 John 8b, Moffatt).*

CHAPTER 15

Other Sheep and Other Shepherds

I. COMMUNICATION TO THE COMMUNITY

Understandably the major focus of attention in this discussion of the shepherding ministry centers upon relationships to and within the flock. However, the Chief Shepherd very pointedly broadened the scope of His (and our) responsibility when He declared, "Other sheep I have, which are not of this fold" (John 10:16). He was referring to the Gentile or heathen world as a potential part of His flock. The implications are very clear. There must be an evangelistic penetration of the non-Christian community. This was discussed in depth in a preceding chapter. But just as clear is the principle taught by both His precept and His example that this penetration must be predicated upon a sound base of confidence which is the product of careful cultivation.

Civic Relationships

Interestingly enough, Jesus did not spend time and effort "fighting city hall." Government was no better then than it is now. Undoubtedly there were inequities in the tax base. But when His critics posed the loaded question "Is it right for us to pay taxes to Caesar or not?" His response was "Give to Caesar what is Caesar's" (Luke 20:22, 25, NIV). This should not be construed as a blanket approval of all that Caesar stood for. But it does indicate that the Christian's stance must be one of involvement rather than aloofness. How else will the leaven of our witness be able to exercise its redemptive influence?

At the same time some practical perimeters should be set to keep the pastor from being too deeply implicated in community affairs. His first priority must always be to his church, and any activities which compromise this primary commitment are suspect. One ironclad rule in this regard is *stay out of politics.* More than one pastor has learned the wisdom of this principle by bitter experience. It is one thing to preach and practice Christian responsibility in electing and supporting officials who are qualified by both ability and integrity. It is another thing to run for office or personally endorse a party or candidate. Both of these latter courses of action have very dangerous, inherent traps and should be studiously avoided. While good laymen can and on occasion should be involved in both, good pastors can't and shouldn't.

However, *ministers must be vigorously and vocally involved in matters of civic morality.* Liquor, gambling, pornography, drug abuse, and other kindred social evils are public enemies and should be identified and denounced as such. Evangelicals, by and large, have been too silent in this regard. While one cannot devote all his time to such endeavors, when a crisis is precipitated by proposed legislation or some flagrant situation arises in the community, the pastor is justified in giving his time and effort to the fight for the right. This falls into the category of causes included in the hymnwriter's challenge:

> *Where duty calls, or danger,*
> *Be never wanting there.*[1]

---

1. George Duffield, Jr., "Stand Up, Stand Up for Jesus."

Service clubs may offer a legitimate opportunity for the shepherd to serve the larger flock of the community. Many of these organizations make complimentary memberships available to ministers. Jay Adams suggests that one may find the right answer to the question "Should a minister be a joiner?" by objectively answering these further questions:

1. Will the contemplated association in any way lead to compromise or confusion of the gospel of Christ?

2. Will the contemplated association cut into my time too deeply to justify it? Will it square with my priorities before God?

3. Will the contemplated association indicate to the community that Jesus Christ is to be identified with the program of this organization?[2]

The man of God cannot afford to project either a holier-than-thou or an unholier-than-thou image. If belonging to the organization will not compromise one's ministerial ideals and will render a service to Christ and the church, the pastor may be justified in joining. Otherwise he may be better off to meet and mingle with businessmen in other situations.

Advertising the Church

Ralph Stoody defines public relations as "Making friends for Christ and his church" while he refers to publicity as "making oneself known."[3] Both are integral parts of good communication to the community. The pastor contributes to both in his civic involvement. However, the message and mission of the church must likewise be communicated. Floyd Craig, an expert in this field, states:

> One of the highest priorities of a church is the communication of its message outside the church. . . . An advertising executive [who is] an active churchman, said: "I know when I have communicated. My client's cash register rings. If it does not ring, I am out of business. But the church never

---

2. Jay C. Adams, *Shepherding God's Flock* (Philadelphia: Presbyterian and Reformed Publishing Co., 1975), p. 55.

3. Floyd A. Craig, *Christian Communicator's Handbook* (Nashville: Broadman Press, 1969), p. 13.

seems to check whether or not it is communicating. It may wake up someday and discover it is out of business."[4]

Larger churches with people qualified in this area would do well to add a public relations committee to their organizational structure. In smaller churches the pastor may have to assume this responsibility. But regardless of who does it, it must be done! It is well-nigh sinful for a church to exist in a community for 10 years or more and be completely unknown to the majority of the people living there.

While the church is more than just a building, outsiders identify the name and ministry of the church with its physical facilities. Therefore, *publicity begins with calling attention to the church building.* Passersby will be favorably impressed with an attractive edifice which is well lighted at night and whose grounds are neatly kept. A tasteful sign which matches the decor of the building should be prominently displayed to identify the church's name. Well-placed directional signs should be placed on major thoroughfares to indicate how the church may be reached. One denominational official declares that after trying to find some churches he believes there is almost a conspiracy among a great number of congregations to keep their locations secret! Didn't Jesus have something to say on the subject of getting gospel light out from under bushel baskets and onto candlesticks? If we really believe that we have the world's only Hope, why are we so backward about getting the church before that world?

Television and radio offer unlimited possibilities for reaching the community with the church's name and message. While air time for TV is costly, this medium makes a maximum impact upon the viewer and warrants the added expense. Radio is still an effective means of reaching the unchurched, and broadcasting rates are generally within reach of the average congregation. Airing the Sunday morning or evening service saves production time and cost. However, when this is done, extra care must be taken to

---

4. Craig, p. 7.

insure that the caliber of music and the format of the service project a good image for the church. The order of service should not become stilted or just a program, but it should reflect the spiritual warmth which characterizes the worship and evangelistic services of the church.

Since the intent of the use of these media is to reach a maximum number of unchurched people, weekday telecasting or broadcasting may be even more productive than that done on Sunday. It should always be kept in mind that *the major objective of these media presentations is to publicize the church and get people to attend its services.* The programming must be suited to this purpose and made attractive to the nonchurched. Dr. James Jauncey makes this perceptive comment about program content:

> One of the reasons for the relative ineffectiveness of religious broadcasting is that much of it uses the direct pitch or sermonic approach and is incredibly dull. Who, in his right mind, wants to listen to or view an hour-long commercial? Perhaps we have made a mistake in assuming that television is an evangelistic method whereas its right place is a *prelude* to evangelism.[5]

In this light, *first-class music should be the main feature.* Nothing is more attractive to the nonchurched than well-presented gospel music. It should be more than entertainment. Each song ought to contain a meaningful spiritual message communicated in listenable, contemporary styling. Then, a short devotional message by the pastor (three to five minutes) will serve to introduce him to the viewing or listening audience. If it is interesting and vital, it will whet their appetites to hear him preach at the church. The whole program should be fast-moving and inspirational and create a desire to experience more of the same at the church.

The local newspaper offers another effective means of advertising. The religion editor is one of the first people the pastor should meet when he comes to the community. His

---

5. James H. Jauncey, *Psychology for Successful Evangelism* (Chicago: Moody Press, 1972), p. 119.

or her friendship should be cultivated over coffee or lunch periodically and with Christmas greetings. Craig observes: "The newspaper is interested in what your church is doing. Your editor is interested in covering the news in the community. Your church and its activities are a part of the news he wants to print. . . . He will print all that he thinks is news."[6]

Here are four ways in which a pastor may improve the quality of material presented to the newspaper and thus guarantee the acceptance of the major part of it.

1. *All stories should be typewritten, double-spaced. Editors do not have time to decode handwritten copy.*

2. *The first sentence should contain the 5 W's—Who, What, When, Where, and Why.* This is standard journalistic practice; and the less rewriting the editor has to do, the more likely he is to use your material.

3. *Keep sentences and paragraphs short.* Reader interest will be maintained best in this way. Newspaper stories are not novels, and the pastor is not an Ernest Hemingway or a Somerset Maugham!

4. *Provide good, clear pictures.* They should be professional quality and genuinely newsworthy. One picture is still worth many hundreds of words.

Advertisements should be bought occasionally to cultivate goodwill with the newspaper. This is their principal source of income, and cooperation at this point will open the door for the maximum amount of free publicity. Advertising revivals and other special events is an art of its own. It is essential, but if it is not done with imagination and reader appeal, it is almost a waste of money. The expertise of advertising salespeople and layout personnel should be employed in the preparation of ads. These should be supplemented by news stories featuring the speakers or musicians. The human interest element gets through best, and an interview by a sympathetic reporter is the best possible newspaper advertising.

---

6. Craig, p. 41.

Another practical public relations tool is the *church news-letter.* This weekly, direct mail communication medium justifies the time and expense involved in its publication if it is well done. Sloppy mimeographing and drab layout can make it more of a liability than an asset. *Good duplicating equipment is a must!* Then adequate time must be spent in gathering and assembling material and producing the newsletter. A good secretary who can care for this responsibility efficiently is worth her weight in gold.

While an \occasional devotional article is in order, the major content should be news. The following items are representative of the type of material which should be included regularly.

1. Reports on recent services and activities
2. Personal items (weddings, funerals, anniversaries, etc.)
3. The hospital and sick roll
4. Statistical report of attendance and finances from the previous Sunday
5. Notices of the coming Sunday's services and other upcoming special events
6. A pastor's column

An exchange of newsletters with other churches will provide fresh ideas for this publication and keep it from becoming stereotyped and uninteresting.

The circulation list should include every potential constituent of the church:

1. Members—both resident and nonresident
2. Families of all Sunday school enrollees
3. Visitors from the community
4. Prospects supplied by members
5. Friends of the church

The mailing list should also include the district superintendent and other denominational officers who are interested in the work of the church. Copies should be mailed to city officials, businessmen, state and national leaders, and other ministers when items will be of special interest to them. Accompanied by an explanatory letter with the particular item clearly marked, this publicity will be a real friend-maker for the church.

II. Relationships with the Larger Flock

Most shepherding takes place in the setting of the local church. However, as we have just noted, there are areas of responsibility in the community to those who do not belong to the family of God. In addition, the pastor has a ministry to those beyond his own congregation who are of the household of faith.

The Christian Community

Happily, there are other churches of the same denomination and of other communions ministering to the spiritual needs of most every community. While it may appear that we are in competition, in the strictest sense we are not. No one church can effectively reach an entire city. The combined efforts of all the flocks only scratch the surface of the total potential. A spirit of cooperation between congregations must be maintained if the whole Kingdom enterprise is to prosper.

Ministerial ethics are imperative if a good working relationship is to be maintained in this larger flock. Nowhere is this more essential than in the matter of a *correct attitude toward other churches' members.* It is true that by their very nature, sheep are prone to stray. Some wander oftener and farther than others. This can pose a potentially serious problem when they stray into another shepherd's fold (particularly if it is of the same denomination). What is a correct attitude toward this situation? These guidelines have proved effective in relating to straying sheep.

1. *Don't call on first-time visitors.* Where the visitor's card clearly indicates that the individual or family belongs to another church in the community, acknowledge the visit with a letter rather than a personal call. The only exception would be if the person specifically asks for a pastoral call. Some visitor's cards have a place where one can request to be put on the mailing list to receive notices of special events. If the party indicates this interest, it is legitimate to honor his request.

2. *If visits continue regularly, inform the individual's pastor.* He has a right to know where his sheep are pasturing. Strained relationships with a brother minister will be avoided if one is able to testify, "I want you to know that I have not called on this person or solicited his attendance." Sometimes the other pastor will be aware of the situation and will encourage you to call. In any event he will have been apprised of the problem and given the opportunity to take remedial action.

3. *When regular attendance indicates that the party intends to change churches, a call is in order.* For various reasons people do seek out another flock. Sometimes these reasons are very legitimate—spiritual hunger, family situations, or a change of residence which places them a long distance from their church. In such cases they should be assured that the fellowship of your church is open to them. If it is discovered that the reason for changing is a petty one such as a misunderstanding with the pastor or members of their church, the part of wisdom is to urge a reconciliation. It may develop that this is a pattern and that they are "church tramps." Such individuals are of dubious value to any church.

4. *Letters of transfer or commendation should be requested by the individual.* If he is not willing to face his pastor with this matter, then he should not be allowed to make this change. This is the layman's responsibility, not the minister's. Here again good relationships with fellow clergymen will be strengthened by such a policy.

The Denominational Flock

The minister who affiliates with a denomination in so doing declares his allegiance to the privileges and responsibilities of the larger flock of his church. This is not narrow or blind sectarianism. His primary commitment is to Christ, the Head, and to His body, the Church which is composed of all Blood-washed, born-again believers. But within this larger frame of reference there is a place for loyal service to Christ through an organized denomination.

History has proved that this is the most effective way of evangelizing the world and of conserving the fruits of evangelism.

One of the subjective by-products of denominational affiliation is the vocational security provided for the minister. Thousands of other local churches with the same doctrinal distinctives are potential pastorates when his tenure is completed in the charge where he presently serves. District superintendents stand ready to assist pastors who wish to move. When physical emergencies arise, medical insurance and special benevolence are available through denominational agencies. When retirement comes, benefits provided by the systematic stewardship of thousands of congregations are available not only to the pastors of large churches but to those who have served small congregations as well.

But *privilege always entails responsibility*. There must be *give* as well as *take!* The key word is *cooperation*. This is still a good word in a day when widespread antiestablishment sentiments have made such concepts unpopular in some quarters. Is any other attitude really Christian? Self-serving ministers who have little or no regard for the larger interests of others in their denomination are derelict in some of their most essential shepherding duties. Representative of these are the following.

1. *Areas of responsibility* adjacent to churches should be honored by pastors serving in the same community. Of course this does not mean that members will be required to attend the nearest church. It is still a free country! Some will choose to drive past a number of other churches to attend the one of their choice. And their desire should be honored. But there should be clearly defined boundaries which identify parishes for the purposes of community surveys, Sunday school bus routes, and other such activities. This is only reasonable and fair. The only possible exception would be in the case of a downtown church located in a commercial zone without any adjacent residential area. In this case permission should be given for the congregation to go "every where preaching the word."

2. *Members who move should be promptly transferred.* No one likes to lose members. But when they are going to move, how wonderful it is to know that in the larger denominational flock there will be another church near them where they may enjoy the same redemptive fellowship. What could be more reprehensible than for a pastor to urge moving members not to transfer their membership and to continue to send their tithe back to his church? The spiritual skeletons of all too many Christians who have failed to unite with a church in their new locality are all too visible in many places. How much better to inform the pastor where they are moving of their new address, request that he call on them immediately, and volunteer to transfer their membership when they are ready to join. Though they are so indicated on the statistical report, *transferred members are not lost.* They are saved to the Kingdom.

3. *Honesty in record-keeping* is also important. When members die or move, their names should be promptly deleted from the roll. One's successor should not have to correct the record. But suppose the membership roll shows such names as well as those of people whose whereabouts are unknown or who have suffered spiritual lapses and no longer attend. Should all these names be dropped immediately? Such action by several pastors can completely erase the evangelistic gains made by the whole district and distort the statistical record. But some pastors reason that they cannot be honest and not take off all "deadwood" the first year. The other side of the coin of honesty is that these inequities did not all occur in the past year. They may well be an accumulation of 10 or 20 years of careless bookkeeping. To take all these names off in one year gives a completely dishonest picture of the year's activity. Of course this major surgery may make it possible for the new pastor to show a sizable gain in members the next year after blaming his predecessor for the previous year's loss. But is this our basic motivation?

A far better method is to *remove a few names each year,* balancing them out with new members who have been received. One of the fringe benefits of this system may be that some "lost sheep" may be located and brought back into the fold if their names are not too quickly deleted. The sage advice of church leaders of other days was that no living member's name should ever be taken from the roll without first making a serious effort to locate him and deal with him about his spiritual condition and then spending a night in prayer for his reclamation. This counsel might well be heeded by every modern-day shepherd!

4. *Participation in denominational activities.* The local flock must not be neglected, but neither must the claims of the church on its district and general levels. This means attendance at *all* denominational meetings from their beginning to their end. Merely putting in an appearance is not sufficient. Drop-in pastors have a way of becoming dropouts! It also entails the accepting of responsibility to serve on boards, committees, and commissions. Another area where pastors' cooperation is imperative is in the operation of summer camps and other youth activities. Counseling a lively group of teenagers is neither a picnic nor a vacation. But these lambs from the larger flock are just as deserving of pastoral care as those from one's own church. Pastor, ask yourself this question: "How efficiently would my denomination function if every pastor's involvement were the same as mine?"

5. *The payment of denominational budgets* is the pastor's fair-share responsibility. This is last but far from least. It has been proved again and again that a pastor's attitude toward these benevolences is the most determinative factor in the church's response to them. When the shepherd commits himself to get the budgets paid, they almost always get paid. When he fails to take this stance, they seldom are paid. How can a minister live with himself and do less? Can I take my salary in good faith when lack of budget payment from my church means that some missionary, some home mission pastor, some college professor, or some retired minister will not receive his? Can I put the physical needs

of my church ahead of the spiritual needs of Christ's "other sheep"?

Sooner or later the pastor who fails to cooperate in these fair-share financial obligations will commit ecclesiastical suicide. One district superintendent acknowledges that he keeps a performance file on 900 pastors in his general area. Along with Sunday school and church growth statistics, he keeps a record of each man's budget payment performance. When a pastor asks him for a church, he consults his record. Indications that he is not a "team man" in keeping faith with denominational financial responsibilities may well eliminate him from consideration. This is not being discriminatory or unfair. It is just not fair to bring a pastor to the district who will not carry his share of the load and thus penalize those who are doing their part.

Relating to Other Shepherds

The ministry is a unique calling, and ministers are a special kind of people. Their relationship to laymen, in and out of the church, is different from any other association. Likewise, there is a distinctive bond between fellow ministers. Happy is the shepherd who takes full advantage of this singular privilege.

The local ministerial association offers an opportunity for enriching fellowship with the clergymen of the community. While their creeds may be poles apart, it is amazing how much common ground brother pastors enjoy. Participation in association-sponsored activities identifies one's congregation as a fully cooperative member of the family of churches. It also gives the pastor valuable exposure in the larger setting of union services and other functions. The shepherd who fails to take part in the work of his association robs himself and his flock of these advantages. He also denies himself the opportunity to propose such valuable interchurch activities as united evangelistic crusades which can be of tremendous value both to the community and to his church. The time invested in the local ministerial association must be carefully monitored so that it does not occupy too large a share of one's schedule. But all things considered, it is time well spent.

Pastoral associations within the denomination are some of the most enriching fringe benefits of this vocation. In larger communities where there are a number of churches of the same denomination, a monthly pastors' fellowship should be inaugurated. The group may choose to meet for breakfast with their wives. A time of devotion together invariably yields rich spiritual benefits. The ladies may then wish to meet separately for their own program. At least occasionally the men may profitably share a time of intellectual stimulation with an assigned paper being read, a book reviewed, or a general discussion of some topic of mutual interest. Then they may wish to disperse to the golf course, tennis court, or other recreational pursuits.

In addition to the very obvious advantages of such an activity, there are also some priceless side effects. Only God knows the frustrations and deep discouragements that a pastor may be undergoing just at the time of the monthly fellowship. The privilege of praying together with fellow ministers and perhaps sharing some of his problems may mean the difference between giving up and going on. Then, too, such a time together provides a clearinghouse for little things which if left to develop could become major issues between pastors and churches. Potential crises may well be averted by open, frank discussion of matters which are bothering some pastors. This should be done with discretion, of course. Principles, not personalities, should be dealt with.

On a larger scale, *district pastors' retreats* provide an occasion for more of the same fellowship opportunities. Such a well-planned event is a real oasis in the schedule of the minister and his wife. Blessedly, more and more districts are going to the format of a relaxed, casual meeting in a recreation area or motel. Preachers are required to let their humanity show by abandoning ties and suits in favor of sport shirts and jackets. Mornings and evenings are given over to inspirational services, often with a general superintendent as the speaker, and separate special interest meetings for the pastors and their wives. Afternoons are dedicated to recreation or relaxation. Such an atmosphere has proved conducive to unusual visitations of the Holy Spirit which have brought much-needed spiritual renewal to shepherds and shepherdesses. Only eternity will reveal how many ministries have been saved by the providential intervention of such a meeting just when pastors were ready to resign.

The pastor who is too busy to attend these ministerial functions is too busy! The "loner" almost invariably eliminates himself by his isolation. Shepherds really do need each other, and in their own best interests as well as those of the Kingdom, they should take full advantage of these personal and professional privileges.

But now at last I am through with my work here (Rom. 15:23, TLB).
But now I go unto Jerusalem to minister unto the saints (Rom. 15:25).

CHAPTER 16

Shepherds Come and Shepherds Go

In order to keep alive the romance and sense of excitement in one's ministry, it is necessary to change flocks and pastures from time to time. The challenge of a new pastorate effectively revives a shepherd's spirits and supplies fresh zest for his work.

Responding to a Call

The parsonage telephone rings. "This is the district superintendent of the _____ District calling. I have just been meeting with the board of the _____ church which is looking for a new pastor. Your name is being given consideration by the board. The church has 200 members, pays a total of $210 per week, and has a very nice four-bedroom parsonage. Do you think you might be interested?"

If one's situation is such that he cannot consider making a move at this time, the ethical answer is a courteous declination: "Thank you for thinking of me, but I am not in a position where I could possibly make a change right now. Perhaps at some later date if an opening were to come, I could give consideration to it." To keep a superintendent and church board dangling when there is no chance of one's accepting a call will understandably lessen the likelihood of receiving a call to that or some other church on that district at a later date. On the other hand, if there has been a growing conviction that one's work may be about done in his present charge, such an inquiry could well elicit a response such as "I appreciate your consideration; and if the board should see fit to nominate me, I will be happy to give the matter prayerful consideration."

Some ministers have the mistaken idea that a successful move must be to a larger church. Nothing could be farther from the truth. Such an attitude smacks too much of an unscriptural image-concern and reduces pastoral ministry to the level of a professional ego trip! On the contrary, what seems to be a step down may in the final analysis prove to be a step up. One of the most gifted young pastors of my acquaintance accepted a call to a much smaller church because the Holy Spirit helped him to see its tremendous potential. In less than a decade it developed into a "superchurch" with a 600 percent membership increase and a 1,000 percent growth in income!

A growing number of church boards are inviting prospective pastors in for an interview before extending a call. This can be mutually beneficial to both the board and the minister under consideration. It gives opportunity for the pastor to state his philosophy of ministry and lay out his general pattern of operation. He may also question the board as to its general goals and willingness to venture. These factors should be given more consideration than the size of the membership and the salary.

The members of the board should be given equal opportunity to probe the prospective pastor. However, *for his own protection he should not go for an interview until he has received a nomination from the church board.* If several ministers meet with the board and then one is nominated, the other candidates may be placed in an embarrassing position. When their churches find out that they have been sufficiently interested in moving to be interviewed by another church board, their effectiveness in their own pastorates may be jeopardized. In the last analysis, a board should rely more on a man's service record and the recommendation of the district superintendent than on the impression which he makes in an interview. Some ministers who have been very successful are unable to "sell" themselves, while others whose credentials are not nearly so good sway a board by their glib speech and sparkling personalities. Once the interview is concluded, there should be a clear understanding that if either the prospective pastor or the board should feel strongly that the call would not be well advised, either should have the privilege of terminating the matter.

The sincere shepherd will be in continuous prayer seeking divine guidance through this whole process. If he does not feel checked at this point and there is reasonable certainty that he would accept the call if he receives a favorable congregational vote, he should give permission for the vote to be announced and taken. Should there be an unusually large number of "no" ballots cast, it would be in order to confer with the district superintendent to see if he feels that they represent personal opposition or if they are simply "traditional negatives." The final decision, of course, must be made on his knees. Nothing less than the certainty of God's approval is sufficient assurance that the move is the right one. A week should be an adequate period of time for this final consideration. If one's answer is affirmative, he should tender his resignation to his own church board before allowing his acceptance to be announced in the church to which he is going. Thirty days' notice should be given to his present charge.

Laying the Foundations

First impressions in the new pastorate are exceedingly important. Since the broadest possible exposure is of great value, it is well to plan to meet the congregation for the first time on Sunday morning. A news story in the local newspaper with a picture of the new pastor will give good publicity to this opening Sunday. An invitation in the church newsletter to all members and friends to meet the new shepherd and his family will help to rally a banner attendance.

The first sermon should be carefully prepared to state the pastor's ideals for his ministry in the new charge, based upon solid scriptural foundations. This message can also serve to acquaint the people with some of the background of their shepherd's conversion and call. Some district superintendents make it a policy to be present to install the new pastor on this day. If so, the details of the service should be worked out with him. Many churches will plan a reception for the new parsonage family at the close of the evening service. This offers a splendid opportunity for getting acquainted with parishioners.

Remembering names is of primary importance. To be in a pastorate for several months and still be unsure of the names of members and regular attendants is a venial if not a mortal sin! People are the same everywhere—they respond to a pastor's personal interest in them. This is unmistakably demonstrated by his calling them by their names. With some ministers this comes more easily than with others. But whether it comes naturally or not, this ability must be cultivated. Concentration on the individual when his or her name is given is the key to making the association.

The first pastoral call will help to cement names and faces in one's memory. This round of calling should be instituted as quickly as possible. It is advisable to make appointments for these initial calls to conserve time and guarantee that people are at home. Grouping calls geographically will save time, too. Since most men and many women work during the daytime, many calls must be made in the evening in order to reach whole families. Older members and young people may be available in the afternoon. A full day of calling on Saturdays will reach many as will Sunday afternoon. *On this first round of calls it is vitally important that the pastor's wife accompany her husband.* She needs to get acquainted with the flock, too, and members need to get to know her. It is not out of order to request the church board to pay for baby-sitting service so that she may be free to make these initial calls.

Attitudes Toward Predecessors

One of the most determinative factors in the early days of one's ministry in the new charge is the way the pastor relates to those who have preceded him as pastor of this church. Wise is the pastor who makes it a policy to *say nothing but positive things about those who have formerly occupied this pulpit and parsonage.* Everything they have done may not be praiseworthy, of course. But neither is everything that the new pastor has done or will do. Every man's record of accomplishment will be uneven. Even the best perform more successfully in some pastorates than in others. But two things will invariably be true about each of your predecessors:

1. If you look carefully, you can find something commendable about each one's work.

2. Every pastor leaves a cadre of strong supporters in the church, especially those whom he has won to the Lord.

Some ministers have the *mistaken idea that to build up their own image it is necessary to tear down that of their predecessors.* Not so! Criticism only alienates those who were their admirers. Compliments, on the other hand, will ingratiate the new pastor with those who still remember former shepherds with appreciation and affection. This is especially true concerning one's immediate predecessor. If he has been extremely popular, his successor identifies himself with his popularity when he praises him. Inviting him back for special occasions is good public relations and capitalizes on the success and goodwill which he has achieved. How much better (and more Christian) this is than to feel threatened by his accomplishments and allow resentments to develop.

But what if the congregation is sharply divided in its estimates of the former pastor? Rather than taking sides, one is well advised to "see no evil, hear no evil, and speak no evil" about him. A positive attitude will promote healing and reconciliation where destructive criticism would only serve to alienate his adherents and deepen the schism. With this kind of pastoral example it is amazing how quickly most churches are willing to let bygones be bygones. Even in the tragic instances where one's predecessor has been forced to leave because of moral breakdown or some other serious ethical failure, the less negative things said the better. No useful purpose will be served by dwelling on the sordid details. Refuse to discuss them. Demonstrate and promote the attitude of forgiveness which Jesus exemplified when He advised the adulteress, "Neither do I condemn thee: go, and sin no more" (John 8:11).

And there is no law against praising one's predecessor in the first report to the district assembly! It is refreshing to hear a preacher pay sincere tribute to the man whom he has followed by giving him proper credit for the achievements for which he is responsible. Such a practice is not only honorable but also promotes good relationships with one's ministerial colleagues who would understandably resent any inferences which were uncomplimentary.

How Long to Stay

The matter of proper tenure is an important one. On the average, more pastors make the mistake of staying too short a period of time than too long. This is especially true in smaller churches. *No great congregation was ever built with a succession of two-year pastors.* The reason some struggling churches have never achieved success is because no pastor has been willing to commit himself to an extended ministry with them which could lead them out of their doldrums into a new day of progress. The Master observed that His sheep knew His voice. This is one of the imperatives of successful shepherding. Pity the poor flock which repeatedly has just gotten to know its shepherd's voice and then has seen him move off to greener pastures. And it takes two or three years before the congregational and community flock develop this confidence in a pastor and are ready to follow him into challenging programs of church growth and development.

On the other hand, it is possible to overstay. A comfortable salary and parsonage in a pleasant community with a congenial congregation may serve to dull a pastor's sensibilities regarding tenure. Staying on just so that one's children may finish their education in the same school is not a worthy enough motive. Sometimes it takes a strongly negative congregational vote to rudely awaken him to the fact that he has stayed too long. And the news of this adverse vote has a way of circulating and making the matter of his placement difficult.

Then there is the matter of congregational adjustment after an overly long pastorate. Lyle Schaller makes this sage observation: "Four-fifths of the pastors who serve the same congregation for over twenty years leave a legacy which greatly handicaps their successors."[1] For this reason many pastors would be reluctant to follow a man who has had unusually long tenure. In some cases churches have gone into a deep sleep after a popular, long-term pastor has left, content to dream about the "good old days" of his ministry (which in fact were probably never as good as they recollect!). Pity the poor shepherd who must endure these fantasies while the work of the Kingdom suffers loss.

If there are perils at both the extremes of too short and too long tenure, how may one determine the correct length of his stay in a pastorate? Here are some guidelines which may help to provide the proper answer to that question.

1. *Tenure will vary in different pastorates.* There is no magic number of service years which will guarantee success in every charge. Some churches respond more quickly to one's leadership than others. Some have been faithfully prepared for harvest by the previous pastor. Others must go through a lengthy cycle of planting, watering, cultivation, and maturation before significant gains can be reaped. It is a travesty for a pastorate to deteriorate into an endurance contest between preacher and people.

---

1. Lyle E. Schaller, *The Pastor and the People* (Nashville: Abingdon Press, 1973), p. 24.

2. *Generally speaking, a 4- or 5-year minimum and a 10- to 12-year maximum are reasonable limits.* Unless some extremely abnormal or critical situation should demand earlier termination, the church has a right to expect that the pastor accepting its call will stay at least a quadrennium. The considerable moving expense involved in bringing him and his worldly goods to the new charge should elicit some moral obligation from the man of God to give at least this minimum term of service. More importantly, any shorter period of time than this does not allow for proper foundation-laying, assessment of basic areas of need, goal-setting, and reasonable achievement. Programwise, "Band-Aids" can be applied in 24 months, but surgery or other major therapy almost invariably requires a minimum of at least twice that amount of time. All too many churches have barely survived a premature "operation" by an impatient physician of souls. Instead of resulting in better congregational health, this malpractice has resulted in the flock's being placed on the critical list immediately and then having a long period of semi-invalidism. *Pastoral patience, thou art a jewel!*

While there are exceptions, of course, experience has proved that the suggested 10- to 12-year maximum term makes sense. This gives adequate time to accomplish most major goals. A man can then have a reasonable sense of accomplishment and feel that his work has been done. If he is truly objective, he will realize that his best work will now be done by facing a new challenge in a new charge. Every pastor benefits from this periodic renewal of the romance of the ministry. If he stays much longer than this, he is prone to become so entrenched in the church and community that the thought of moving will become increasingly traumatic. Then, he also needs to face the fact that a change of shepherds once in a decade will prove beneficial to the sheep. Lloyd Douglas, once a pastor himself, observed that every minister basically has just one message; and if he stays too long, he robs the congregation of the privilege of hearing another man's message. While this may be an oversimplification, there is a valid principle here. A new shepherd will bring fresh inspiration to the flock with his new message and methods.

3. *When goals have been achieved, go!* Every pastor should have both immediate and long-range goals. The former should be publicly announced; the latter restricted to the circle of lay leadership (it being somewhat presumptive to launch a six-year program on a one-year call!). The successful realization of short-range goals should provide a platform of confidence on which to build a long-term program. The latter demands a generous supply of pastoral perseverance. Dr. Glen Whitlock comments:

> He needs to be the kind of person who can tolerate goals that are long-range and those that cannot be immediately achieved. He needs to be the kind of person who can encounter frustration and temporary failure, and be able to rebound rather than to capitulate to defeat.[2]

The achieving of such goals demands an exemplary dedication on the part of the pastor. Before committing his congregation to a project of the magnitude of a major building program, he must commit himself to stay until the venture is completed. This will include the stabilization of the financial considerations to the satisfaction of the lending institution from which a loan has been secured. Or the pastor may have challenged the congregation to undertake a multiple-staff ministry. To resign before this program has become financially secure and before the personnel involved have had a reasonable tenure is a breach of faith with both the church and the undershepherd. Fidelity to such goals is imperative. When they have been achieved, it may well be time to start setting goals somewhere else.

4. *Continued church growth should be the basic condition of continued tenure.* There are several growth indicators. *Sunday school attendance* is one of these. However, one must read these records carefully. With all due respect for

---

2. Whitlock, *From Call to Service*, p. 88.

promotional efforts, it is possible for a few busloads of boys and girls enticed by the promise of free hamburgers or plane rides on a special rally day to completely distort average attendance statistics. Nowhere in the church can this year's boom more quickly become next year's bust (or vice versa). *Financial income* is another indicator which must be properly assessed. For example, in an inflationary period a 10 percent increase in total giving actually may not represent a gain but only the maintaining of the status quo.

Church membership growth by profession of faith is the most reliable and vital life sign of the congregation's health. Net gains will not always be sensational. Natural attrition will see to that. And in some years exodus will exceed evangelism. But if the growth graph levels off for more than one year (or two years at the most) after he has had a reasonable tenure, the shepherd should begin to question whether his usefulness has come to an end. Although the church is not pressuring him to leave, and his wife may be nicely situated in a well-paying teaching position, his final accountability is to the Chief Shepherd, who confronts his lack of productivity with the searching question "Why cumbereth . . . [he] the ground?" (Luke 13:7).

5. *Leave when things are going best, not worst.* This is contrary to our natural disposition. We pray for calls when problems seem to outnumber promises. And when a spiritual tide is on and statistics are up, we could care less about whether another church desires our services. But interestingly, most calls come when you don't really need them. This is understandable. Church boards searching for pastors are naturally interested in shepherds who are achieving in their present pastorates. The sweet smell of success has a way of getting around, and so it is logical that these men find themselves in demand.

If one finds himself somewhere between the suggested minimum and maximum tenure limits and has achieved his most urgent goals, he might well give serious consideration to calls which come while he is enjoying his best days.

The situation can change abruptly. The whole operation may go into reverse, and the next years may be as frustrating and counterproductive as the earlier ones were fruitful and fulfilling. And the pastor's popularity poll can take a disastrous drop in a short period of time. The same people who publicly declared a few months ago that they would die if he left can drastically change their opinions and just as publicly insist that the church will die if he doesn't leave. Under these circumstances good calls can become as scarce as the proverbial hen's teeth.

6. *When in doubt, seek the counsel of the district superintendent.* He is the pastor's pastor. His background of experience as well as his position make him a qualified counselor. He is in a unique position to advise a pastor as to whether he feels his work is done or not. If he urges you to stay and see a situation through, you can continue on with the assurance of his confident support. If he indicates that you may possibly have achieved your most important objective, he will undoubtedly pledge his best efforts to assist you in making a change of pastorates. *This is not ecclesiastical politics!* It is simply availing yourself of the assistance of a knowledgeable, sympathetic fellow minister in making a very crucial decision.

7. *Settle the matter on your knees.* All of the foregoing factors should be fed into one's mental computer and carefully weighed. But in the last analysis the question of greatest consequence is "What is God's will in this matter?" Weighing all the evidence will help to determine the answer. Prayer will make it absolutely certain. Just as you found God's will in accepting the call to this pastorate, so you can depend on His clear release when your work is done. A period of fasting and prayer always enabled me to secure a sense of divine direction when I was faced with this crucial decision. Nothing less than this certainty of God's leadership will provide the necessary assurance for facing the future with quiet confidence.

Preparation for Parting

Going is just as important a process as coming. Once the decision has been made, resignation should be made to the district superintendent and church board as quickly as possible. Word of their shepherd's departure should not reach the flock from other sources. Thirty days' notice should be given before one actually leaves. This gives opportunity for the congregation to make pastoral arrangements, and a smooth transition can be made. And under no circumstances should the departing pastor be involved in naming his successor. This should be left strictly to the district superintendent and the church board. Even if members solicit suggestions from the outgoing shepherd, he should courteously but firmly decline.

The congregation has a right to expect adequate pastoral care during this last month of a pastor's tenure. The mechanics of moving will make special demands upon one's time, of course, but the church should not suffer because of inattention. If vacation time is due, it should be taken in the interim between pastorates.

This month will provide adequate time to update the records of the church for your successor. Shoddily kept membership and financial records are a poor legacy to leave behind. Current addresses and phone numbers will be invaluable to the new pastor as he undertakes his assignment. A complete list of sick and shut-in parishioners as well as a list of prime prospects will also be most helpful.

One of the most important endeavors of this last month is *the severing of all ties with the congregation.* This is not easy. They have been deepened and strengthened with the close associations of the years. But they must be cleanly and completely broken in the best interests of the church. Nothing you can do will more effectively condition the congregation for the coming of the new pastor than this. What untold damage has been done to the Kingdom by pastors who have insisted on maintaining communication with their former parishioners. *Nothing is more unethical!*

An excellent practice when leaving is to print an open letter to members and friends of the church in the newsletter such as the following:

Dear Members of the Church Family,

Resigning as your pastor has been one of the most difficult decisions I have had to make. Our years together have been among the happiest and most rewarding which my family and I have known. There is only one real reason why we are leaving. God has made it plain that my work as your pastor is done. He has another place of service for me, and He has another pastor for you.

It has been a wonderful privilege to be your pastor. You have opened your hearts and your homes to me. I shall never forget you. But now Rev. _____ will be your new shepherd. Open your hearts and homes to him. Lavish the same love and affection on him and his family that you have on us. He is a great pastor, and you will have no problem transferring your loyalties to him. He will marry your young people and bury those who pass on. Please do not ask me to come back for weddings and funerals. I will have a new flock to shepherd and will not be able to return.

Do not expect me to come back to visit you. If you write to me, please do not expect an answer. In fairness to your new pastor I cannot maintain communication with any members of the church. This may sound harsh. Please understand that it is not intended to be. We shall always treasure the happy memories of these years of association with you. But they must only live in memory.

Be assured of our personal interest in the ongoing of the church under your new pastor's leadership. Your best days are ahead! As you give him your full cooperation and support, he will lead you forward into the realization of many of the hopes and dreams which we shared.

Yours and the Saviour's,

This letter should also be read from the pulpit on one of your last Sundays. Then no one can misunderstand how you feel about this matter. And then keep these commitments. Make no exceptions. *When you leave, leave!* Give your successor every opportunity to win the full loyalty of his new flock without competition from its former pastor. Only return at his invitation. Lean over backwards to do unto him as you would have your successor do unto you.

When Retirement Comes

This same principle should apply when one takes leave of his last pastorate to enter retirement. While the natural inclination might be to settle in this community where you have served, experience has proved that it is better to cut the ties and move to another area. John C. Banker advises:

> Leave the community in which you have concluded your ministry. It is always possible that you are an unflawed and unfaulted saint who could not possibly be the focus of any trouble for the new pastor. If by chance you are, it is possible that your wife may not be![3]

How much better to choose a new community where there is a good possibility of being involved in some part-time ministry which will not affect your successor. Locating adjacent to a cluster of churches increases the likelihood of being called upon for pulpit supply work. Vacationing pastors welcome the opportunity to have a sensible, seasoned retiree preach in their absence. Then there is the possibility of being pressed into service by a district superintendent who needs an interim pastor for a church. Congregations which are without the services of a pastor for an extended period of time benefit from the pulpit and parish care of an older minister.

The matter of when to retire is dependent upon one's physical health and other contributive circumstances. Some men can maintain their effectiveness to age 70 or longer. However, Banker makes sense when he suggests: "Retire before you have to and move to your new home while you and your wife are healthy enough to make new friends. It isn't easy to make new friends if you arrive in a new community on a stretcher."[4]

---

3. Banker, *Personal Finances*, p. 111.
4. *Ibid.*, p. 114.

The choice of where to retire should take into consideration where your wife will be happy. She has faithfully followed her shepherd-husband where he has felt called, and she deserves the opportunity of helping to choose the place where you will spend your last years. If she isn't happy, you won't be for long!

Then *grow old gracefully*. Keep optimistic. Make up your mind to take a positive, constructive attitude toward the church and the new generation of shepherds. Nothing is sadder than to see a retired minister who has grown bitter and critical in his declining years. Nothing is more blessed than a sweet-spirited senior shepherd whose life is a source of encouragement to young pastors and whose very presence is a benediction. What better way to conclude one's ministry of shepherding?

Bibliography

Adams, Jay C. *Shepherding God's Flock*. Philadelphia: Presbyterian and Reformed Publishing Co., 1975.

Anderson, Martin. *A Guide to Church Building and Fund Raising*. Minneapolis: Augsburg Press, 1959.

Archibald, Arthur Crawley. *Man to Man*. Nashville: Broadman Press, 1955.

Banker, John C. *Personal Finances for Ministers*. Philadelphia: Westminster Press, 1968.

Barclay, William. *Daily Celebration*. Edited by Denis Duncan. Waco, Tex.: Word Books, 1971.

----. *In the Hands of God*. New York: Harper and Row, 1966.

Barth, Karl. *The Preaching of the Gospel*. Translated by B. E. Hooke. Philadelphia: Westminster Press, 1963.

Benjamin, Paul. *How in the World?* Lincoln, Ill.: Lincoln Christian College Press, 1973.

Benson, Dennis C. *The Now Generation*. Richmond, Va.: John Knox Press, 1969.

Blackwood, Andrew Watterson. *Pastoral Work*. Philadelphia: Westminster Press, 1945.

Boreham, Frank William. *A Tuft of Comet's Hair*. New York: Abingdon Press, 1926.

Bowie, Walter Russell. *Where You Find God*. New York: Harper and Row, 1968.

Brister, C. W. *Pastoral Care in the Church*. New York: Harper and Row, 1964.

Brooks, Phillips. *Lectures on Preaching*. New York: E. P. Dutton, 1891.

Buttry, Lucas Wayne. *The Calling Program of the Local Church*. Butler, Ind.: Higley Press, 1956.

Chapman, James Blaine. *The Preaching Ministry*. Kansas City: Beacon Hill Press, 1947.

Cleland, James T. *Preaching to Be Understood*. New York: Abingdon Press, 1965.

Craig, Floyd A. *Christian Communicator's Handbook*. Nashville: Broadman Press, 1969.

Davis, Henry Grady. *Design for Preaching.* Philadelphia: Fortress Press, 1958.

Dicks, Russell Leslie. *Pastoral Work and Personal Counseling.* New York: The Macmillan Co., 1944.

Dittes, James E. *The Church in the Way.* New York: Charles Scribner's Sons, 1967.

Dobbins, Gaines Stanley. *Evangelism According to Christ.* Nashville: Broadman Press, 1949.

Doon, James L. *Journal of the National Conference on Church Architecture*, April 22-29, 1965.

Edge, Findley Bartow. *The Greening of the Church.* Waco, Tex.: Word Books, 1971.

Eisenhower, Dwight David. *At Ease.* New York: Doubleday, 1967.

Finney, Charles Grandison. *Charles G. Finney: an Autobiography.* New York: Fleming H. Revell Co., 1903.

Fisher, Charles William. *Evangelistic Moods, Methods, and Messages.* Kansas City: Beacon Hill Press of Kansas City, 1967.

Fisher, Wallace E. *Preaching and Parish Renewal.* Nashville: Abingdon Press, 1966.

Forsyth, Peter Taylor. *The Church and the Sacraments.* London: Independent Press, 1917, 1955.

----. *Positive Preaching and the Modern Mind.* Grand Rapids, Mich.: Wm. B. Eerdmans Publishing Co., 1964.

Frey, Edward Snively. *This Before Architecture.* Jenkintown, Pa.: Religious Publication Co., 1963.

Gibbs, Mark. "They Deserve a First-Class Education." *Theological Education*, vol. 4, no. 1 (autumn, 1967), pp. 23-24.

Gilmore, J. Herbert. *When Love Prevails.* Grand Rapids, Mich.: Wm. B. Eerdmans Publishing Co., 1971.

Hahn, Ferdinand. *The Worship of the Early Church.* Translated by David E. Green. Edited by John Reumann. Philadelphia: Fortress Press, 1973.

Hammarskjöld, Dag. *Markings.* Translated by Leif Sjöberg and W. H. Auden. New York: Alfred A. Knopf, 1964.

Harner, Nevin Cowger. *Youth Work in the Church.* New York: Abingdon Press, 1942.

Haselden, Kyle. *The Urgency of Preaching.* New York: Harper and Row, 1963.

Havner, Vance. *Living in Kingdom Come.* Westwood, N.J.: Fleming H. Revell Co., 1967.

----. *That I May Know Him.* New York: Fleming H. Revell Co., 1948.

Hendrix, Olan. *Management and the Christian Worker.* Fort Washington, Pa.: Christian Literature Crusade, 1970.

Hiltner, Seward. *Ferment in the Ministry.* Nashville: Abingdon Press, 1969.

Holck, Manfred. *Money Management for Ministers.* Minneapolis: Augsburg Press, 1966.

Howe, Reuel L. *Partners in Preaching.* New York: Seabury Press, 1967.

Howse, William Lewis. *The Church Staff and Its Work.* Nashville: Broadman Press, 1959.

Hutchinson, Eliot D. *How to Think Creatively.* New York: Abingdon Press, 1949.

Irving, Roy G., and Zuck, Roy B., eds. *Youth and the Church.* Chicago: Moody Press, 1968.

Jackson, Edgar Newman. *Group Counseling.* Philadelphia: Pilgrim Press, 1969.

Jauncey, James H. *Psychology for Successful Evangelism.* Chicago: Moody Press, 1972.

Johnson, Paul Emmanuel. *Psychology of Pastoral Care.* Nashville: Abingdon Press, 1953.

Jones, Eli Stanley. *Conversion.* New York: Abingdon Press, 1959.

Jowett, John Henry. *The Preacher, His Life and Work.* New York: George H. Doran Co., 1912.

Judy, Marvin T. *The Multiple Staff Ministry.* Nashville: Abingdon Press, 1969.

Keller, W. Phillip. *A Shepherd Looks at Psalm 23.* Grand Rapids, Mich.: Zondervan Publishing House, 1970.

Kennedy, Dennis James. *Evangelism Explosion.* Wheaton, Ill.: Tyndale House Publishers, 1970.

Kennedy, Gerald Hamilton. *The Seven Worlds of the Minister.* New York: Harper and Row, 1968.

Kennedy, James William. *Minister's Shop-Talk.* New York: Harper and Row, 1965.

Kerr, Hugh Thomson. *The Christian Sacraments.* Philadelphia: Westminster Press, 1944.

LeTourneau, Richard. *Management Plus*. Grand Rapids, Mich.: Zondervan Publishing House, 1973.

Lloyd-Jones, D. Martyn. *Preaching and Preachers*. London: Hodder and Stoughton, 1971.

Manual, Church of the Nazarene. Kansas City: Nazarene Publishing House, 1972.

Mills, Edgar W., and Koral, John P. *Stress in the Ministry*. Washington, D.C.: Ministry Studies Board, 1971.

Moffatt, Gene E. *The Anatomy of the Ministry*. Atlanta: Pendulum Books, 1966.

Morse, John E. *To Build a Church*. New York: Holt, Rinehart, and Winston, 1969.

Niebuhr, H. Richard, in collaboration with Daniel Day Williams and James M. Gustafson. *The Purpose of the Church and Its Ministry: Reflections on the Aims of Theological Education*. New York: Harper and Brothers, 1956.

Norris, Mike. "Midweek Innovations." *Preacher's Magazine*, October, 1974, pp. 8-10.

Noyse, Morgan Phelps. *This Ministry: The Contribution of Henry Sloane Coffin*. New York: Charles Scribner's Sons, 1946.

Oman, John B. *Group Counseling in the Church*. Minneapolis: Augsburg Press, 1972.

Pattison, Thomas Harwood. *For the Work of the Ministry*. Philadelphia: American Baptist Publication Society, 1907.

Purkiser, W. T. *The Gifts of the Spirit*. Kansas City: Beacon Hill Press of Kansas City, 1975.

----. *The New Testament Image of the Ministry*. Kansas City: Beacon Hill Press of Kansas City, 1969.

Pusey, Nathan M., and Taylor, Charles L. *Ministry for Tomorrow*. New York: Seabury Press, 1967.

Quayle, William Alfred. *The Pastor Preacher*. Cincinnati: Jennings and Graham, 1910.

Randolph, David James. *The Renewal of Preaching*. Philadelphia: Fortress Press, 1969.

Rank, Otto. *Will Therapy and Truth and Reality*. Translated by Jessie Taft. New York: Alfred A. Knopf, 1936.

Read, David Haxton Carswell. *Religion Without Wrappings*. Grand Rapids, Mich.: Wm. B. Eerdmans Publishing Co., 1970.

Redding, David A. *What Is the Man?* Waco, Tex.: Word Books, 1970.

Rees, Paul Stromberg. *Don't Sleep Through the Revolution.* Waco, Tex.: Word Books, 1969.

Richards, Lawrence O. *A New Face for the Church.* Grand Rapids, Mich.: Zondervan Publishing House, 1970.

Rochelle, Jay C. *Create and Celebrate.* Philadelphia: Fortress Press, 1971.

Rouch, Mark A. *Competent Ministry.* Nashville: Abingdon Press, 1974.

Sanders, John Oswald. *Spiritual Leadership.* Chicago: Moody Press, 1967.

Sangster, William Edwin. *Power in Preaching.* New York: Abingdon Press, 1958.

Schaeffer, Francis. *True Spirituality.* Wheaton, Ill.: Tyndale House, 1971.

Schaller, Lyle E. *The Pastor and the People.* Nashville: Abingdon Press, 1973.

Scherer, Ross P., and Wedel, Theodore O. *The Church and Its Manpower Management.* New York: National Council of Churches of Christ in the U.S.A., 1966.

Schlesinger, Arthur M. *A Thousand Days.* Boston: Houghton Mifflin Co., 1965.

Shanafelt, Ira L. *The Evangelical Home Bible Class.* Kansas City: Beacon Hill Press of Kansas City, 1969.

Shoemaker, Helen (Smith). *I Stand by the Door: the Life of Sam Shoemaker.* New York: Harper and Row, 1967.

Southard, Samuel. *Pastoral Evangelism.* Nashville: Broadman Press, 1962.

Speakman, Frederick B. *The Salty Tang.* New York: Fleming H. Revell Co., 1954.

Stevenson, Dwight Eshelman. *The False Prophet.* New York: Abingdon Press, 1965.

----. *In the Biblical Preacher's Workshop.* Nashville: Abingdon Press, 1967.

Stevick, Daniel B. *Language in Worship.* New York: Seabury Press, 1970.

Stewart, James Stuart. *Heralds of God.* New York: Charles Scribner's Sons, 1946.

Sweazey, George Edgar. *Effective Evangelism.* New York: Harper and Brothers, 1953.

Towns, Elmer L. *Evangelize Through Christian Education.* Wheaton, Ill.: Evangelical Teacher Training Assoc., 1970.

Tozer, Aiden Wilson. *Of God and Men.* Harrisburg, Pa.: Christian Publications, 1960.

Trueblood, David Elton. *The Future of the Christian.* New York: Harper and Row, 1971.

----. *The Incendiary Fellowship.* New York: Harper and Row, 1967.

----. *The Validity of the Christian Mission.* New York: Harper and Row, 1972.

Turnbull, Ralph Gale, ed. *Evangelism Now.* Grand Rapids, Mich.: Baker Book House, 1972.

Wedel, Leonard E. *Building and Maintaining a Church Staff.* Nashville: Broadman Press, 1966.

White, James F. *New Forms of Worship.* Nashville: Abingdon Press, 1971.

Whitesell, Faris Daniel. *The Art of Biblical Preaching.* Grand Rapids, Mich.: Zondervan Publishing House, 1950.

Whitlock, Glenn E. *From Call to Service.* Philadelphia: Westminster Press, 1968.

Widber, Mildred C., and Ritenour, Scott Turner. *Focus: Building for Christian Education.* Philadelphia: Pilgrim Press, 1969.

Wise, Carroll Alonzo. *The Meaning of Pastoral Care.* New York: Harper and Row, 1966.

Yutang, Lin. "My Steps Back to Christianity." *Reader's Digest,* October, 1959, pp. 58-61.